What scholars say about this book

'The notion of a synthesis between Gramsci and Freire in relation to adult education is a complex one and Peter Mayo steers a coherent and insightful route through complexity.'

Professor Sallie Westwood, University of Leicester

'This study represents, to my knowledge, the most thorough attempt to date to analyse comparatively the full range of English-language writings of these two critical figures as regards their application for the practice of adult education.'

Professor Budd L. Hall, OISE/University of Toronto

'Peter Mayo's book addresses the much-ignored links between Antonio Gramsci's popular education projects and his insights regarding working-class culture, ideological hegemony and class consciousness. He also offers the most thorough comparison to date of Gramsci's perspective on education and social transformation with the approach of Paulo Freire, the most widely heralded contemporary popular educator.'

Professor David W. Livingstone, OISE/University of Toronto

'Peter Mayo has helped adult educators greatly in his close examination of Gramsci and Freire. Connecting the thought of these two monumental thinkers, Mayo clarifies the powerful legacies left to educators who teach for social justice. They make the road by walking and Mayo in his own right reveals the road ahead.'

Professor Ira Shor, College of Staten Island

'The needs and aspirations of society are nowadays defined in purely economistic terms; education has been reduced to training and the acquisition of marketable skills. Peter Mayo engages in a critical reflection on the alternative visions of Antonio Gramsci and Paulo Freire, for whom the interests of the oppressed and subaltern social groups have priority over the omnivorous greed of capital.'

Professor Joseph A. Buttigieg, University of Notre Dame

'The works of Antonio Gramsci and Paulo Freire are fundamental contributions to the study of the politics of culture and education in this century. Peter Mayo explores the potential complementarity and theoretical intersections in Gramsci and Freire, offering a fascinating book which is an important addition to the specialized bibliography, a must to read.'

Professor Carlos Alberto Torres, UCLA

About the Author

Dr Peter Mayo was educated at the Universities of Malta, London and Alberta before moving to the Ontario Institute for Studies in Education (University of Toronto) for his doctorate. He is currently Lecturer in the Faculty of Education at the University of Malta, where he specialises in the sociology of education and adult and continuing education. He serves on the editorial advisory committee of *Convergence* and the *Canadian Journal for the Study of Adult Education*, and is also reviews editor of the *Mediterranean Journal of Educational Studies*. His books include *The National Museum of Fine Arts* (Midsea, Malta, 1995) and *Beyond Schooling: Adult Education in Malta*, co-edited with Godfrey Baldacchino (Mireva, Malta, 1997).

Gramsci, Freire and Adult Education

Possibilities for Transformative Action

PETER MAYO

ZED BOOKS
London & New York

Global Perspectives on Adult Education and Training

Series Editors: Budd Hall with Carol Medel-Anoneuvo
and Griff Foley

Series Advisors: Peggy Antrobus, Phyllis Cunningham, Chris Duke,
Patricia Ellis, Matthias Finger, Heribert Hinzen, Agneta Lind,
Peter Mayo, Derek Mulenga, Jorge Osorio, Lalita Ramdas, Te Rippowe,
Nelly P. Stromquist, Rajesh Tandon, Carlos Alberto Torres,
Alan Tuckett, Shirley Walters, Makoto Yamaguchi,
Karen Yarmol-Franko, Frank Youngman and Abdelwahid Yousif

This new series is designed to provide for the first time a genuinely global basis to the theory and practice of adult education and learning worldwide. A key goal is to introduce readers to issues, debates and understandings related to centrally important areas in adult education and training, particularly but not exclusively in the majority (or third) world, and to provide a forum where practitioners from the South, women, and other social groups historically under-represented in AET, can find a voice. To this end, the new series will contribute to redressing an imbalance in the literature whereby our understanding and debates in adult education and training in the English-speaking world have been unduly dominated by bodies of knowledge and theoretical perspectives drawn from experience in the USA and Britain and relatively unrepresentative of class, race and gender.

Among the issues of immediate and vital interest to adult educators throughout the world which new titles in this series will address are: popular education, adult learning and civil society, post-colonial perspectives, women's perspectives, informal learning in peoples' struggles, worker education, environmental adult education, participatory research, the political economy of adult education, indigenous knowledge and adult learning, and the impact on them of globalization and other social trends.

Titles already available

Shirley Walters (ed.), *Globalisation, Adult Education and Training: Impacts and Issues*

Peter Mayo, *Gramsci, Freire and Adult Education: Possibilities for Transformative Action*

Griff Foley, *Learning in Social Action: A Contribution to Understanding Informal Education*

Moacir Gadotti and Carlos A. Torres (eds), *Popular Education in Latin America: A Reader*

In preparation

Matthias Finger and Jose Asun, *Learning Our Way Out: Adult Education at the Crossroads*

Griff Foley, Budd L. Hall, Rajesh Tandon and Michael Welton, *Adult Learning, Globalization and Civil Society*

Frank Youngman, *The Political Economy of Adult Education and Development*

For full details of this list and Zed's other subject and general catalogues, please write to: The Marketing Department, Zed Books, 7 Cynthia Street, London N1 9JF, UK or email Sales@zedbooks.demon.co.uk Visit our website at: http://www.zedbooks.demon.co.uk

Gramsci, Freire and Adult Education was first published by
Zed Books Ltd, 7 Cynthia Street, London N1 9JF, UK,
and Room 400, 175 Fifth Avenue, New York, NY 10010, USA in 1999

Distributed in the USA exclusively by St Martin's Press, Inc.,
175 Fifth Avenue, New York, NY 10010, USA

Typeset in Baskerville by Lucy Morton & Robin Gable, Grosmont
Cover designed by Lee Robinson/AdLib Designs
Printed and bound in the United Kingdom
by Biddles Ltd, Guildford and King's Lynn

A catalogue record for this book is available from the British Library

Library of Congress Cataloging-in-Publication Data
Mayo, Peter, 1955–
    Gramsci, Freire, and adult education : possibilities for
transformative action / Peter Mayo.
        p.   cm.
    Includes bibliographical references and index.
    ISBN 1–85649–613–9. — ISBN 1–85649–614–7 (pbk.)
    1. Adult education—Social aspects.   2. Adult education—
Philosophy.   3. Gramsci, Antonio, 1891–1937.   4. Freire, Paulo,
1921– .   I. Title.
LC5225.S64M39   1998
374′.001—dc21   98–30388
                                                        CIP

ISBN 1 85649 613 9 (Hb)
ISBN 1 85649 614 7 (Pb)

Contents

Acknowledgements

There are a number of people whose support and assistance, with regard to the development of this book, I should like to acknowledge. In the first place, I should like to thank my wife, Josephine, and two daughters, Annemarie and Cecilia, for their love, patience and support throughout the entire period in which I worked on this, including my period of Ph.D studies in Toronto. The basis for the book is a Ph.D thesis for which I carried out work as a graduate student in the then Department of Sociology in Education (now the Department of Sociology and Equity Studies in Education) at the Ontario Institute for Studies in Education/University of Toronto. In this regard, I must acknowledge the excellent guidance provided by my Ph.D thesis supervisor, David W. Livingstone, who made me reflect on issues which I would not otherwise have developed in this work. Important advice was also given to me by the other two members of my Ph.D committee, Angela Miles and Budd L. Hall. The Master's thesis in Sociology of Education which I wrote at the University of Alberta served as the foundation for this piece of work. It was there that I first explored the points of convergence and contrast in the work of Gramsci and Freire which I consider relevant to adult education. It is therefore appropriate for me to acknowledge the input of the four members of the committee for this Master's thesis: M. Kazim Bacchus, Carlos A. Torres, Raymond A. Morrow and Derek Sayer. Carmel Borg, a close friend and collaborator on a number of projects, is another person to whom I am indebted. Carmel read some of the draft chapters, and over the years he has discussed with me issues relevant to the development of this work. In this context, I am also indebted to two other good friends and collaborators, Godfrey Baldacchino and Toni Xerri. Throughout this project, I have derived invaluable intellectual and emotional stimulus from friends in different parts of the world, notably in Malta, especially in the Department of Foundations in Education at the University of Malta; and in Canada, particularly in Edmonton and Toronto. These friends are too numerous to mention individually, and there is always the danger that I would leave out somebody important.

Finally I have made use of or developed, in this book, material which I had published in a number of journals. I should like to thank the various editors or publishers of these journals for having granted me authorisation to do so. Full reference to the original published sources is provided in the first footnote of the relevant chapters. The journals are: *Alberta Journal of Educational Research* (vol. XL, no. 11), *Canadian Journal for the Study of Adult Education* (vol. 8, no. 2), *Humanity & Society* (vol. 18, no. 3), *International Gramsci Society Newsletter* (no. 4, April 1995), *International Journal of Educational Development* (vol. 15, no. 4), *International Journal of Lifelong Education* (vol. 13, no. 2; vol. 16, no. 5), *Mediterranean Journal of Educational Studies* (vol. 2, no. 2) and *Studies in the Education of Adults* (vol. 25, no. 1).

CHAPTER I

Introduction

The last decade or so has witnessed the propagation of a hegemonic discourse in adult education. This discourse is essentially
technical–rational and focuses primarily on 'what works'. It reflects
a concern with marketability at the expense of, for instance, social
justice. Among other things, it propagates the creation of programmes aimed at providing a 'flexible' and 'adaptable' workforce. This workforce is to be capable of learning and relearning
the skills for employment required in an age characterised by the
threat of the 'flight of capital' across different geographical boundaries. This is all part of the intensification of that globalisation
process[1] which, as indicated by Marx and Engels in the *Communist
Manifesto* of 1848,[2] has always been a key feature of capitalism.

The intensification of this process of globalisation constitutes
the means whereby capitalism reorganises itself to counter the
tendency of the rate of profit to fall, owing to the 'crises of over-
production'.[3] In his writings on 'Americanism and Fordism',
Gramsci points to the need for capitalism to reorganise itself
periodically to counter such a tendency. Taylorisation constituted
the earlier means in this regard.[4] The intensification of globalisation is the latest form of capitalist reorganisation.[5] And yet there
is ample documented evidence to show that this process of intensification has brought in its wake mass poverty in various parts of the
world, predominantly in the so-called 'Third World'. Accounts of
the effects of neo-liberalism, which provides most of the ideological
underpinning to the process of global capitalist restructuring in

the industrially underdeveloped world, make depressing reading.[6] It is the neo-liberal ideology which underlies much of the discourse concerning adult education in this day and age. Since the early 1980s, it provided the dominant hegemonic discourse surrounding economic development and public policy and was very much a feature of the Pinochet regime's ideology in Chile,[7] Thatcherism, Reaganomics[8] and, of course, the IMF's and World Bank's structural adjustment programmes in much of the industrially underdeveloped world.[9] It is now also a feature of parties in government which have historically been socialist. The presence of this ideology on either side of the traditional political spectrum in Western democracies testifies to the *hegemonic* nature of neo-liberalism.

The presence of the neo-liberal ideology in adult education, as well as in other spheres of activity, can easily lead one to think and operate within the logic of capitalist restructuring. This process is generally characterised by such features as that of converting what were once public goods (adult education among them) into consumption goods, as the 'ideology of the marketplace' holds sway. Neo-liberal thinking brings in its wake increasing privatisation and related cuts in public spending, together with increased user charges and cost recovery policies, therefore limiting popular access to health, education and other social services. It also leads to a decline in real incomes, which turns the whole question of 'choice' into a farce as people who cannot afford to pay for educational and health services are fobbed off with an underfunded and therefore poor-quality public service in these areas. It also entails a deregulation of commodity prices and the shift from direct to indirect taxation.[10]

However, the present scenario is also characterised by other features, many of which have a direct bearing on adult education. A popular cliché in the education of adults has been that of 'participation'. This is generally held to be an important concept within the progressive paradigm of thinking concerning production and learning. This particular conception of the process of participation has its roots in the various experiments which were intended to provide an alternative to the traditionally hierarchical forms of capitalist production. These experiments ranged from the process of self-management experienced in the former Yugoslavia and, until recently, the Malta Drydocks, to the process of worker-ownership one finds in cooperatives. The literature on education contains accounts and critiques of learning programmes related to some of these experiences.[11]

Yet it has always been one of the strengths of capitalism, a reflection of its dynamism, to appropriate a once oppositional concept and gradually dilute it in such a way as to make it an integral feature of the dominant discourse. Take the current fetish of Total Quality Management. It involves the creation of 'worker–management' teams, arguably the one approach to employee participation that has been gaining currency. In this process of 'pseudo-participation', management encourages employees to contribute to the handling of little else apart from 'tea, towel and toilet' issues at the workplace, possibly ensuring their loyalty and greater productivity in the process, without allowing them real involvement in corporate decision-making and the development of corporate strategy.

The concept of participation has been appropriated in a neo-liberal context even outside the sphere of production, in the larger public domain. Only recently, I attended a meeting in my home country focusing on a new project of 'community development' in an area of the island (the Cottonera area) commonly regarded as 'depressed'. Five cabinet members addressed this meeting, emphasising the need to place the onus for community development on the people themselves and not rely on 'government handouts'. The project is still in its initial stages and one must wait and see before passing judgement. While I have always felt that grassroots empowerment should be a feature of any genuine democracy, I would argue that this does not mean that the state abdicates its responsibility for ensuring quality provision of services, guided by the principles of equity and entitlement. We are being exposed, globally, to a discourse centring around such concepts as 'empowerment' and 'active democratic citizenship',[12] widely used in the adult education field, which, unfortunately, can easily prove insidious in that it can reflect another process of New Right misappropriation. As Margaret Ledwith argues, it can reflect 'the New Right misappropriation of a language of liberation ("empowerment", "active citizenship", etc.) as a way of offloading social responsibilities onto the family, the individual and the community',[13] especially in a scenario characterised by stringent budgets.

In this regard, the literature on Paulo Freire's work as Education Secretary in São Paulo, to which I shall be referring shortly and later on in the book, can be instructive. Here community empowerment took on the form of a partnership between social movements and the state.

One other feature of the adult education debate which deserves some consideration is the postmodern paradigm of thinking. It has gained currency in the adult education literature, as elsewhere.[14] I feel that adult educators can no doubt derive several insights from writers whose work falls within this paradigm, certainly in terms of the challenges they pose to those whose liberatory discourse is rooted within the Enlightenment project,[15] with one of the constant dangers being that this discourse becomes a 'totalising' one. There are, however, strands of postmodern thought which are characterised by a nihilistic and paralysing streak.[16] Paula Allman and John Wallis argue, in their critique of postmodernism, in the context of a debate on radical adult education and 'critical intelligence', that this has led to 'the impasse in radicalism'.[17] Freire and other contemporary writers have often used the term 'reactionary postmodernity'[18] in this context. The exponents of this type of postmodernist writing ensnare us with their ludic[19] mystifications. As Valerie Scatamburlo has argued, in a heartfelt tribute to Freire, these exponents are bent on 'proclaiming the implosion of subjects or treating them as mere functions of discourse, as entities which float aimlessly in a sea of ever-proliferating signifiers'.[20] There are those who proclaim the end of the grand narratives – that is to say, the end of antagonistic grand ideologies.[21]

At the heart of this thinking lies a negation of the idea that one can work collectively for human emancipation. In one of his last works, Freire concludes that, according to this ideology,

> We therefore don't have to continue to propose a pedagogy of the oppressed that unveils the reasons behind the facts or that provokes the oppressed to take up critical knowledge and transformative action. We no longer need a pedagogy that questions technical training or is indispensable to the development of a professional comprehension of how and why society functions. What we need to do now, according to this astute ideology, is focus on production without any preoccupation about what we are producing, who it benefits, or who it hurts.[22]

And yet the scenario of mass impoverishment in various parts of the world caused by the ruthless dismantling of social pro- grammes, the ever widening gap between North and South, the concomitant displacement of people from this very same South and Eastern Europe to create a 'third world' in the 'first world', as well as the persistence of structures of oppression in terms of class, gender, race, ethnicity, sexuality and ability/disability strike me as being among the several reasons why we should still be preoccupied with *how* (my addition to Freire's statement) as well as 'what we are producing, who it benefits or who it hurts'. These are reasons why we should be concerned with engaging in edu- cational *processes* that are not meant to consolidate 'what is' but are driven by a vision of 'what should and can be'. In short, I feel that the above are some of the many reasons why we need to retain an emancipatory vision of adult education, one that reflects the will to contribute to the creation of a world which, in Freire's words, is 'menos feio, menos malvado, menos desumano' (less ugly, less cruel, less inhumane).[23]

We are faced with the question which Freire, arguing that there is no such thing as a neutral education, has been posing to us ever since his work first captured the imagination of educators world- wide: on whose side are we when we teach/act? Drawing on Freire, Jane Thompson, as editor of a book providing a radical debate on adult education, posits the existence of two forms of education, neither of which is 'value-neutral':

> there is no such thing as a neutral education process. Education either functions as an instrument which is used to facilitate the integration of generations into the logic of the present system and bring about con- formity to it, or it becomes the 'practice of freedom', the means by which men and women deal critically and creatively with reality and discover how to participate in the transformation of their world.[24]

The statement certainly echoes the familiar contrast in Freire between domesticating and liberating education.[25] The choice one makes in this regard depends on one's values. My specific values have led me to choose the second and infinitely more arduous path. It is therefore with the transformative and emancipatory dimension of adult education that this book is concerned. It has been written with the conviction that people can educate, learn and work collectively for change both outside and *within* institutions, both state-controlled and non-governmental. In this respect, I share the view expressed by Michael Welton several years ago: 'Resistance to and transformation of societal structures emerges from the adult population, and is premised upon men's and women's ability to learn new ways of seeing the world and acting within it.'[26]

My choice of the phrase 'within institutions' indicates, with respect to the Freirean statement formulated by Jane Thompson, that an option in favour of transformative education also entails that we *engage* with the logic of the system. We do this for a variety of reasons, not least of which being that we first need to survive in order to be able to transform. For many, survival means earning a living within the system itself. Most importantly though, we have to engage with the logic of the system in order to be effective. Both Gramsci and Freire move us in this direction. The first does so with his strategy of 'war of position', so central to the concept of 'hegemony', to be discussed in detail in Chapter 2. The second does so with his constant insistence that we be 'tactically inside and strategically outside the system'. In this respect, I feel that it would be more realistic to view the 'two educations' posited in the Thompson quotation as ends of a continuum where living and working critically would entail one's readiness to experience the tension involved in trying to move towards the 'transformative end' of the continuum while being pushed towards the other end by the material forces with which we contend daily.

Engaging critically and dialectically with the logic of the system implies a readiness to live with the tension to which I have just referred. Such an engagement is born out of a conviction that the system and its institutions are not monolithic entities but offer spaces wherein such struggles can occur. In keeping with the Gramscian conception of social transformation, this book has been written with the conviction that dominant forms of thought and practice can be challenged in the vast and amorphous arena of struggle that is civil society.

'Civil society' has been given a lot of prominence in a section of the adult education literature, where it has often been romanticised, conceived of as an arena of popular oppositional politics.[27] Of course, this conception is arguably at its strongest among dissidents writing/acting in the context of a totalitarian state.

Korsgaard makes this point with reference to the positive connotations accorded to civil society by Eastern European intellectuals
in the 1980s and the African National Congress in South Africa.[28]
My use of the term 'struggle' suggests that I follow Gramsci's
conception of civil society. According to this conception, civil
society is regarded as an area that, for the most part, consolidates,
through its dominant institutions, the existing hegemonic arrangements, but which also contains sites or pockets, often within the
dominant institutions themselves, wherein these arrangements are
constantly renegotiated and contested. As Stuart Hall underlines,
when elaborating on Gramsci's conception of hegemony, 'periods
of settlement are unlikely to persist forever. There is nothing
automatic about them. They have to be actively constructed and
positively maintained.'[29]

The above concepts from Antonio Gramsci and Paulo Freire
will be developed further in this book, where they will be considered within the context of the overall view of social change that
can be gleaned from their large, and in Gramsci's case often fragmentary and scattered, corpus of writings. Both were engaged in
projects which, though different, were conceived of and carried
out within the context of an unmistakably left-wing politics of
social transformation and, therefore, an ongoing struggle against
systemic, structural and symbolic forms of oppression. Both regarded forms of adult education as having an important role to
play in such a struggle.

There is a clear convergence between, and an element of complementarity about, their thought, which I seek to demonstrate in
this work. In this regard, I ought to mention at the outset that
Gramsci exerted an influence on Freire's thought, Marcela Gajardo
having introduced him to the Sardinian's *Letteratura e Vita Nazionale*
(Literature and National Life) in 1968, when Freire was in exile in
Chile.[30] Freire has acknowledged Gramsci's influence on his thinking in various places, particularly in his reply to discussants at the
Institute of Education, University of London in the Autumn of
1993:

> I only read Gramsci when I was in exile. I read Gramsci and I discov-
> ered that I had been greatly influenced by Gramsci long before I had
> read him. It is fantastic when we discover that we had been influenced

by someone's thought without even being introduced to their intellectual production.[31]

Much earlier, Freire had stated that Gramsci influenced him profoundly 'with his keen insights into other cultures'.[32] The ideas of Antonio Gramsci figure prominently in his conversational books.[33] Furthermore, when discussing his formative years,[34] Freire mentions Gramsci, together with Fanon, Memmi and Vygotsky, as an important source of influence on him. One also ought to underline that Freire's work is very much part of the tradition of popular education in Latin America which 'draws primarily from alternative Humanist Marxist interpretations offered by individuals like Antonio Gramsci'.[35] One should also bear in mind the great reception Gramsci's work had in Latin America and its influence on the New Left there, a point stressed by Faundez in his book.[36]

Furthermore, Gramsci's concepts and formulations figure prominently within the political party of which Freire was a founding member: the Partido dos Trabalhadores (PT), the Workers' Party.[37] Both Gramsci and Freire express what can be regarded as complementary views, from which a synthesis can be established. My intention, in this book, is to move towards a synthesis of their insights concerning adult education. I feel that this synthesis can provide theoretical signposts for transformative adult education. However, the build-up towards this will be a gradual one. Before engaging with their ideas, it seems appropriate, at this early stage, to provide biographical sketches of the two figures in question.

Antonio Gramsci

Antonio Gramsci (1891–1937) originated from Sardinia, an impoverished island with a largely agrarian economy, a strong sense of identity (*Sardismo*), high levels of illiteracy and a widespread belief in superstition and magic. Giuseppe Fiori, quoting Antonio's brother Gennaro, indicates that their father's family 'was typical of the better-off southern class that supplies the state bureaucracy with its middle-rank officials'.[38] As for his mother's family, they are described as having been 'middling folk, quite nicely off by the standards of our villages'.[39]

Gramsci was disabled, having suffered from what would now be diagnosed as Potts Disease. In fact, he was never 'more than four and three quarters feet tall'.[40] The official family explanation of his disability was that it was caused by a fall from a maid's arms. This, however, has been widely interpreted as an attempt by the family to conceal the truth in an environment, characterised by superstition, where disabled people were assumed to be possessed by evil spirits.[41] The situation concerning disabled people was to have an effect on Gramsci's thinking with respect to Sardinia, the *mezzogiorno* and 'folklore'. The last mentioned was to be given pejorative connotations in his writings.

Because of his poor health, Gramsci, who spent his infancy enjoying nature and playing with the children of peasants and shepherds, started school rather late, at the age of seven-and-a-half.[42] When Gramsci was still young, his father was arrested and imprisoned on a charge of petty embezzlement. Gramsci consequently had to interrupt his schooling to enter the world of paid employment.[43] He eventually resumed his schooling, moving through the various *licei*. On 26 July 1910, he published his first article, in *l'Unione Sarda*.[44] Later, Gramsci was to win a scholarship, offered by the Collegio Carlo Alberto of Turin to poor students from the former Kingdom of Sardinia.[45] The scholarship enabled him to leave the agrarian environment of Sardinia and take up university degree studies in Italy's industrial heartland, Turin. His studies for a *laurea* at the University of Turin focused on a variety of subjects, including philosophy, literature, art criticism, philology and linguistics. He was a talented student, especially in philology, his area of specialisation, and linguistics.[46] The professors he came in contact with included Umberto Cosmo, Annibale Pastore,[47] Luigi Einaudi[48] and Pietro Toesca.[49]

Home of Fiat and the recipient of a large amount of immigrant labour from the South, Turin had a very militant working class, ever ready to take to the streets. Gramsci was to describe it as 'Italy's Petrograd'.[50] He soon became politically active within the ranks of the Italian Socialist Party (PSI). Abandoning his studies due to physical ailments and lack of funds, he devoted himself to revolutionary politics and engaged in the education of workers both as a journalist and as an adult educator. He wrote for *Il Grido del Popolo* and the Turin edition of *Avanti!* As an adult educator, he gave talks at worker education circles[51] and founded the *Club Vita Morale*. His writings included theatre reviews, focusing on performances of Shakespeare, Chekhov, Ibsen and Pirandello (he later wanted to develop an entire study on the Sicilian play-wright, claiming to have contributed to the popularisation of his theatre and to have written enough, between 1915 and 1920, to put together a volume of two hundred pages[52]). They also included polemical pieces, social and political commentary, and the 'Sotto la Mole' column in *Avanti!*[53] In 1917 Gramsci became editor of *Il Grido del Popolo* and on 1 May 1919 published, with Angelo Tasca, Umberto Terracini and Palmiro Togliatti, the first edition of *L'Ordine Nuovo*, initially a review of socialist culture, later to become a daily and then a fortnightly publication.[54]

Over the following year, the factory council movement came into being. It was conceived of by Gramsci as an educative agency promoting socialist relations of production which were to prefigure the socialist state.[55] This year saw a general strike staged by factory workers. Subsequent action included a workers' occupation of the Fiat factories, with Gramsci greatly involved in the movement promoting this insurgent activity.[56] In this particular action, the workers were isolated, with little support forthcoming from the rest of the country.[57] They finally had to give in, swayed by Giovanni Agnelli's promises of better conditions – promises which were not kept following the Fascist rise to power in subsequent years.[58] Vague promises of a new 'industrial co-partnership' by Prime Minister Giovanni Giolitti[59] and of legislation for 'workers' control' were made.[60]

Meanwhile, Gramsci had become an important figure in the communist faction of the PSI and subsequently a member of the central committee of the newly formed Communist Party of Italy (PCI), following the split from the PSI which occurred at the Seventeenth Congress of the Socialist Party in Livorno in January 1921.[61] That same month, Gramsci, together with Professor Zino Zini and others, founded the Institute of Proletarian Culture, a section of the Lunacharsky-led *Proletkult* in Moscow.[62] The Institute in Italy had a very short life (1921–22)[63] as did many of Gramsci's adult education initiatives, which one should therefore be careful not to romanticise. Gramsci had written on the idea of developing a proletarian cultural association, inspired in this regard not only by the *Proletkult* but also by the *Clarté* movement associated with Romain Rolland and Henri Barbusse.[64] The former had coined the phrase 'pessimism of the intellect, optimism of the will', which was reproduced in every copy of *L'Ordine Nuovo* and is often erroneously attributed to Gramsci himself.

In 1922, the Fascists came to power. Gramsci was in Moscow at the time. There he met Julia Schucht, whom he married and with whom he had two sons, one of whom, Giuliano, he was never to see. The Fascist rise to power led to a series of reprisals against communist leaders. Gramsci kept contact with the PCI from abroad, even proposing the title *L'Unità* for the party daily, which it still bears today. Gramsci returned to Italy on the eve of Giacomo Matteotti's assassination. There followed a period of intense activity on behalf of the party, including adult educational work. This involved the setting up of the party's correspondence school and the preparation and writing of study materials.[65] Gramsci was also involved, during this period, in the formulation of the famous *Tesi di Lione* (Lyon Theses), which laid out the policy to be followed by the PCI. He collaborated in this with Palmiro Togliatti.[66]

In 1926, Gramsci was arrested, despite his parliamentary immunity. He was imprisoned at the Regina Coeli in Rome, later sent to the island of Ustica, then brought back to the San Vittore prison in Milan; he was subsequently taken back to Regina Coeli for the trial of the leaders of the PCI and finally sent south to the Casa Penale di Turi. The mass trial, at which Gramsci was sentenced to twenty years', four months' and five days' imprisonment, took place between 28 May and 4 June 1928.[67] The prosecutor was to proclaim at this trial: 'For twenty years we must stop this brain from functioning.'[68] But his statement could not have been further off the mark.

Gramsci was exposed, both before and after his trial, to great physical and psychological suffering, including isolation, excruciating journeys from one prison to another, often from almost one end of the peninsula to the other (there was a frustrating long wait and a few false departures before crossing from Palermo to Ustica[69]), and the inhuman physical surroundings to which he was confined. Nevertheless, Gramsci still found the energy for organisational work, at least in the early stages of imprisonment. His adult education work had continued among the prisoners at Ustica where, together with Amadeo Bordiga and others, he helped set up a *scuola dei confinati* (school for prisoners). Help was also forthcoming from his long-time friend Piero Sraffa (Professor of Economics at the University of Cagliari, and later Cambridge University), who established, at a Milan bookshop, an open account for books to be forwarded to Gramsci.[70] The school had a well-developed programme consisting of various levels.[71] In a letter, following his departure from Ustica, Gramsci advocated that there should be three levels, the final level being more of a circle than a school, with participants preparing and giving talks (as *relatori*) on specific topics.[72] The overall programme included the teaching of different languages. Gramsci himself was both teacher and student at this school, teaching history and geography and enrolling in the German language course.[73] But Gramsci's activities as teacher and learner in this school did not last long since he was on the island for only a short period of time, from 7 December 1926 until 20 January 1927.[74]

Removed from the daily engagements of party politics, Gramsci availed himself of the solitude of incarceration to produce a corpus of very profound writing. This includes numerous letters, addressed to family members and friends, wherein he reflects on a variety of issues. Antonio Santucci lists the names of Gramsci's correspondents: Giuseppe Berti (political detainee at Ustica); Virginio Borioni (another political detainee at Ustica); Gramsci's younger brother, Carlo; his first son Delio (Delka); his second son, Giuliano (Julik); his elder sister, Grazietta; his other sister Teresina; his mother, Giuseppina (or Peppina); Clara Passarge (his landlady in Rome); his wife, Julia (Julca) Schucht; Julia's sister, Tatania (Tania) Schucht; Piero Sraffa.[75]

The most enduring part of Gramsci's work in prison, however, is his attempt to develop a large piece of work *für ewig* (for eternity), involving studies on a variety of topics. He tells Tania, in a letter dated 19 March 1927, that he has been tormented by this idea, a 'phenomenon' found among prisoners, in keeping with a complex conception of Goethe which greatly preoccupied Pascoli.[76] The fragmentary notes for this study were contained in notebooks; together, these constitute what is generally regarded as a masterpiece of twentieth-century political thought. Gramsci started working on the first notebook on 8 February 1929, having obtained permission to write in the cell.[77]

Gramsci's sentence was eventually reduced and, following recommendations by visiting doctors, he was allowed to be transferred to a clinic due to the precarious condition of his health. He was eventually released from prison in April 1937, in what was to be the last month of his life, which he spent at the Quisisana Clinic in Rome. He died in the early hours (4.10 a.m.) of 27 April after being stricken, two days earlier, by a cerebral haemorrhage.[78] He had been planning to request expatriation to the USSR to be reunited with his wife and children.[79] There were more security guards at his funeral than family members, of whom there were only two persons: his sister-in-law Tatania and his younger brother Carlo.[80]

Paulo Freire

Paulo Reglus Neves Freire (1921–1997)[81] is widely considered to have been one of the greatest thinkers on education this century.[82] His thinking on education, born out of practice in Brazil and a variety of countries and regions throughout the world, is expressed in a number of books, articles and video/audio tape-recordings, spanning a period of over thirty years. His work was primarily in the area of the education of adults, but he has written on education in general, including initial education and higher education.[83]

Freire was born in Recife in the state of Pernambuco, in the north-east of Brazil. It is one of the most impoverished regions in the country. Although born into a middle-class family, he experienced hunger as a result of the impact that the Great Depression of 1929 had on Brazil. He states that this experience of hunger made him 'connect' with the lives of those living in poor neighbourhoods in the city's outskirts.[84]

Freire lived in a region characterised by semi-feudal relations of production which *campesinos* (peasants) had to accept to gain access to land. The rural landowning class is engaged in a historical alliance with the national indigenous bourgeoisie located in the south-east, the São Paulo area.[85] The situation was one of stark contrast in access to material goods and power, in a country whose fortunes have been guided by colonial and neo-colonial interests.

The hunger which Freire had suffered hampered his progress at school, but he recovered the lost ground and eventually studied law. His career as a lawyer was shortlived.[86] In 1947, he started work in the Social Service of Industry (SESI) and remained there for ten years.[87] He was Director of the Division of Education and Culture[88] and was part of the first SESI education committee which its first president, Cid Sampaio, put together.[89] Here he established contact with poor children and their parents. This formative experience was to influence Freire's ideas on education and was to be strongly reflected in the doctoral dissertation in education, subsequently his first book, which he successfully defended in 1959 at what was then the University of Recife, later the Federal University of Pernambuco.[90]

Freire also worked in adult literacy within the context of the Popular Culture Movement. He established a connection between 'reading the word and the world', which became the distinctive feature of his pedagogical approach. He was very successful in this regard in an experiment which occurred in the town of Angicos in Rio Grande do Norte.[91] The populist government of João Goulart invited him to plan and carry out a similar project on a national scale. This project, however, was abruptly brought to an end by the multinationals-backed military coup of 1964.

Because of the success of his 'pedagogy of the oppressed', which was political also in the sense that it rendered people literate and therefore eligible to vote, Freire began to be regarded by the country's reactionary forces as a potential threat to the status quo. The post-1964 military regime, which worked in the interests of multinational companies and the landowning class thriving on a latifundium system, considered Freire a 'subversive'. He was immediately arrested and later forced into exile.

Freire moved to Bolivia for a brief stay and then went to Chile, where he was engaged in literacy work among *campesinos* as part of the agrarian reform programme initiated during the period of government led by the Christian Democrat, Eduardo Frei. Freire spent five years there working for UNESCO and the Chilean Institute for Agrarian Reform.[92] There he worked with a number of intellectuals, including his close collaborator Marcela Gajardo.[93]

From Chile, he moved to Mexico and then to the United States, and specifically to Massachusetts, where he lived, for the greater part of a year, in a relatively poor neighbourhood.[94] There he supervised the translation of two of his books, led independent seminars and taught at Harvard,[95] his appointment being at Harvard University's Center for Studies in Development and Social Change.[96] In Massachusetts, he established contact with a variety of intellectuals, including Jonathan Kozol, a close friend.[97]

Freire left the USA for Switzerland in January 1970,[98] where he worked for the World Council of Churches. As part of his work there, he served as consultant on education to the governments of such former Portuguese colonies in Africa as Guinea-Bissau, São Tomé e Príncipe, Cape Verde and Mozambique. In Geneva, he was involved in the establishment of the Institute of Cultural Action.[99]

Freire's thinking until then, as captured in his works, betrayed several influences. Hegel and Marx[100] are two very important sources of influence. Freire, however, draws on a broad range of writings, including the work of Leszek Kolakowski, Karel Kosik, Erich Fromm, Antonio Gramsci, Karl Mannheim, Pierre Furter, Teilhard de Chardin, Frantz Fanon, Albert Memmi, Lev Vygotski and Amilcar Cabral, and the Christian Personalism theory of Tristian de Atiade and Emanuel Mounier. Freire's work reveals two dominant strands: Marxism and Liberation Theology.

Freire, himself a 'man of faith',[101] was certainly influenced, in the genesis of his ideas, by the radical religious organisations which made their presence felt in Brazil in the late 1950s and early 1960s. There are strong similarities between his emancipatory views on education and the education document produced by the Latin American bishops at the 1968 Episcopal Conference in Medellín, Colombia, which represents a landmark in the development of Liberation Theology.[102]

After his return to Brazil following sixteen years of exile, he was actively engaged in political work on behalf of the Workers' Party (PT), of which he was a founding member. This was one of the three parties constituting Brazil's political left.[103] Freire acted as consultant for the literacy campaigns in Grenada and Nicaragua.[104]

In 1986, Freire became a widower, having suffered the loss of Elza, the schoolteacher from Recife whom he married in 1944, with whom he had three daughters and two sons and from whom he derived great inspiration.[105] Elza (her maiden name was Elza Maia Costa Oliveira) collaborated on several projects with her husband. In 1985, they were both awarded, by the Association of Christian Educators in the USA, the prize of outstanding Christian educators.[106] On 27 March 1988, Freire married Ana Maria (Nita) Araújo, an educationist in her own right and daughter of one of his former teachers.[107]

A year later, in 1989, Freire was appointed Secretary of Education in the PT municipal government of São Paulo during Luisa Erundina de Sousa's term of office as mayor. In this post, Freire carried out several reforms in the public sector, with respect to both schooling and adult education.[108] He was responsible for 654 schools comprising 700,000 students, as well as being engaged in a programme of adult education and literacy training (Mova SP)[109] which involved, as much as possible, mass organisations and other stakeholders in the educational enterprise.[110]

Following his retirement as Education Secretary in 1991, Freire remained active in a variety of ways, delivering keynote addresses at conferences, carrying out workshops and continuing to develop and articulate his ideas in a number of books and works. From the mid-1980s onwards, he had been co-authoring works and engaged in 'talking books' (dialogical books) with a number of writers and educators, including the radical adult educator Myles Horton[111] (founder of the Highlander Folk High School, Tennessee), the Brazilian Dominican friar and theologian, Frei Betto,[112] the exiled Chilean philosopher, Antonio Faundez,[113] and American critical pedagogue, Ira Shor.[114] There was also strong collaboration between Paulo Freire and the Massachusetts-based scholar Donaldo P. Macedo, originally from Cape Verde.[115] Freire's writing continued unabated. In 1996 he published, as letters to his niece, a series of reflections on his youth, childhood, exile and contemporary debate.[116] Other volumes were published in the final year of his life. In addition, a number of books have been or are planned to be published posthumously.[117]

Freire had been looking forward to a trip to Cuba in May 1997 to collect an award from Fidel Castro. In the early hours of 2 May, however, having been admitted to São Paulo's Albert Einstein Hospital because of heart problems, Paulo Freire breathed his last.

His widow, Ana Maria Araújo Freire, stated that his agenda for 1997 was all planned. He had started to write another book, and he planned to co-write three others, one on the 'deterministic fatalism of neoliberalism'.[118] He was to receive another six honorary degrees, from different countries, to add to the thirty-five he had already been awarded.[119] Shortly before his death, Paulo Freire is reported to have said: 'I could never think of education without love and that is why I think I am an educator, first of all because I feel love.'[120]

Existing Literature on Gramsci and Freire in Adult Education

The importance of these two theorist–activists for the development of a theory of transformative adult education has been highlighted by a number of writers in the field. Writers who have provided some of the most sustained accounts on radical adult education would dwell at considerable length on the work of at least one of these two figures and make passing references to and often insightful comments on the other.[121] The same can be said with respect to works dealing with educational or social theory in general, Paul Ransome's study on Gramsci and Raymond A. Morrow and Carlos Alberto Torres' chapter on the 'two Gramscis' being obvious examples.[122]

Literature on Gramsci and adult education

In 1997, conferences and seminars were held in Italy to commemorate the sixtieth anniversary of Gramsci's death, and his educational ideas were given due prominence in these events. There was an entire workshop on the theme of 'New Forms of Hegemony: Media, Education and Conformism', chaired by Luciana Castellina, at a conference on Gramsci held in Naples in October 1997. Meanwhile, an activity for schools, 'Gramsci and the Learning Society', was held in Rome in May, with the involvement of the Associazione Democratica degli Insegnanti (the Democratic Association of Teachers).[123]

There has, of course, been a burgeoning literature on Gramsci not only in Italy but in many parts of the world, as the compilation of essays edited by Eric Hobsbawm, *Gramsci in Europa e in America*, amply demonstrates.[124] Gramsci's impact on a variety of fields has been tremendous; and, as with Freire, publications focusing on his life and ideas continue to be produced. Complete volumes on Gramsci and education have been produced by Mario Alighiero Manacorda, Angelo Broccoli, Harold Entwistle, Timothy Ireland, Italia de Robbio Anziano and Atilio Monasta.[125] Manacorda has also edited an anthology of Gramsci's educational writings.[126] Most of these volumes analyse Gramsci's pedagogical ideas in their broader context and certainly beyond the context of schooling. Gramsci's work is often an important source of reference in English-language books that contribute to the radical debate on adult education.[127] The Torres and La Belle books deal with the impact of Gramsci on non-formal education in Latin America and the Caribbean.[128]

There are, however, works which deal at greater length with Gramsci's ideas and their relevance to adult education. One of the earliest articles in this respect is probably that by Tom Lovett, who dwells on community education among the working class in Northern Ireland.[129] Harold Entwistle made one of the first major contributions in the English language in his well-researched book *Antonio Gramsci: Conservative Schooling for Radical Politics*, which draws on a variety of primary and secondary Italian sources.[130] The chapter on adult education deals with Gramsci's writings on political education, the formation of intellectuals,[131] culture, the factory councils and technical and vocational education. The book aroused controversy for its interpretation of Gramsci's view of schooling – one that is, however, shared by others, notably the Brazilian philosopher Dermeval Saviani[132] and, among later writers on the issue, Guy B. Senese.[133] Timothy Ireland's monograph *Antonio Gramsci and Adult Education: Reflections on the Brazilian Experience* is, however, the first full-scale publication in English devoted exclusively to the relevance of Gramsci's ideas to adult education.[134] It deals specifically with his influence on popular education in Brazil.

Gramsci features not only in volumes entirely dedicated to his work but also in scholarly papers, which frequently appear in the adult education literature. Examples of such papers include those by W. John Morgan,[135] who provides, in the second of his two journal articles, a comparative piece involving Gramsci and Raymond Williams. Paul F. Armstrong[136] emphasises the importance of informal political education occurring at the workplace and the community, as does Diana Coben,[137] who highlights, among other things, the importance for Gramsci of political adult education in enabling learners to move from 'common sense' to 'good sense'. This is a key aspect of Gramsci's pedagogical views; as such, the chapter 'Political Education and Common Sense', in Walter Adamson's *Hegemony and Revolution*, that entitled 'Political Consciousness: Education and the Intellectuals', in Paul Ransome's *Antonio Gramsci*, and Federico Mancini's discussion paper on the Factory Councils are all important reading material for anyone interested in this aspect of Gramsci's contribution to adult education theory.[138] All three contributions will, of course, be referred to in the course of the discussion in this book.

Ursula Apitzsch, a sociologist from the Goethe University in Frankfurt, who has written extensively on Gramsci in German and Italian[139] and on migration and ethnicity, has published a paper in an adult education journal on Gramsci's views regarding migration and the South.[140] She regards Gramsci's views on this issue as very relevant to the current debate on multiculturalism. Meanwhile, Paula Allman and John Wallis are the joint authors of a lengthy paper focusing on the appropriation of Gramsci's ideas within the *New Times* project and the use that is made of his thought within radical and left-leaning educational practice in Britain.[141]

Literature on Freire and adult education[142]

The literature relating Freire specifically to adult education has been vast.[143] Of course, there are works on Freire which relate not only to adult education but to education and social commitment in general. Some appear as articles in journals or as introductions to Freire's books. One of the most memorable, in my view, is Henry Giroux's introduction to *The Politics of Education*, subsequently republished in one of Giroux's own books.[144] Giroux is one of the leading North American exponents of critical pedagogy, and has written perceptive pieces on Freire, including chapters in his own books. The most recent article focuses on Freire's relevance for a postcolonial politics.[145]

Freire's recent death has led to an increase in the number of publications throughout the world commemorating his work. The American journal of Culture and Education, *Taboo*, for instance, dedicated a substantial part of its Fall 1997 volume to tributes from various parts of the world. These tributes range from pieces focusing on Freire's contribution to educational thinking to others based on personal anecdote, including one by his second wife, Nita.[146] *Convergence*, the journal produced by the International Council for Adult Education (ICAE), has put together a special issue dedicated to the memory of Freire, one of the organisation's past honorary presidents and a distinguished contributor to the journal. Another collective work is a special issue of the *New Zealand Journal of Adult Learning*, put together by Brian Findsen and Peter Roberts, which contains a range of different perspectives on Freirean theory and practice.[147]

There have been and will continue to be fora devoted to Freire's work in a number of countries, the most notable being the one held in São Paulo, Brazil at the end of April 1998, organised by the Instituto Paulo Freire. Tributes to Freire were published in journals, annual Adult Education readers and national newspapers worldwide, including the *New York Times* and the *Guardian*. In my native Malta, for instance, all the Sunday newspapers carried features on Paulo Freire soon after his death.

It has to be said that publications and conferences celebrating Freire's ideas and evaluating their relevance to different fields and forms of social activism never ceased throughout the last twenty years or so. Freire himself produced a considerable output of published work, as will be evident from the references and quotations throughout this book. Some of this work has only just seen or has yet to see the light of day.[148] Furthermore, there are works that Freire wrote in either Portuguese or Spanish which are currently being translated into English. In addition to Freire's own work, which includes several articles published in a variety of journals, and ideas expressed on video and audio tape, the last seventeen years or so have witnessed a series of studies concerning the application of Freire's ideas in different contexts. This includes work edited by Ira Shor and a study focusing on the community adult learning project in Gorgie Dalry, Edinburgh, Scotland.[149] We have seen the publication of three comprehensive critical studies in English,[150] as well as a number of edited volumes. One of the best-known edited works is *Literacy and Revolution*, the collection put together in Australia by Robert Mackie.[151]

Arguably, the two books edited by Peter McLaren – *Paulo Freire: A Critical Encounter*, with Peter Leonard, and *Politics of Liberation: Paths from Freire*, with Colin Lankshear – are the most comprehensive and up-to-date edited volumes of papers in English on Freire. They include some memorable pieces from a variety of sources, revised and updated – most notably Peter McLaren's own review essay of Freire's *Politics of Education*, which appeared in *Educational Theory*, Kathleen Weiler's much-cited paper from the *Harvard Educational Review*, and Carlos Alberto Torres' piece from the University of Botswana publication *Education with Production*, extended to include a discussion on the reforms brought about by Paulo Freire as Education Secretary in São Paulo.[153] McLaren argues, in his paper, that Freire allows us a reprieve from the kind of nihilism and paralysing politics found in postmodernist thought, thus touching on one of the themes developed in the early part of this introduction. Weiler's paper, wherein she seeks to fuse Freire's ideas with those representing different strands within feminism, appears alongside others relating Freire's work to issues associated with social movements, notably the one by bell hooks in *Politics of Liberation*.[154] Weiler's paper on a specific form of oppression joins others in the same vein, including an excellent piece by Asgedet Stefanos on women in specific African contexts, notably Guinea-Bissau (an important context for some of Freire's writings) and her native Eritrea.[155] Many references to papers included in these two edited collections, as well as in those discussed earlier, will be made throughout this book.

Bringing Gramsci and Freire together

The literatures on both Freire and Gramsci are indeed burgeoning. There are those who refer, rather cynically, to the existence of a veritable 'industry' with respect to the work of each. Most of the studies in question, while focusing almost entirely on one of the two authors, make passing reference to the other since, as I shall attempt to demonstrate, the connections between the two are great.

And there exists a literature that seeks to bring the ideas of the two authors together. Marjorie Mayo's *Imagining Tomorrow* contains a chapter in which competing perspectives on adult education are discussed.[156] The market-led perspectives, dealt with at the outset of this introductory chapter, are contrasted with those focusing on adult education for social transformation. With respect to the latter perspective, she focuses at some length on the work of Gramsci, Freire and Ettore Gelpi.[157] Diana Coben has also written a book on the two writers.[158] This study had not been published when the present book went to press; nevertheless it appears, from personal communication I have had with the author, that her study provides an interesting contrast to the position taken in this book and in some of the literature cited in this subsection. In Coben's work, 'The linkage of Gramsci's and Freire's ideas in the adult education literature is considered and broadly rejected.'[159]

With respect to attempts to bring the ideas of Gramsci and Freire together, I would mention my own work and Paula Allman's chapter in the 1988 *Reader* edited by Tom Lovett.[160] Most recently, there has been the publication of a book by Margaret Ledwith advocating transformative action in the area of community development rooted in critical pedagogy, a work inspired, to a large extent, by the writings of Antonio Gramsci and Paulo Freire, to which an entire chapter is devoted.[161] Other works include those by Paul Ransome and Peter Leonard; these, however, do not deal specifically with adult education.[162]

In her chapter on education for socialism in Lovett's *Reader*, Allman draws on the ideas of Gramsci and Freire, alongside those of Ivan Illich, in the context of a sustained discussion on ideology. This is an issue that Allman and participants in the diploma course she coordinated at the University of Nottingham had to contend with as they sought signposts for a socialist approach to adult education. Allman sees adult education as part of the 'prefigurative work' which, as Gramsci insisted, has to precede every revolution.

The task Gramsci set himself, and consequently the task to be faced in a Gramsci-inspired process of adult education, involves a *dialectical* engagement with the 'material conditions present at the time of analysis, i.e. an insistence on conceptualizing the dialectic movement of material and social forces'.[163] This involves an analysis of the material expressions of ideology present in our relations and practices. Freire's dialogical process of *praxis* serves as a most appropriate pedagogical vehicle for this transformative learning to take place.

As this overview of the pertinent literature will have shown, Paula Allman has written extensively on both Gramsci and Freire, and developed courses at the University of Nottingham where the inspiration has been Gramscian–Freirean. Her work and writing in this regard has often been in tandem with her colleague John Wallis. Our views on Gramsci and Freire have converged. Together, we have provided a brief first attempt at drawing out the implications of the insights derived from Gramsci and Freire for socially committed adult education in an age characterised by the intensification of globalisation.[164]

My engagement in the project carried forward in this book started in Edmonton, Canada, in the autumn of 1986. As a graduate student at the University of Alberta, taking a class on the History of Sociological Thought, taught by Professor Raymond Allan Morrow, I worked on a term paper in which the ideas of these two figures were compared. The comparison followed a preliminary discussion centring around a selection from Marx, particularly his early writings. This preliminary attempt at comparing their ideas with respect to education eventually evolved into a Master's thesis with the focus being narrowed to adult education.

Years later, after having worked in adult education in my native Malta, I returned to this project, during my Ph.D. studies in sociology at the Ontario Institute for Studies in Education, Toronto. There, under Professor David W. Livingstone's supervision, I was encouraged to develop the comparative project further. The challenge was for me to work towards a synthesis of some of their ideas with a view to discovering signposts for transformative adult education. Much of the literature referred to in this subsection (Coben's book seems to be a notable exception) indicates the relevance of these two figures for a transformative project and stresses the convergence of their ideas in this regard. I feel that what is now required is a comprehensive book-length analysis of their work, incorporating an attempt to synthesise the

ideas gleaned from their writings, with due consideration given to
the limitations in their work for a contemporary project. It is this
sort of work that I attempted in Toronto. A substantial part of this
work constitutes the basis for this book. Most of my published
papers, dealing with this subject, derive from my Master's and
doctoral theses. Since they too provide the basis for this book,[165]
the arguments I develop in them need not be repeated at this
stage.

Many of the writers referred to above advocate a process of
adult education with a transformative edge, the approach that is
also being proposed in this book. What would such an approach
entail?

Transformative Adult Education

I would describe a theory of transformative adult education as
one which recognises the political nature of all educational interventions. It is also a theory which calls for socially transformative
adult educational initiatives that focus, in J.E. Thomas's words,
'upon change at the roots of systems'[166] and therefore not on the
symptoms of what are perceived as structurally determined forms
of oppression.

These considerations give rise to a series of questions which, to
my mind, should form the basis of an assessment of the potential
that an educationist's work can have for incorporation in a theory
of transformative adult education. It is my view that an alternative transformative pedagogical theory should be grounded in a
critique of mainstream educational systems. The question that
arises, therefore, is: does the work contain a 'language of critique'?[167] By a 'language of critique' I mean a process of analysis
which ties educational systems to systemic and structural forms of
domination in the wider society, without denying these systems a
'relative autonomy'. It also entails a form of dialectical engagement which exposes the contradictions that lie behind the veneer
created by the dominant, hegemonic discourse. This constitutes a
process of what Freire would regard as 'unveiling'. A related
question would be: in what way is the view of education posited
in the work different from conventional, mainstream ones? This

question calls for an assessment of the extent to which education is politicised in the work and, therefore, the extent to which the author/s concerned expose it as not being 'neutral', relating it to the dominant power interests and configurations in society.

The next stage would be to determine whether the work contains, to use another prominent Giroux phrase, a 'language of possibility', or, more comprehensively, whether it exists within the contours of what Roger I. Simon would regard as a 'project of possibility': 'an activity determined by both real and present conditions and certain conditions still to come'.[168] Does the work allow room for agency? And I would submit that, when dealing with the issue of agency in adult education, a 'critically conscious agency',[169] one should enquire: with whom does the agency lie? The question can, in my view, be answered in terms of an identification of the type of adult educator who can act as an agent of social transformation. Furthermore, are there particular subaltern groups, victims of oppressive social relations, with whom the agency for social transformation lies? This question leads one to explore the issues of class, gender, race, ethnicity and other forms of social differentiation.

The following questions are also pertinent. Are there larger agencies that can promote the cause of these subordinated groups most effectively? If so, does the work being examined recognise and draw out the implications for the role which radical adult education can play within the context of this larger agency? This brings us to issues of party and social movements, the latter increasingly being considered in the literature[170] as important agents of social change. One also notices the existence of a growing literature in the area of 'adult education and social movements'.[171]

In terms of transformative adult education, one would perforce have to determine in what ways the kind of pedagogy being proposed is different from that which prevails in contemporary society, and what the ramifications would be for such a change in pedagogical approach. Progressive adult education tends to lay special emphasis on process, on the nature of social relations taking place within the learning situation. How far along the democratic continuum are these social relations?

Then there is, in *Pedagogy of the Oppressed,* Freire's own dichotomy regarding what a progressive teacher does under conditions of dialogical education and what a traditional teacher does under conditions of 'banking education'. This immediately brings to the fore the issue of social relations. I also consider the issue of social relations to be an important one because this is an area in which power manifests itself. In my view, forms of power should not be reified, viewed as 'things', but should be regarded as complex sets of social relations. One can challenge the power structure by attempting to change some of the social relations that give rise to it. And educational initiatives, complemented by similar initiatives in other sites of social practice, can make an important contribution in this regard.

However, progressive teaching also has to contend with the issue of content: whose knowledge is considered legitimate and why? Which knowledge forms part of the 'cultural arbitrary' (Bourdieu) or, put simply, the cultural preferences of dominant groups? This, too, has become a feature of practice and theory inspired by democratic and critical pedagogical ideals. One of the central themes in the book is therefore the issue of 'cultural production'.

Furthermore, one can speak of a tradition in the adult education field, and, of course, other fields (e.g. critical pedagogy), according to which education is seen as a process which is not limited to schooling. It involves a variety of sites of pedagogical practice. There is a recognition that education should be viewed in its wider context, beyond the boundaries of formal institutions, and in its widest sense as a concept. There is also a recognition that processes of learning, whether in support of or against the existing power relations in society, take place in different instances and different settings throughout our life. This point will be stressed further when I discuss hegemony in the section on Gramsci. An effective strategy of counter-hegemonic adult education should therefore involve as wide a range of social practices as possible.

I attempt, in the expository chapters on Gramsci and Freire, to examine how far these theorists go in providing us with material concerning each of these three aspects of the pedagogical process – namely, social relations, sites of practice and content. I would argue that all three elements are interrelated in a process of radical adult education, and that it would perhaps be foolish to consider them separately. The interrelationship can best be explained with regard to Freire's concepts of 'banking education' and 'cultural invasion'. Banking education, characterised by hierarchical social relations of education, creates the conditions for cultural imposition (cultural invasion) to take place. Those being educated are denied the possibility of bringing their own culture to bear on the classroom proceedings. Their culture is not valorised; it is not engaged with in a manner which implies a recognition of its value; and it is not allowed to constitute an integral part of the general learning process taking place. However, although I recognize the important interrelation of these terms, in the interest of clarity they are presented separately in the exposition that follows.

Chapter 2 constitutes an updated exposition of Gramsci's ideas that are relevant to adult education, with reference to both primary and significant secondary material, including Italian sources. With Gramsci, one has to draw on an exceedingly large corpus of scattered and often cryptic pieces dealing with a wide range of issues. Some of the ideas relevant to adult education are implicit. Despite the fact that Gramsci was himself directly involved in different forms of adult education, his *oeuvre* reflects a commitment to a much larger project than simply radical, political adult education. And yet one can draw out further implications for transformative adult education practice from his large corpus of social theory. The cryptic nature of the writings often creates problems, since it leaves these writings open to a variety of interpretations. Showstack Sassoon argues, in a post-structuralist vein, that Gramsci 'produced an archetypal open text that the reader must recreate each time she or he reads it'[172] – a position, regarding the reading of texts, which Freire would no doubt have endorsed.[173]

Chapter 3 deals with Paulo Freire, and here the task of exposition will be somewhat easier. Unlike the Italian theorist, Freire 'speaks for himself' in so far as ideas relevant to adult education are concerned. In this chapter, I seek to provide an updated account of Freire's ideas, indicating their evolution over the years, and the different contexts from which they emerged.

Chapter 4 comprises a comparative analysis of the ideas expressed by Gramsci and Freire which are relevant to adult education. A complementarity thesis is posited in this chapter which provides the framework for a synthesis of their ideas. The comparison of their ideas, in terms of their differences, complementarity and convergences, is preceded by another comparison, one which deals with the specific contexts in which the two theorists operated.

The comparative analysis is followed by a short chapter (Chapter 5) in which the limitations of their ideas for a contemporary project of transformative adult education is underlined. Importance is attached to the issues of race, gender, sexuality and class relations (including relations between peasants and industrial working class) as well as to the issues of mobile global capital and of gaining access to and critically appropriating information technology.

Chapter 6 is an attempt at a synthesis project in which I shall draw on literature not only from Gramsci and Freire but also from within the areas of critical pedagogy, cultural studies, feminism/s, anti-racist education and, of course, adult education. This discussion is concluded in Chapter 7 by an attempt to identify some of the contexts in which the specific pedagogical approaches, advocated throughout this book, can be developed.

Notes

1. See the collection of essays on globalisation, adult education and training in Walters, 1997, the first volume in the Zed Books global adult education series. See, in particular, the essay by Korsgaard, 1997. Another recommended piece is Miles, 1998. As for the connection between globalisation and education in general, see, among others, Comeliau, 1997 and McGinn, 1996, 1997 and the rest of the 'Open File' in *Prospects*, vol. XXVII, no. 1, and the special issue of the *Alberta Journal of Educational Research*, vol. XLII, no. 2. See also Ross and Trachte, 1990 and Amin, 1997 for more general discussions on globalisation grounded in political economy.

2. I am indebted to Paula Allman for drawing my attention to this point as we worked on a joint SCUTREA paper – cf. Allman and Mayo, 1997.

3. Allman and Wallis, 1995a.

4. See Hoare and Nowell Smith, in Gramsci, 1971b: 280. Argument reproduced from Allman and Mayo, 1997: 8.

5. See Foley, 1994 with respect to the implications of such reorganisation for capitalism.

6. See Boron and Torres, 1996; Pannu, 1996; Mulenga, 1996; McGinn, 1996.

7. International guidelines for a market economy were introduced in Chile in 1975, with most of the influential members of the relevant ministry having been products of the University of Chicago and having been strongly infuenced by Milton Freidman – Quiroz Martín, 1997: 39.

8. Pannu, 1996.

9. Pannu, 1996; Boron and Torres, 1996; Mulenga, 1996. Text virtually reproduced from Allman and Mayo, 1997: 7.

10. Boron and Torres, 1996; Pannu, 1996; Mulenga, 1996; McGinn, 1996. Text virtually reproduced from Allman and Mayo, 1997: 6.

11. See, for example, Vanek, 1977; Ornelas, 1982; Tonkovic, 1985; Crane, 1987; Baldacchino, 1990; Zammit, 1995–96; Mayo, 1997b; Spencer, 1998a.

12. 'Adult Education and Active Democratic Citizenship' is the focus of a research network within the European Society for Research on the Education of Adults, henceforth ESREA. The network incorporates a variety of perspectives on active democratic citizenship.

13. Ledwith, 1997: 148.

14. See, for example, Westwood, 1991b; Usher and Edwards, 1994; Plumb, 1995; Usher, Bryant and Johnston, 1997; Briton, 1996; M.C. Clark, 1997; Edwards and Usher, 1997.

15. See Westwood, 1991b.

16. See McLaren, 1994.

17. Allman and Wallis, 1995a: 31. See also the discussion in Allman and Wallis, 1997: 118, 119.

18. See, for instance, Freire, 1998a: 14.

19. I borrowed this term from McLaren, 1995: 100.

20. Scatamburlo, 1997: 56.

21. See, for example, Fukuyama, 1992.

22. Freire, 1996: 84.

23. In Gadotti and Torres, 1997: 100.

24. Thompson, 1980: 26; cited in M. Mayo, 1995: 5.

25. Freire, 1972b.

26. In Torres, 1988: 273; the original source is Welton, 1987.

27. I have been inspired to address the concept of 'civil society' critically by an informal discussion I had at SCUTREA '97 with Angela Miles from the Ontario Institute for Studies in Education/University of Toronto. Joseph Buttigieg of Notre Dame University, Indiana, argued along the same lines in his presentation on the category of the subaltern in Gramsci's *Quaderni*, at the International Gramsci Conference held at Palazzo Serra di Cassano, Naples, in October 1997. See the discussion on 'civil society' by Korsgaard (1997).

28. Korsgaard, 1997: 22.

29. Hall, 1996: 424.

30. Morrow and Torres, 1995: 457. In the 1950s and 1960s, Hector

Agosti and others published, in Argentina, translations of Gramsci's prison writings, with José Aricó producing *Literatura y vida nacional* in 1961 – Fernández Díaz, 1995: 143.

31. Freire, 1995: 63, 64. I am indebted to M. Mayo (1997) for drawing my attention to this point.

32. Freire, 1985: 182.

33. Cf. Freire and Faundez, 1989; Horton and Freire, 1990.

34. Horton and Freire, 1990: 36.

35. La Belle, 1986: 47.

36. Freire and Faundez, 1989.

37. See Coutinho, 1995: 135.

38. Fiori, 1970: 10.

39. Fiori, 1970: 10.

40. Germino, 1990: 1; Lepre, 1998: 4.

41. Germino, 1990: 1; Lepre, 1998: 4.

42. De Robbio Anziano, 1987: 10.

43. Fiori, 1970: 15, 25; Lepre, 1998: 7.

44. Santucci, in Gramsci, 1996: xxxii.

45. De Robbio Anziano, 1987: 12; Lepre, 1998: 11.

46. Hoare and Nowell Smith, in Gramsci, 1971b: xx.

47. Hoare and Nowell Smith, in Gramsci, 1971b: xxi.

48. Buttigieg, 1992: 67.

49. Buttigieg, 1992: 67; Caprioglio, in Gramsci, 1976: 21.

50. Adamson, 1980: 50.

51. Buttigieg, 1992: 68.

52. Gramsci, 1996: 56.

53. Buttigieg, 1992: 68.

54. Santucci, in Gramsci, 1996: xxxiv, xxxv.

55. Gramsci, 1977: 65, 66.

56. Buttigieg, 1992: 74.

57. See, for instance, Lawner, 1973: 28; Hoare, in Gramsci, 1977: x; Adamson, 1980: 60; Ransome, 1992: 85, 86; Germino, 1990: 112.

58. See entry on Fiat in Encarta '98.

59. Ransome, 1992: 86.

60. Germino, 1990: 108.

61. See Buttigieg, 1992: 75.

62. Manacorda, 1970: 38; Buttigieg, 1992: 75.

63. Caprioglio, in Gramsci, 1976: 216.

64. Broccoli, 1972: 49.

65. Buttigieg, 1992: 83.

66. Santucci, in Gramsci, 1996: xxxv.

67. Spriano, 1979: 49.

68. Hoare and Nowell Smith, in Gramsci, 1971b: lxxxix; De Robbio Anziano, 1987: 13; Buttigieg, 1992: 88.

69. See letter to Piero Sraffa, 2 January 1927, in Gramsci, 1996: 28, 29.

70. Buttigieg, 1992: 86.

71. Gramsci, 1996: 27; Manacorda, 1970: 69.

72. See Gramsci's letter to Giuseppe Berti of 4 July 1927, in Gramsci, 1996: 95.

73. Gramsci, 1996: 30; Manacorda, 1970: 70.

74. Santucci, in Gramsci, 1996: xxxvi.

75. Santucci, in Gramsci, 1996: xxxix–xli.

76. Gramsci, 1996: 55. The reference here is to Pascoli's *Per Sempre* (Forever) contained in his *Canti del castelvecchio* – Santucci, in Gramsci, 1996: 58.

77. Santucci, in Gramsci, 1996: xxxvi.

78. Spriano, 1979: 115, 116.

79. Spriano, 1979: 108.

80. Buttigieg, 1992: 1.

81. This biographical sketch draws from Mayo, 1997a.

82. For good biographical accounts, see Taylor, 1993; Gerhardt, 1993.

83. See Escobar et al., 1994.

84. Freire, 1996: 21.

85. Ireland, 1987: 12.

86. Freire, 1994: 15, 16.

87. Freire, 1996: 81; see also Freire, 1994.

88. See Gadotti, 1994: 5–7.

89. Freire, 1996: 81.

90. Freire, 1994: 16, 17; Freire, 1996: 87.

91. Gadotti, 1994: 15.

92. Shaull, 1970: 12.

93. Freire, 1994: 51.

94. Kozol, 1997: 176, 177.

95. Kozol, 1997: 176, 177.

96. McLaren, 1997: 34.

97. Kozol, 1997: 177. Kozol wrote the Foreword to Freire, 1978.

98. Kozol, 1997: 177.

99. McLaren, 1997: 34.

100. See Torres, 1994a on Hegel's influence on Freire and, for instance, the numerous articles by Allman (see list of references) on the Marxian influence on Freire's thinking.

101. He stated this in a forum, featuring also Augusto Boal and Peter McLaren, at the Pedagogy of the Oppressed Conference held at the University of Nebraska, Omaha in March 1996.

102. See Retamal, 1981; Elias, 1994; Cooper, 1995; Lange-Christensen, 1996.

103. Da Silva and McLaren, 1993: 38.

104. R.M. Torres, 1986; Jules, 1993; Arnove, 1986; Carnoy and Torres,

1987.

105. Adaptation from Denis Collins's *Paulo Freire: His Life, Works and Thought*, Internet entry on Paulo Freire. See Collins, 1977.

106. Gadotti and Torres, 1997: 98.

107. Araújo Freire, 1997: 6.

108. Regarding this experience, see Freire, 1991, 1993; Torres, 1993, 1994b; O'Cadiz et al., 1997.

109. Gadotti and Torres, 1997: 98.

110. Freire, 1991, 1993; Torres, 1993, 1994b.

111. Horton and Freire, 1990.

112. Freire and Betto, 1985.

113. Freire and Faundez, 1989.

114. Shor and Freire, 1987.

115. Macedo has translated several works by Freire, was one of the translators of Freire, 1998, co-edited Freire et al., 1997 and co-authored books and pieces with Freire – Freire and Macedo, 1987, 1993, 1995, 1998.

116. Freire, 1996.

117. Freire and Macedo, 1998; Freire et al., 1997; Freire, 1998a, 1998b.

118. Araújo Freire, 1997: 10.

119. Araújo Freire, 1997: 10.

120. In McLaren, 1997: 38.

121. See, for example, Youngman, 1986; Torres, 1990a.

122. Ransome, 1992; Morrow and Torres, 1995.

123. I am indebted to Giorgio Baratta for this information, personal communication, 15 August 1997.

124. The volume focuses on the reception of Gramsci in France, Spain, Britain, Russia, the United States, Brazil and the rest of Latin America. Hobsbawm, 1995.

125. Manacorda, 1970; Broccoli, 1972; Entwistle, 1979; Ireland, 1987; De Robbio Anziano, 1987; Monasta, 1993a. The last mentioned is also the author of a piece on Gramsci in English – see Monasta, 1993b.

126. Gramsci, 1972.

127. See Thompson, 1983; Youngman, 1986; La Belle, 1986; Torres, 1990a; Green, 1990; M. Mayo, 1995, 1997. Most of the present discussion on Gramsci in the English-language adult education literature derives from an article on the subject published in the *International Gramsci Society Newsletter* – Mayo, 1995b.

128. Gramsci's influence in Latin America is very strong. For informative and perceptive accounts of the reception of Gramsci's work in Latin America, see Aricó, 1988; Fernández Díaz, 1995; Coutinho, 1995 and Melis, 1995. So far as literature on education is concerned, a major source in English is Morrow and Torres, 1995.

129. Lovett, 1978. The source for this information is Jackson, 1981: 81.

130. Entwistle, 1979.

131. On this issue and its relevance to adult education, see Hommen, 1986.

132. See Da Silva and McLaren, 1993.

133. Senese, 1991. Entwistle's interpretation of Gramsci led to a number of reactions in education journals, note especially those expressed by Henry Giroux, Douglas Holly and Quintin Hoare in a review symposium, centring around the book, published in a 1980 issue of the *British Journal of Sociology of Education*: 307–25. It also led to reactions in the literature on adult education, notably a couple of articles in the widely circulated *Convergence* – see Alden, 1981; Jackson, 1981.

134. Ireland, 1987.

135. Morgan, 1987, 1996.

136. Armstrong, 1988.

137. Coben, 1994, 1995.

138. Adamson, 1980; Ransome, 1992; Mancini, 1973.

139. Apitzsch, 1995.

140. Apitzsch, 1993.

141. Allman and Wallis, 1995b.

142. This section draws considerably on Mayo, 1997c.

143. See, for instance, Grabowski, 1972; Lloyd, 1972; Haviland, 1973; Kekkonen, 1977; Kidd and Kumar, 1981; Youngman, 1986; Jarvis, 1987a; Allman, 1988, 1994, 1996; Cunningham, 1992; Kirkwood and Kirkwood, 1989; Moriarty, 1989; Taylor, 1993; Mayo, 1993a, 1995c, 1997a; Allman and Wallis, 1997.

144. Giroux, 1988.

145. Giroux, 1988; 1996.

146. Steinberg, Kincheloe and Hausbeck, 1997.

147. Peter Roberts – personal communication.

148. See, for instance, Freire and Macedo, 1998; Freire et al., 1997; Freire, 1998.

149. Shor, 1987; Kirkwood and Kirkwood, 1989.

150. Taylor, 1993; Elias, 1994; Gadotti, 1994.

151. Mackie, 1980.

152. McLaren, 1986; Torres, 1982; Weiler, 1991.

153. See also on this subject, Torres, 1994b; O'Cadiz, Wong and Torres, 1997.

154. hooks, 1993.

155. Stefanos, 1997.

156. M. Mayo, 1997.

157. Ettore Gelpi, the former head of UNESCO's Lifelong Education Unit, provides formulations on the concept of Lifelong Education which demonstrate an awareness of the structural constraints that influence our life chances and the educational choices we make. Such writing stands in contrast to the more uncritical accounts of Lifelong Learning underpinned

by the neo-liberal, market-driven ideology, which Murphy, 1997 so cogently critiques with respect to the EU's policy in this regard.

158. Coben, 1998.

159. Publishers' blurb in Coben, 1998, conveyed to me by the author prior to the book's publication.

160. Allman, 1988.

161. Ledwith, 1997.

162. Ransome, 1992; Leonard, 1993.

163. Allman, 1988: 105.

164. Allman and Mayo, 1997.

165. Mayo, 1994a; 1994b; 1994c; 1996.

166. Thomas, 1991: 11.

167. Giroux, 1985: xiv.

168. Simon, 1992: 162.

169. Allman, 1988: 95.

170. Bocock, 1986: 12, 13; Sklair, 1995.

171. Lovett, 1988; Finger, 1989; Arvidson, 1993; Welton, 1993; Miles, 1989, 1997, 1998.

172. The article in question, 'Gramsci's Subversion of the Language of Politics', was published in *Rethinking Marxism* 3, Spring 1990, pp. 14–25. This information is derived from Diskin, 1993.

173. Freire has argued that the act of reading a text involves a rewriting of that text in the reader's mind. I personally heard him forcefully make a statement to this effect during the forum with Augusto Boal and Peter McLaren at the 'Pedagogy of the Oppressed' conference in Omaha, Nebraska on 23 March 1996.

CHAPTER 2

Antonio Gramsci and Adult Education

Antonio Gramsci sought, in his scattered writings, often written under adverse circumstances, to formulate a revolutionary strategy for social transformation in Western Europe.[1] In terms of affiliation, Gramsci was first a socialist and eventually a communist militant whose ultimate goal was proletarian revolution. His political project was, therefore, comprehensive, extending far beyond the analysis and discussion of educational issues. However, one may argue that education, in its wider context and conception, played an important role in his overall strategy for social transformation. It is accorded an important role in his particular formulation of the concept of hegemony, which he borrowed from Lenin.[2]

The Contested Terrain: Hegemony and Education

Hegemony has been defined, in the strictly Gramscian sense, 'as a social condition in which all aspects of social reality are dominated by or supportive of a single class'.[3] I go along with this definition. However, since my concerns, with respect to exploring possibilities for a theory of radical adult education, extend beyond class, I would substitute the phrase 'dominant groups' for 'a single class.' I do this to stress the multiple facets of power (not necessarily unrelated) in a given society.

These aspects of social life are generated among and made acceptable to people through the exercise of influence and the

winning of consent.[4] This involves a process of 'learning'. For
Gramsci, every relationship of hegemony is essentially an educational relationship.[5] The agencies that, in his view, engage in this
educational relationship are the institutions forming civil society,
which constitute the cultural bedrock of power. These are ideological social institutions such as law, education, mass media,
religion and so forth. Gramsci argues that, in Western society, the
state is surrounded and propped up by a network of these institutions, which are conceived of as 'a powerful system of fortresses
and earthworks' that makes its presence felt whenever the state
'trembles'.[6] As such, social institutions such as schools and other
educational establishments are not 'neutral'; rather, they serve to
cement the existing hegemony, and are therefore intimately tied
to the interests of the most powerful social groups, especially the
bourgeoisie.

Implicit throughout Gramsci's writings on the state and civil
society is a critique of educational establishments. Contained in
these writings are elements of an analysis of the politics of education in the Western capitalist social formation. Education is
perceived as playing an important role in cementing the existing
hegemony. It is crucial in securing consent for the ruling way of
life, one which is supportive of and supported by the prevailing
mode of production. Compulsory initial learning, mandated by
the capitalist Italian state, during the years of Fascist rule, is
problematised by Gramsci in his critique of the *Riforma Gentile* and
the kind of streaming it was intended to bring about. His critique
of the Fascist regime's proposed separation between 'classical' and
'vocational' schools strikes me as being well within the radical
tradition of opposing any kind of differentiation on the basis of
'merit', on the grounds that the whole process, in effect, is one of
selection made on the basis of class. He argued for the provision
of a broad education, with a strong humanistic basis, for all
children. It had to be an education which would not jeopardise a
child's future as a result of early and narrow professional specialisation.[7] Gramsci insisted that professional schools should not be
'incubators' of 'small monsters' narrowly instructed for a specific
occupation, lacking in 'general ideas', a 'general culture' and 'a
soul', while being in possession only of an 'infallible eye' and a
'firm hand'.[8] These concerns, regarding narrow vocational spe-

cialisation at an early age, anticipate much of the contemporary criticism of the 'new vocationalism'.

Agency

Gramsci's writings are imbued with the 'language of critique'. Is there a 'language of possibility'? I would submit that such a language makes its presence felt throughout Gramsci's work. Gramsci was no economic determinist. Indeed, his work is generally regarded as having marked a decisive break with the official Marxism of the time.[9] He rejected the views regarding social change which emerged from the Second International – views one associates with such key figures as Plekhanov, Bukharin, Kautsky and the Italian Achille Loria.[10] Gramsci's ideas in this respect also contrasted with the positive-determinist views of social change espoused by several Italian trade unionists and socialists at the time. These people advocated a policy of reformism, which Gramsci rejected.[11] He likened the fatalism that such views generated to a 'theory of grace and predestination'.[12]

Gramsci was aware of the limitations of certain aspects of Marxist thought. For him, these limitations characterise the early phase that any process of intellectual reform must go through before it can be elaborated into a 'superior culture'. This, after all, had applied to the Lutheran reform and Calvinism which first gave rise to a *popular culture* and only much later developed a *superior culture*.[13] In contrast to those Marxists whose works are characterised by evolutionary economic determinism, Gramsci's writings, including his early work, convey a strong sense of *agency*. In an early article, entitled *La Rivoluzione Contro il Capitale* (The Revolution against *Das Kapital*), Gramsci argued that the Bolshevik Revolution proved Karl Marx wrong:[14]

> But events have overcome ideologies. Events have exploded the critical schemas determining how the history of Russia would unfold according to the canons of historical materialism. The Bolsheviks reject Karl Marx, and their explicit actions and conquests bear witness that the canons of historical materialism are not so rigid as one might have thought and has been believed.[15]

Angelo Broccoli[16] argues that one of the reasons why the young Gramsci was attracted to the works of Benedetto Croce was simply because the Neapolitan philosopher affirmed human values in the face of the sense of acquiescence and passivity conveyed by positivism and which Gramsci associated with the mechanistic and deterministic theories of the Second International and of such people as Plekhanov. 'For Croce, man was the unique protagonist of history. His thought stimulates action – concrete "ethical-political" action – which is the creation of new history.'[17]

This sense of agency can be discovered in Gramsci's theoretical formulations concerning hegemony and the state. For Gramsci, hegemony is characterised by a number of features: it has a non-static nature (it is constantly open to negotiation and renegotiation, and therefore to being renewed and re-created); it is incomplete, selective;[18] and there exist moments wherein the whole process undergoes a crisis.[19] This indicates that there can be room for counter-hegemonic activity, which can be very effective at highly determinate moments. There are also excluded areas of social life that can constitute a terrain of contestation for people involved in such counter-hegemonic activities.

War of position

For Gramsci, the terrain wherein hegemony can be contested is the very terrain that supports it, namely that of civil society, which is conceived of as a site of struggle. He argued that, because it is propped up by the institutions of civil society, the state cannot be confronted head-on by those aspiring to transform it in order to develop a new set of social relations. Gramsci refers to that kind of confrontation as a 'war of manoeuvre'. The process of transforming the state and its coercive apparatus must, in Gramsci's view, precede, rather than follow, the seizure of power.[20] People working for social transformation – in this case, the proletariat seeking to transform the bourgeois state – had to engage in a 'war of position', a process of wide-ranging social organisation and cultural influence. It is through this process that the group creates, together with other groups and sectors of society, a *historical bloc*, the term Gramsci uses to describe the complex manner in which classes or their factions are related.[21]

[E]very revolution has been preceded by an intense labour of criticism, by the diffusion of culture and the spread of ideas among masses of men who are at first resistant and think only of solving their own immediate economic and political problems for themselves who have no ties of solidarity with others in the same condition.[22]

The primacy of cultural activity for the revolutionary process is therefore affirmed by Gramsci, an idea which reflects the influence of a number of people, notably Angelo Tasca, a syndicalist of Turin[23] and one of Gramsci's socialist friends who had emphasised the importance of cultural activity for the working class in a speech delivered at the Socialist Youth Congress in Bologna in 1912.[24] Gramsci wrote, in *Il Grido Del Popolo*:

Socialism is organization, and not only political and economic organization, but also, especially, organization of knowledge and of will, obtained through cultural activity.[25]

As a crucial area of civil society, adult education can play an important role in this 'war of position', entailing wide-ranging counter-hegemonic cultural activity.[26] Indeed, there is historical evidence to show that it has played such a role in a pre-revolutionary context, albeit one which, according to Gramsci's distinction between 'war of manoeuvre' and 'war of position', should have lent itself more to the former than the latter strategy. Accounts of the Nicaraguan revolution[27] indicate how popular education, carried out by, among others, Catholic priests belonging to the 'liberation wing' of the Church, helped create the climate for revolution prior to the Sandinista seizure of power in 1979.

Industrial democracy and the new state

In the revolutionary climate that prevailed in Turin prior to the Fascist takeover, Gramsci's *Ordine Nuovo* group directed a lot of its energies towards the factory council movement, which was, in effect, conceived of as an adult education movement through which workers were 'educated' as producers rather than simply as 'wage earners'[28] and initiated into the process of industrial democracy. The factory council was conceived of as a 'politically educative institution',[29] the means whereby the workplace would be converted into a veritable 'school of labour', to use the term[30] borrowed from Marx. For Gramsci, the factory councils were intended to provide the means whereby the proletariat could 'educate itself, gather experience and acquire a responsible awareness of the duties incumbent upon classes that hold the power of the state.'[31] This was to constitute an important step for the working class in the direction of 'exercising leadership before winning Government power'.[32] This movement brought Turin close to a revolution, the main reason for its ultimate failure being that its activity was not carried out in the context of the kind of alliance which was later called for by Gramsci through his elaboration of the Sorelian concept of the 'historical bloc'. Gramsci noted, in retrospect, that the insurgents in Turin were isolated.[33]

While on the issue of agency, it would be pertinent at this stage to determine who, in Gramsci's view, are the agents of social change. With respect to adult education, the issue can be discussed by identifying those who would be the adult educators and whether there exists a potential target learning group with whom the responsibility for agency lies. In Gramsci's view, the agents who play a pivotal role in this 'war of position' are the intellectuals.

Intellectuals

Intellectuals can be of two types. First, there are the 'great' intellectuals, such as those who helped 'prevent the splits in the Agrarian bloc' in the South from 'becoming too dangerous and causing a landslide'.[34] This bloc constitutes the means whereby 'the southern peasant is tied to the big property-owner' and 'acts as an intermediary and overseer for northern capital and the big banks'; its sole purpose being 'to preserve the *status quo*'.[35] These 'great intellectuals' include Gramsci's mentor, Benedetto Croce, who helped fashion the cultural climate of the age, a climate commensurate with the hegemonic group's interests.[36] One other important intellectual of this type was Giustino Fortunato. According to Gramsci, Croce and Fortunato 'can be regarded as the most industrious reactionaries of the peninsula'.[37] The second type are the subaltern intellectuals, such as teachers, priests (Gramsci outlines major differences between Northern and Southern priests and in the degree of 'moral correctness' they exhibit[38]) or functionaries, who, by and large, work in favour of the prevailing political system.[39]

Gramsci suggests a new way of looking at intellectuals. He writes of 'organic intellectuals': cultural or educational workers who are experts in legitimation. They emerge 'in response to particular historical developments', as opposed to 'traditional intellectuals' whose 'organic' purpose is over as society enters a different stage of development.[40] With regard to organic intellectuals, Gramsci writes:

> Every social class, coming into existence on the original basis of an essential function in the world of economic production, creates with itself, organically, one or more groups of intellectuals who give it homogeneity and consciousness of its function not only in the economic field but in the social and political field as well: the capitalist *entrepreneur* creates with himself the industrial technician, the political economist, the organiser of a new culture, of a new law, etc.[41]

Regarding traditional intellectuals, Gramsci writes:

> But every 'essential' social class emerging into history from the preceding economic structure, and as an expression of one of the developments of this structure, has found, at least in all history up till now, intellectual categories which were preexisting and which, moreover, appeared as representatives of an historical continuity uninterrupted even by the most complicated and radical changes in social and political forms.[42]

In Edward Said's words, 'organic intellectuals are actively involved in society, that is, they constantly struggle to change minds and expand markets.'[43] The organic intellectuals can, if they are organic to the dominant class/group (e.g. managers), serve to mediate the ideological and political unity of the existing hegemony.[44] Alternatively, if they are organic to the subordinated group or class aspiring to power, they engage in the war of position that enables it to secure the alliance(s) necessary to succeed. If they are organic to a subaltern group, part of the task is to contribute to an 'intellectual and moral reform',[45] which Gramsci felt was necessary in his native Italy to lay the foundations for a socially more just society. The reform for which Gramsci yearned in Italy was one that would have the sort of impact on the peninsula that the Protestant reform had had on Northern Europe.[46] It had to be a reform which involved the masses, with its roots firmly embedded in popular consciousness. It therefore had to be different, for example, from the kind of reform brought about by Crocean idealism, a reform which did not affect large masses and disintegrated as soon as the first counter-offensive was mounted.[47] Organic intellectuals committed to the subaltern had to help bring about such a reform. They had to form a vital component of the 'Modern Prince', that collective structure, 'organism' or 'mass party' which would enable them to become 'qualified' (well formed) political intellectuals or *dirigenti* (those who provide direction).[48]

Adult educators engaging in counter-hegemonic cultural activity are, according to the Gramscian conception, to be understood as intellectuals organic to the 'subaltern' groups aspiring to power. This implies that they should be politically committed to those they teach. Unless this is the case, there can be no effective learning. One of the reasons why Gramsci did not believe that the Italian 'popular universities' – institutions similar to those of the WEA (Workers' Education Association) in the UK[49] – operated in the interest of the proletariat was that the intellectuals involved were not organic and therefore committed to this class.[50] The popular universities were regarded as typical reformist and philanthropic institutions where the dissemination of culture among the masses was not carried out within the context of an attempt to transform their social and cultural conditions.[51] Furthermore, he also questioned the approach to learning adopted by the teachers, who failed to connect with the learners' background and framework of relevance. Gramsci stated that 'more care is taken to impress than to teach effectively'.[52] For this latter purpose, Gramsci argued that it is imperative for the working class, to whose cause he was committed, to produce its own intellectuals or else assimilate traditional intellectuals, the process of assimilation being a crucial aspect of the 'war of position' itself. It is most likely that a social group's endeavours, in this regard, would be characterised by a combination of both processes.

The industrial working class and peasants

As for the issue of whether there exists in Gramsci a social category with whom the responsibility for agency lies, one can argue that, despite his first-hand knowledge of the peasant-dominated South, it was to the industrial proletariat, located in Turin, that he turned for revolutionary potential. Although he attempted to deal, in some depth, with the *Southern Question*[53] and advocated a historical bloc characterised by a 'national-popular' alliance between the proletariat and the peasantry, he ascribed to the former the role of leadership (*direzione*) in the alliance:

> we favoured a very realistic and not at all 'magic' formula of the land for the peasants; but we wanted it to be realised inside the framework of the general revolutionary action of the two allied classes *under the leadership* of the industrial proletariat [emphasis added].[54]

Gramsci's view can easily be regarded, by such writers as Laclau and Mouffe, as an essentialist[55] one, hardly removed from the classical Marxist tradition of ascribing agency to the proletariat, hailed as the 'universal class' with a historic mission to accomplish. This is not to say that he did not ascribe agency to other groups or movements. Indeed, it has been pointed out that Gramsci attached importance to national liberation movements as active agents in history.[56] However, most of Gramsci's writings that are relevant to adult education focus on the educational needs of the industrial working class. The issue of adult literacy, an important concern for anyone dealing with adult education in the Southern Italian regions, where illiteracy was widespread, is paid only lip service in Gramsci's writings. A very short piece on adult literacy, explaining the causes of peasant-class resistance to compulsory education, is, to my knowledge, the only piece on the issue.[57] In short, there is an identification in Gramsci's writings of a specific adult education clientele; this can be explained by the fact that these writings are the product of his first-hand experience as activist, organiser and adult educator. These experiences were confined to the city of Turin. He wrote specifically about the area in which he was directly involved.

A discussion on the issue of agency in Gramsci's writings would be incomplete without reference to the fact that he conceived of his proposed revolutionary and educational activities within the framework of a movement or alliance of movements. These movements constitute the larger agency in relation to which socially transformative activities would be carried out. Arguably, the greatest period of revolutionary ferment in Gramsci's life was that of the factory council movement.[58] What we discover is that, during this period, cultural action is carried out within the context of a movement coordinated by the *Ordine Nuovo* group. This appears to suggest that a 'war of position' would have a good chance of success if carried out within a movement. The inference that one draws from Gramsci's factory council experience is that this must be a movement which, unlike the one in Turin, should be broad enough to extend its activities into various spheres of social life and beyond the locality in question. Gramsci's bitter final experiences with the Turin factory council movement,[59] as well as subsequent writings that address the need for the creation of a historical bloc, appear to point to this. *L'Unità*, the name of the PCI (now the PDS) daily chosen by Gramsci (who is also recognised as the paper's founder[60]), conveys the idea of an alliance – a unity of all the popular forces in a new historical bloc, achieved through the acquisition of a large consensus.[61]

Sites of Practice, Social Relations and Content

What type of adult educational activity does Gramsci propose? I shall discuss this issue from the standpoints of sites of practice, social relations and content.

Sites of practice

In keeping with the idea of a 'war of position' – that is to say, a cultural offensive on all fronts – Gramsci's writings convey the idea that different sites of social practice can be transformed into sites of adult learning. In point of fact, his scattered writings reflect a lifelong effort to engage in counter-hegemonic activities in all spheres of social life. Gramsci comes across in these writings as an indefatigable organiser and educator who would leave no space unexplored to educate members of the 'subaltern' classes. The routes are many, including circles, clubs and associations directly linked to the political organisations of the working class, namely unions and parties.[62] The area of industrial production becomes an important site of learning. These workplace educational experiences are to be sustained, according to Gramsci, by cultural centres or circles. The *Club Vita Morale*, which he helped organise in 1917 and wherein workers read books and gave presentations to each other,[63] was one such centre. Another centre was the short-lived Institute of Proletarian Culture, which, as indicated in Chapter 1, was inspired by ideals similar to those of the Russian *Proletkult*[64] and Rolland and Barbusse's[65] group revolving around *Clarté*. Barbusse had in fact delivered a lecture on the movement at Turin's *Casa del Popolo* in December 1920.[66]

Some of Gramsci's writings reveal a yearning, on his part, for the creation of a cultural association for workers, one which creates space wherein workers can debate all that is of interest to the working-class movement. Gramsci wrote that such an institution 'must have class aims and limits. It must be a proletarian institution seeking definite goals.'[67] He also felt that such an association would cater for the need to integrate political and economic activity with an organ of cultural activity, so that 'the proletarian movement will gain in compactness and in energy for conquest'.[68] Gramsci may have been inspired, in this respect, by the writings of Anatoli Lunacarskij, who had an article on the issue translated into Italian and published in *Il Grido del Popolo*, a periodical for which Gramsci wrote. Lunacarskij[69] had insisted on the creation of a network of socialist cultural circles. The importance of these circles must have been recognised by Gramsci for a long time. Indeed there is evidence that in 1916 the young Gramsci had delivered talks to workers' study circles in Turin on a variety of topics, including Marx, the Paris Commune, Romain Rolland and the French Revolution.[70] His engagement as an adult educator therefore started at an early age, during which time he was also greatly involved in journalism.[71]

The ongoing commitment by Gramsci to explore opportunities for proletarian adult education is reflected in his efforts, despite obvious physical and external constraints, to create and teach (albeit for a short time) at the Ustica 'Prison School'.[72] This idea spread to all other prisons in Italy where political detainees could be found.[73] For Gramsci, therefore, transformative education can take place in a variety of sites of social practice, and this strikes me as being well within the tradition of radical, non-formal adult education, particularly the tradition which incorporates the efforts of social-change-oriented movements. These efforts within the

various sites were also sustained by such media as cultural reviews, which Gramsci, no doubt drawing on his own experience
as a journalist, must have regarded as important sources of informal adult education. *L'Ordine Nuovo*, the periodical which Gramsci,
Umberto Terracini and Palmiro Togliatti launched on 1 May 1919,
was intended as a review of socialist culture[74] and therefore an
important source of adult education. It constituted the means
whereby cultural productions of the period were analysed from
the standpoint of the 'subaltern' class, whose interests the review
purported to represent. Such a review must therefore have been
intended as an important vehicle to assist the Turin workers in
critically appropriating elements of the dominant culture, as well
as elaborating the more emancipatory aspects of popular culture,
with a view to creating a new proletarian culture.

Social relations

Allowing for the fact that there are scattered references to adult
education in Gramsci's letters and cultural writings, I would argue
that his greatest contribution to the development of theory in this
area lies in his writings on the factory council movement. The
emphasis in these writings is on the acquisition of industrial democracy, the backbone of the workers' state. According to John
Merrington, this is one area where 'democracy was crucially denied
in a capitalist society'.[75] The sense of democracy is conveyed
throughout Gramsci's writings on the factory council movement,
with their emphasis on the generation of an environment characterised by a 'collaboration between manual workers, skilled workers, administrative employees, engineers and technical directors'.[76]
Through such collaboration, workers were to experience 'the unity
of the industrial process' and see themselves 'as an inseparable
part of the whole labour system which is concentrated in the object
being manufactured'.[77] As such, they were to acquire complete
mental control over the production process in order to 'replace
management's power in the factory'.[78] Furthermore, the knowledge acquired at the workplace would, according to Gramsci, lead
to a greater understanding of the workings of society: 'At this
point the worker has become a producer, for he has acquired an

awareness of his role in the process of production at all levels, from the workshop to the nation to the world.'[79]

One assumes that the educational programme which the factory councils had to provide, in order to render workers capable of exerting such control, would mirror the spirit of democracy and collaboration it was intended to foster at the workplace and eventually in the envisaged democratic workers' state.[80] For the kind of environment generated by the factory councils was intended to prefigure that of the socialist state:

> The Socialist State already exists potentially in the institutions of social life characteristic of the exploited working class. To link these institutions, co-ordinating and ordering them into a highly centralized hierarchy of competences and powers, while respecting the necessary autonomy and articulation of each, is to create a genuine workers' democracy here and now – a workers' democracy in effective and active opposition to the bourgeois State, and prepared to replace it here and now in all its essential functions of administering and controlling the national heritage.[81]

The democratisation of relations in the sphere of production must therefore have been regarded as an important step towards democratising those wider social relations that constitute the state. The state is here conceived of by Gramsci not as a 'thing', a reified object, but as a relation of production.[82] In my view, the logical conclusion to be drawn from the foregoing is that the social relations of adult education, involving worker-educators and worker-learners, had to be participative and radically democratic if the councils were to prove effective in their prefigurative work.

That Gramsci was concerned with mitigating hierarchical relations between those who 'educate' and 'direct' and those who learn can be seen from his writings concerning hegemony and the role of intellectuals. He advocates a relationship which has to be 'active and reciprocal', one whereby 'every teacher is always a pupil and every pupil a teacher'.[83] I take this to mean that Gramsci favoured a relationship between intellectuals and masses wherein the former act in a directive capacity with the latter, on the basis of their theoretical formation, and at the same time allow them some directive capacity. They would therefore learn from the masses in a reciprocal manner. In her excellent biography of

Gramsci, Laurana Lajolo indicates how he himself engaged in this process during discussions with workers at the *Club Vita Morale* or at his *Avanti!* office. She remarks that, during the heated discussions which took place, Gramsci did not do much talking, limiting himself to offering suggestions regarding ethical conduct, requesting the clarification of certain views or making some objections with a view to preventing contradictory arguments. His was the attitude of the Socratic teacher, a patient educator who refutes rhetoric and demagoguery.[84]

The same applies to his views concerning educators. In his piece on the 'Common School' – which led certain authors to argue that he advocated a conservative education,[85] or elements of such an education,[86] for working-class empowerment – Gramsci refers to the teacher who limits himself or herself to a straightforward transmission of facts as 'mediocre'.[87] This teaching was closely associated with the 'old school'. However, according to Gramsci, the old school has its merit, not to be found in the *Reforma Gentile*. It was, nevertheless, considered 'wayward' enough by Gramsci to justify the struggle for its replacement.

The point Gramsci seems to be making is that dialogue and other elements of a participative education not grounded in information and rigour would be detrimental to the working class. Any such dialogue would be merely rhetoric. He highlighted the merits of the conveyance of facts, an aspect of the old school, in reaction to what he perceived as the emerging practice of carrying out dialogue in a vacuum. The implication for adult educators seems to be that a certain degree of instruction needs to be imparted to render any dialogical educational process an informed one. This point is topical in today's debate on adult education, where it is argued that mere facilitation, without critical analysis, keeps the learner locked in the same paradigm of thinking.[88] The inference that I would draw from the foregoing, for a theory of transformative adult education, is that the adult educator can enhance a participative and dialogical education by conveying information within the context of democratic social relations.

The pedagogy is directive (it is intended towards a political goal) and the organic intellectual/adult educator is equipped with a body of knowledge and theoretical insight which, nevertheless, needs to be constantly tested and renewed through contact with the learners/masses. This explains Gramsci's advocacy of a dialectical relationship between adult educators/organic intellectuals and the learners/masses. The reciprocal educational relationship which he advocates and which was cited earlier, 'exists throughout society as a whole and for every individual relative to other individuals. It exists between intellectual and non-intellectual sections of the population.'[89]

Content

Gramsci focuses in his writings on both aspects of the conventional and problematic 'high' and 'low' culture divide. In this respect he recalls Lenin, who in a polemic with Lunacarskij and the *Proletkult* movement, a movement he criticised for its negation of existing cultural ties with the past,[90] argued:

> Proletarian culture is not something that has sprung from nowhere, it is not an invention of those who call themselves experts in proletarian culture. That is all nonsense. Proletarian culture must be the result of the natural development of the stores of knowledge which mankind has accumulated under the yoke of capitalist society, landlord society and bureaucratic society.[91]

Referring in his piece on education to the traditional school, Gramsci argues that pupils learnt Greek and Latin for no immediate practical reasons but 'to know at first hand the civilization of Greece and Rome – a civilization that was a necessary pre-condition for our modern civilization: In other words, they learnt them to be themselves and know themselves consciously.'[92] This particular aspect of 'high culture', therefore, constituted for Gramsci the means of knowing the pre-condition for the kind of civilization the proletariat seeks to create. This issue, which needs to be addressed critically, is one I shall return to later.

The study of these classical subjects or 'dead languages' provided the rigour necessary for those who belonged to society's *ceti intelletuali* (strata of intellectuals). This is not to say, however, that Latin and Greek would remain relevant to the new school that Gramsci felt should replace the old.[93] Gramsci is explicit in this regard: 'It will be necessary to replace Latin and Greek as the fulcrum of the formative school, and they will be replaced.'[94] And the search should be for a more relevant area of study to provide pupils with similar rigour. According to Gramsci, this is not a straightforward task:

> But it will not be easy to deploy the new subject or subjects in a didactic form which gives equivalent results in terms of education and general personality-formation, from early childhood to the threshold of the adult choice of career.[95]

It would not be stretching the point to infer that the same would apply to the education of adults. There would be a constant search for areas of study and inquiry that would develop, in adult learners from the subaltern classes, the sort of qualities Gramsci identifies in his discussion on the 'Common School': 'diligence, precision, poise (even physical poise), ability to concentrate on specific subjects'.[96]

Gramsci's focus on both aspects of the 'high' and 'low' cultural divide occurs as part of a constant search for a synthesis of the potentially emancipatory elements found in both spheres. This, for Gramsci, was to provide the basis for a new culture. It is perhaps for this reason that he expresses a keen interest, in the *Quaderni* (Notebooks), in the way areas of popular culture are incorporated by the dominant culture. He expresses great interest in works, like Dostoyevsky's novels, which draw on the serial, and therefore popular, fiction to produce 'artistic' fiction and, in so doing, reveal the interplay between the 'popular' and the 'artistic'.[97] This process was of interest to Gramsci 'because of its bearing on the question of how a dominant class can become hegemonic'.[98] Gramsci laments the deterioration of serial fiction in Italy and argues that the proletariat should develop this form of popular cultural production by creating a body of writers who are 'artistically to serial literature what Dostoyevsky was to Sue and Soulie',[99] the last two authors being writers of popular literature. This literature must have been considered by Gramsci capable of providing working-class members with a set of meanings relevant to the revolutionary project he had in mind. One example Gramsci cites is Giovagnoli's 'Spartacus',[100] an image of a 'freedom fighter' that has always appealed to Marxist movements. Gramsci therefore identifies the popular serial fiction as an area worth focusing on in an attempt to create a new literature, part of a new proletarian culture, which has its roots firmly in the popular but which is also the product of an interplay between the popular and dominant forms of artistic expression.

Several elements of the 'canon' were considered by Gramsci to be relevant to the needs of the working class. This explains the enthusiasm he shows in some of his reviews for plays and writings by established figures which contain themes and moral actions that, he felt, resonate with the experiences of members of the subaltern groups. For instance, he seems to have seen in the figure of Ibsen's Nora Helmer, the protagonist in *A Doll's House*,[101] the prototype for the 'new feminine personality', on which he dwells elsewhere in his writings.[102]

The inference I draw from the foregoing is that such knowledge should feature in a programme of cultural preparation of workers developed on Gramscian lines. This knowledge, however, should not be treated as unproblematic. The process involved is one of critical appropriation.

> Creating a new culture does not only mean one's own individual 'original' discoveries. It also, and most particularly, means *the diffusion in a critical form of truths already discovered*, their 'socialisation' as it were, and even making them the basis of vital action, an element of co-ordination and intellectual and moral order. [emphasis added][103]

The notion of critical appropriation of existing knowledge is central to the emergence of a new 'subaltern' and, in Gramsci's case, proletarian culture. The issues of critical and selective appropriation of the dominant culture, in order to transform it, constitute the basis of Henry Giroux's and Michael Apple's critiques[104] of Harold Entwistle's book.

The issue of mastering the dominant culture in order to transform it is also developed in other aspects of Gramsci's work. For instance, Gramsci advocates mastery of the dominant hegemonic language by members of the 'subaltern' classes so that they do not remain at the periphery of political life. This has implications for adult literacy programmes. In the short piece dealing with illiteracy, referred to earlier, he emphasises the need for peasants to learn the standard language to transcend their insular environment characterised by *campanilismo* (parochialism).[105]

> If it is true that every language contains the elements of a conception of the world and of a culture, it could also be true that from anyone's

language, one can assess the greater or lesser complexity of his conception of the world. Someone who only speaks dialect, or understands
the standard language incompletely, necessarily has an intuition of the
world which is more or less limited and provincial, which is fossilized
and anachronistic in relation to the major currents of thought which
dominate world history. His interests will be limited, more or less corporate and economistic, not universal.[106]

Moreover, Gramsci also felt that the subaltern classes would
achieve greater unity through the ability to speak a common language, one which, however, is not 'artificial', 'mechanical' and
'ahistorical' – features which Gramsci attributes to Esperanto.[107]
Such unity would not be achieved if various regional groups within
the subaltern classes confine themselves to speaking their own
particular dialect.

For Gramsci, it is not only the dominant culture that has to be
mastered in processes of adult education but also knowledge of
history. As with the canon, which has its roots in the past, history
too needs to be confronted, mastered and transformed. History
should be a feature of working class adult education. He states:

> If it is true that universal history is a chain made up of efforts man has
> exerted to free himself from privilege, prejudice and idolatry, then it is
> hard to understand why the proletariat, which seeks to add another
> link to the chain, should not know how and why and by whom it was
> preceded or what advantage it might derive from this knowledge.[108]

I consider the issue of a critical appropriation of the dominant
culture to be central to an exploration of the potential contribution that Gramsci's writings can make to the development of a
theory of radical adult education. There are, however, other issues,
in so far as content is concerned, emphasised by Gramsci. The
earlier discussion on workplace democracy highlights the importance Gramsci attached to the workers' sharing of knowledge of
the entire production process and of their learning economic and
administrative skills.

Being first and foremost a Marxist, Gramsci must have considered important the process of education through praxis. And
the notion of praxis that comes across in his writings is one that
entails an absolute fusion between education and the world of
production. It is for this reason that he revealed a fascination for

forms of art that stressed the relationship betwen human beings and industry. Indeed, his letters to Trotsky on Futurism are indicative of his preoccupation with this issue. The Futurist movement sought to bring an end to *fin de siècle* bourgeois cultural residues,[109] equating artistic modernism with industrialism. Gramsci states that the movement's cultural reviews were read by members of the working class, and praises its members for having 'grasped sharply and clearly that our age, the age of big industry, of the large proletarian city and of intense and tumultuous life, was in need of new forms of art, philosophy, behaviour and language.'[110] The Futurist poet and ideologue Filippo Marinetti was also invited by the factory council coordinators to explain the new movement's ideas to workers.

Of course, this faith in the Futurist movement eventually turned sour on Gramsci as many of its adherents aligned themselves with the Fascist cause, a fact which he acknowledges in a letter to Trotsky.[111] However, his initial enthusiasm for the movement indicates his interest in art forms that stress the relationship between human beings and industry. It is this interest which led him to affirm, somewhat idealistically, that

> The worker studies and works; his labour is study and his study is labour. In order to be a specialist in his work, the worker on average puts in the same number of years that it takes to get a specialised degree. The worker, however, carries out his studies in the very act of doing immediately productive work.... Having become dominant, the working class wants manual labour and intellectual labour to be joined in the school and thus creates a new educational tradition.[112]

Conclusion

Antonio Gramsci saw in the education and cultural formation of adults the key to the creation of counter-hegemonic action. He considered such processes essential for subordinated social groups to engage successfully in the 'war of position' necessary to challenge the bourgeois state and transform it into one that represents broader interests. It is for this reason that I regard Gramsci's work of great relevance for the development of a theory of radical adult education. The challenge is to build upon his insights in order to develop an adult education strategy that will contribute to the transformation of society into one that represents the interests of all those groups of people who, under present circumstances, occupy a subordinated position in the power structure.

Notes

1. A shorter version of this chapter appears as a section in Mayo, 1994a.

2. Morrow, 1987; Morgan, 1987.

3. Livingstone, 1976: 235. The emphasis on 'all aspects of social life' indicates that hegemony extends beyond the concept of ideological domination to denote 'a whole body of practices and expectations' – Williams, 1976: 205. Paula Allman regards this interpretation of hegemony as not so much signifying something that extends beyond ideology as representing a broadening of the latter concept itself. She argues that Gramsci was 'the first Marxist, this century, to expand the concept of ideology by locating its expression not just in ideas and thought but also in the material relations, practices and fabric of society, some of which but not all of which could be directly traced to the social relations of production' – Allman, 1988: 100.

4. Morgan, 1987: 299.

5. Gramsci, 1971b: 350.

6. Gramsci, 1971b: 238.

7. Gramsci, in Manacorda, 1970: 32.

8. See Gramsci, in Manacorda, 1970: 32.

9. Diskin, 1993: 18.

10. Broccoli, 1972: 28; Merrington, 1977: 144; Adamson, 1980: 45.

11. Clark, 1977: 52.

12. Gramsci, 1957: 75.

13. This is virtually a literal translation of the point made, in Italian, in Sergio Caruso's essay – Caruso, 1997: 85, 86.

14. Cf. Lojacono, 1977: 8; Clark, 1977: 51; Adamson, 1980: 45. The reference to Karl Marx, wherein Gramsci apparently hits out at what he must have regarded as the rigid economism of the canons of historical materialism, is somewhat disconcerting. Was the young Gramsci really attributing such rigidity to Marx himself? Walter Adamson argues that, for Gramsci, the real enemy, in this respect, 'was not Karl Marx, not even the Karl Marx of *Capital*. His real enemy was the vulgarised Marxism which had become prominent in the Second International' – Adamson, 1980: 45. In her discussion of the same piece, Anne Showstack Sassoon regards the Second International's interpretation of Marx as the target of

his attack – Showstack Sassoon, 1987: 29. One ought to bear in mind, however, that Marx's early manuscripts, wherein he appears less rigid, attaching great importance to the interplay between agency and structure, were not accessible to Gramsci.

15. Gramsci, 1977: 34.
16. Broccoli, 1972: 28.
17. Fiori, 1970: 239.
18. Williams, 1976.
19. La Belle, 1986: 49; Carnoy, 1982: 88.
20. Lawner, 1973: 49.
21. Showstack Sassoon, 1982: 14.
22. Gramsci, 1977: 12.
23. Marks in Gramsci, 1957: 192.
24. Clark, 1977: 49.
25. Gramsci in Clark, 1977: 53.
26. Cf. Armstrong, 1988: 257, 258.
27. Cf. Arnove, 1986; Arnove, 1994.
28. Merrington, 1977: 158.
29. Merrington, 1977: 158.
30. Welton 1991: 25; Welton, 1993: 220. Michael Welton distinguishes between 'schools of labour' and 'labour schools'. He defines the former as 'the socially organised workplaces, embedded in networks of economic, social and political control'. Labour schools are 'those spaces workers themselves, their leaders or sympathetic pedagogues open up for reflection on the meaning of their work and culture' and these include fora, journals, periodicals, university extension programmes, the WEA etc. – Welton, 1991: 25; 1993: 220.
31. Cited in Merrington, 1977: 159.
32. Gramsci, 1971b: 57.
33. Adamson, 1980: 60.
34. Gramsci, 1957: 47.
35. Gramsci, 1957: 45.
36. De Robbio Anziano, 1987: 28.
37. Gramsci, 1957: 47.
38. Gramsci, 1957: 44.
39. De Robbio Anziano, 1987: 28.
40. Ransome, 1992: 198.
41. Gramsci, 1957: 118.
42. Gramsci, 1957: 119.
43. Said, 1994: 4.
44. Merrington, 1977: 153.
45. Caruso, 1997.
46. Caruso, 1997: 73, 74.
47. Gramsci, in Caruso, 1997: 81.

48. Mastellone, 1997: xxxiii, xxxiv.

49. Hoare and Nowell Smith in Gramsci, 1971b: 329.

50. Broccoli, 1972: 41.

51. Manacorda in Gramsci, 1972: xv.

52. Gramsci, 1988: 67.

53. Cf. Gramsci, 1964: 797–819.

54. Gramsci, 1957: 30; Gramsci, 1964: 799.

55. It is in the sense defined by Laclau and Mouffe (1985) that I am using the term 'essentialist' in this book. 'Essentialism', according to this usage, refers to a situation where one asserts the primacy of one form of social differentiation in the process of social change.

56. Bocock, 1986: 106.

57. Gramsci, 1964: 235, 236; Gramsci, 1988: 67, 68.

58. Cf. Clark, 1977.

59. One of the reasons the movement failed is because it did not extend beyond Turin, and its activities were not supported by other sectors of the labour movement, including trade unions.

60. The fact that the newspaper was founded by Antonio Gramsci is acknowledged on the front page of each issue, just beneath the masthead.

61. Amendola, 1978: 39. The relevant sentence in Amendola's original Italian text reads: 'non a caso il giornale del partito comunista lo voleva chiamare "L' Unità" che non é l'unità di un partito, é l'unità di forze sociali, di un blocco storico che si deve formare attraverso la conquista di un largo consenso' – Amendola, 1978: 39.

62. Almost literally translated from the Introduction in Italian by Manacorda, in Gramsci, 1972: xv.

63. De Robbio Anziano, 1987: 124.

64. Caprioglio, in Gramsci, 1976: 216.

65. Broccoli, 1972: 47.

66. Buttigieg, 1992: 75.

67. Gramsci, 1985: 21.

68. Gramsci, 1985: 22.

69. Lunacarskij, 1976: 362 .

70. Buttigieg, 1992: 68.

71. Buttigieg, 1992: 68.

72. De Robbio Anziano, 1987: 125.

73. Lawner, 1973: 68.

74. Festa, 1976: 12.

75. Merrington, 1977: 158.

76. Gramsci, 1977: 110.

77. Gramsci, 1977: 110.

78. Gramsci, in Mancini, 1973: 5.

79. Gramsci, 1977: 111; Gramsci, in Manacorda, 1970: 46.

80. Cf. Gramsci, 1977: 66.

81. Gramsci, 1977: 65.

82. Corrigan, Ramsay and Sayer, 1980.

83. Gramsci, 1971b: 350.

84. Lajolo, 1985: 35. The relevant passage in Lajolo's book reads as follows: 'Durante le accese discussioni del "Club di Vita Morale", Gramsci non parla molto: preferisce dare suggerimenti di comportamento etico, o chiedere precisazioni e avanzare obiezioni al fine di evitare il procedimento contradittorio dei ragionamenti, con l'atteggiamento del maestro socratico, dell'educatore paziente ed appassionato, che rifiuta i discorsi retorici e demagogici.'

85. Harold Entwistle, 1979, stresses the conservative aspects of Gramsci's views regarding schooling with a view to critiquing exponents of the 'new sociology of education' who draw on Gramscian concepts. Guy B. Senese, 1991, also imposes a conservative reading on Gramsci in his critique of critical pedagogy exponents ('possibilitarians'), notably Henry Giroux, Stanley Aronowitz and Peter McLaren. These three writers also draw on Gramsci in their work.

86. De Robbio Anziano, 1987.

87. Gramsci, 1971a: 141; Gramsci, 1971b: 36.

88. Cf. Brookfield, 1989: 209, 210.

89. Gramsci, 1971b: 350.

90. Broccoli, 1972: 65.

91. Lenin, cited in Entwistle, 1979: 44; Lenin in Broccoli, 1972: 66.

92. Gramsci, 1971b: 37.

93. Manacorda, in Gramsci, 1972: xxix.

94. Gramsci, 1971b: 39.

95. Gramsci, 1971b: 39, 40.

96. Gramsci, 1971b: 37.

97. Forgacs and Nowell Smith, in Gramsci, 1985: 12.

98. Forgacs and Nowell Smith, in Gramsci, 1985: 344.

99. Gramsci, 1985: 102.

100. Gramsci, 1985: 102.

101. Cf. Gramsci, 1964: 246, 247; Gramsci, 1985: 72.

102. Cf. 'Americanism and Fordism', in Gramsci, 1971b: 296; cf. Simon, 1982: 90.

103. Gramsci, 1971b: 325.

104. Giroux, 1980: 312; 1988: 201, 202; Apple, 1980: 437, 438.

105. Gramsci, 1964: 236.

106. Gramsci, 1971b: 325. I am indebted to Adamson, 1980: 151, for drawing my attention to this quotation.

107. Gramsci, 1985: 29.

108. Gramsci, 1971b: 41.

109. Forgacs and Nowell Smith, in Gramsci, 1985.

110. Gramsci, 1985: 51.

111. Gramsci, 1985: 52.

112. Gramsci, 1985: 43.

CHAPTER 3

Paulo Freire and Adult Education

Paulo Freire is widely regarded as one of the leading figures in the area of critical pedagogy,[1] that particular type of pedagogy which is concerned with issues concerning social difference, social justice and social transformation.[2] Unlike Gramsci, Freire writes primarily from the standpoint of an educationist rather than a political analyst. Despite his late involvement as Education Secretary in São Paulo on behalf of the Brazilian Workers' Party (PT), his writings do not contain formulations for a comprehensive party strategy. For the most part, they concentrate on issues pertaining to education, even though these issues are discussed within the framework of wider and more general discussions concerning forms of oppression and possibilities for social transformation. Like Gramsci, however, Freire underlines the strong relationship that exists between education and politics: 'It is impossible to deny, except intentionally or by innocence, the political aspect of education.'[3]

Political Pedagogy

Freire's writings are therefore grounded in a critique of traditional educational methods. Giroux's phrase, the 'language of critique', as well as its corollary, 'the language of possibility', were used in relation to this aspect of Freire's work:

> Freire has appropriated the unclaimed heritage of emancipatory idea in those versions of secular and religious philosophy located within the

corpus of bourgeois thought. He has also critically integrated into his work a heritage of radical thought without assimilating many of the problems that have plagued it historically. In effect, Freire has combined what I call the language of critique with the language of possibility.[4]

Drawing on his experiences in Latin America, Freire, in his early writings, projects a vision of society as characterised by relations of power and domination. The focus is on the ideological means whereby those in a position of privilege and power (the oppressors) exert their control over those whom they exploit (the oppressed); the social relations that are constitutive of such power are prescriptive in nature. This process of prescription is facilitated by a variety of means, including traditional mainstream education. Mainstream education is characterised by what Freire calls 'banking education,'[5] a top-down approach to knowledge transmission, through which the teacher is the sole dispenser of knowledge and the students are its passive recipients.[6] It constitutes a non-reflective mode of learning.[7]

> Education thus becomes an act of depositing, in which the students are the depositories and the teacher is the depositor. Instead of communicating, the teacher issues communiqués and makes deposits which the students patiently receive, memorize, and repeat. This is the 'banking' concept of education, in which the scope of action allowed to the students extends only as far as receiving, filing and storing the deposits.[8]

Under such conditions, the learner is 'object' rather than 'subject' of the learning process. Deference to authority, an uncritical consumption of knowledge and an immersion in what Freire calls the 'culture of silence' are the likely outcomes of such a process. The prescriptive mode of pedagogy destroys any sense of relationship that the educatee may have with the material to be learnt, thereby constituting a process of cultural alienation. It also facilitates what Freire calls 'cultural invasion', since the learner becomes vulnerable to ideas imposed from above (ideas related to the dominant culture) and from without (ideas disseminated as part of a process of 'cultural imperialism').[9]

Given this affirmation of the strong connection between education and dominant political interests, Freire argues that education cannot be neutral. It is perhaps this aspect of his work which renders it diametrically opposed to conventional, mainstream educational theories. He demands of educators an important choice: 'Educators must ask themselves for whom and on whose behalf they are working.'[10] This is a recurring theme throughout Freire's writings. In one of his later publications in English, for example, he argues that neutrality is a 'convenient alternative to saying that one is siding with the dominant'.[11]

As with other radical educators, Freire advocates commitment to the cause of social transformation, an issue that is given prominence in a transcribed conversation with Myles Horton where the experiences of popular educators in Nicaragua, who risk life and limb for the cause of liberation, are reflected upon.[12] Drawing on his experience as an observer during the elections in Nicaragua, Horton dwells on the courage shown by popular educators who were targets of Contra attacks. This underlines the nature of the commitment entered into by popular educators in various parts of Latin America: the context for Freire's early literacy experiences. The commitment is possibly at its greatest in conflict-ridden areas such as was the case in Nicaragua during the Contra war, and in El Salvador. Julio Portillo indicates the nature of the danger facing El Salvadorean popular educators, in an interview with John L. Hammond:

> Then in 1981 and 1982, educators who were members of ANDES were forced to leave the country for exile, because the Duarte government was hunting us down. In the first eight months of the Duarte government in 1980, 180 teachers were killed, and 97 were kidnapped and are still missing.[13]

Similar views are expressed by Maria Zuniga, a popular educator in the area of health education in Nicaragua:

> both health and education were attacked by the counter-revolution, especially at the beginning of the War in 1982 and in 1983 and 1984. Many people who were *Brigadistas* or were popular educators or popular health educators were a target for the counter-revolutionary forces. Popular education and popular health programmes were the first and most important ones of the Revolution.... And so the first people who were attacked were the teachers and the health workers. And many health workers disappeared, or were killed, as were teachers. They were kidnapped and never found. Some were taken away to the Contra camps and others were killed. I can't remember how many casualties were suffered but there were many victims among those kinds of workers.[14]

Such commitment would also be called for in Brazil, where activists like union leader Chico Mendes and land-hungry peasants are often the victims of rural violence. In a report written in 1992, the Pastoral Land Commission (CPT) pointed out that since 1964, the year of the military coup, 1,684 Brazilian rural workers had been murdered.[15]

Agency: Liberation Theology and Marxism

The stress on commitment indicates a conviction on Freire's part that social transformation is possible. This makes his work of great relevance for the purposes of establishing the bases for a theory of radical adult education. The message conveyed throughout Freire's writing is one of hope: a vision that, in Henry Giroux's words, is the product of 'the spirit and ideological dynamics that have both informed and characterised the Liberation Theology movement that has emerged primarily out of Latin America'.[16]

Freire is scathing in his critique of those particular forms of religion that deny people agency and the feeling that, collectively, they can make a difference. In Freire's view, traditional forms of religion serve to preserve the status quo. Writing specifically about the traditionalist Church, he argues:

> The traditionalist church, first of all, is still intensely colonialist. It is a missionary church, in the worst sense of the word – a necrophiliac winner of souls; hence its taste for masochistic emphasis on sin, hell-fire, and eternal damnation. The mundane, dichotomized from the transcendental, is the 'filth' in which humans have to pay for their sins. The more they suffer, the more they purify themselves, finally reaching heaven and eternal rest.[17]

It is an institution which prevents the oppressed from under-standing the structural and systemic bases of oppression and, as a result, conveys a sense of helplessness. Oppression is explained in terms of 'God's will':

> They resort (stimulated by the oppressor) to magical explanations or a false view of God, to whom they fatalistically transfer the responsibility for their oppressed state.... A Chilean priest of high intellectual and moral caliber visiting Recife in 1966 told me: 'When a Pernambucan

colleague and I went to see several families living in shanties [*mocambos*] in indescribable poverty, I asked them how they could bear to live like that, and the answer was always the same: 'What can I do? It is the will of God and I must accept it.'[18]

Opposed to this kind of religious practice is a theology which emphasises the role of human agency in the permanent struggle against oppression and social injustice for the creation of the Kingdom of God on earth.[19] In Freire's view, this is a theology from the margins dealing with concerns of the margins, which presents 'an immense challenge to the evangelising mission of the church',[20] and is espoused by what he calls 'the prophetic church':

> It is the prophetic church. Opposed and attacked by both traditional-
> ist and modernizing churches, as well as by the elite of the power
> structures, this utopian, prophetic, and hope-filled movement rejects
> do-goodism and palliative refoms in order to commit itself to the domi-
> nated social classes and to radical social change.[21]

The sense of agency that this theology conveys is underlined here. Freire's sense of agency derives not merely from Liberation Theo-logy,[22] but also from other sources, including Marxist humanist thought,[23] Hegelian dialectics and phenomenology.[24] Because he accords great importance to the transformative potential of human agency, Freire repudiates the overly deterministic and mechanistic theories of reproduction associated with 'vulgar Marxism'. He argues:

> I believe that many people under the Marxist banner subscribe to purely
> mechanistic explanations by depending on a fatalism that I sometimes,
> humorously, call liberating fatalism. This is a liberation given over to
> history. Hence, it is not necessary to make any effort to bring about
> liberation. It will come no matter what. I don't believe in this fatalism,
> of course.[25]

Democratic Education

As in the section on Gramsci, I consider it pertinent at this stage to enquire: who or what produces agency? Freire regards adult education – and in particular, given his Latin American back-ground, that kind of adult education known as 'popular education'[26] – as an important source of agency. Needless to say, adult educators play an important role in this context, conceived of by Freire as democratic educators. Their task is to promote learning through dialogue. This process is contrary to the notion of the teacher as the sole dispenser of knowledge and is intended to render the learners active participants in the process of their own learning, to render them 'subject'. The culture of the learners increasingly becomes the basis of the learning process.

Praxis

Through a 'pedagogy of the question'[27] rather than a prescriptive pedagogy, the educator enables the learners to reflect on the codified versions of their 'reality' (their own world of action) in a process of praxis. The codification serves its purposes in distancing the learners from their world of action so that, through reflection, the educatees begin to see it in a different, more critical light. The concept of praxis is described by Freire thus: 'But men's activity consists of action and reflection: it is praxis, it is transformation of the world.'[28] In Freire's view, any separation of the two key elements in the process of praxis (i.e. action and reflection) is either mindless activism or empty theorising, the latter being what Peter Jarvis would call 'armchair reflectivity'.[29] The two elements ought, in Freire's view, to be inextricably intertwined. Freire's approach seeks to combine the two, having praxis at its core. The process involved is traditionally referred to as *conscientização* (conscientisation), a term that was originally used by Catholic radicals in the 1960s[30] and that, according to Freire, was rendered popular by Archbishop Helder Camara.[31] It is also a term that Freire stopped using after 1974. He felt that it had been loosely used in a manner which stripped it of its actual significance.[32] Yet Freire never lost the sense of its significance and worked to clarify it in lectures, workshops and seminars.[33] He is quoted as having said, regarding the term:

> As soon as I heard it, I realised the profundity of its meaning since I was fully convinced that education, as an exercise in freedom, is an act of knowing, a critical approach to reality.[34]

In an interview with Carlos Alberto Torres, he explains:

Conscientization is the deepening of the coming of consciousness. There can be no conscientization without coming first into consciousness.... To work, therefore, in a conscientizing posture, whether with Brazilian peasants, Spanish-Americans or Africans, or with university people from any part of the world, is to search with rigor, with humility, without the arrogance of the sectarians who are overly certain about their universal certainties, to unveil the truths hidden by ideologies that are more alive when it is said they are dead.[35]

'Coming into consciousness' refers to the process of 'taking distance' from objects, something which 'presupposes the perception of them in their relations with other objects.'[36] Furthermore, he defines the deepening of this process as 'learning to perceive social, political, and economic contradictions, and to take action against the oppressive elements of reality'[37] – all part and parcel of being critically literate. The process of 'gaining distance' is central to the pedagogy involved. In his discussion of 'paradigms of nonformal education', Carlos Alberto Torres states, with respect to conscientisation,

In its most radical version, the specificity of conscientisation resides in the development of critical consciousness as class knowledge and practice, that is, it appears as part of the 'subjective conditions' of the process of social transformation.[38]

The class factor is important in the Latin American popular education context, even though race and gender factors came into play as the process of Freire-inspired consciousness-raising began to be adapted in the contexts of various, often interrelated, struggles world wide. The specificity of conscientisation, one may argue, borrowing from Torres,[39] lies in the development of critical consciousness as the knowledge of historically subordinated groups – subaltern knowledge.

For the sake of brevity, I reproduce Dennis Goulet's succinct description of the process of *conscientização* from his excellent introduction to one of Freire's early English-language publications:

- participant observation of educators 'tuning in' to the vocabular universe of the people;
- their arduous search for generative words at two levels: syllabic richness and a high charge of experiential involvement;
- a first codification of these words into visual images which stimulate

people 'submerged' in the culture of silence to 'emerge' as conscious makers of their own 'culture';

- the decodification by a 'culture circle' under the self-effacing stimulus of a coordinator who is no 'teacher' in the conventional sense, but who has become an educator–educatee – in dialogue with educatee–educators too often treated by formal educators as passive recipients of knowledge;
- a creative new codification, this one explicitly critical and aimed at action, wherein those who were formally illiterate now begin to reject their role as mere 'objects' in nature and social history and undertake to become 'subjects' of their own destiny.[40]

Dialogue

Because the process throughout is a dialogical one in which the educator learns from the educatees in the same way that the latter learn from her or him, the roles of educator and learner become almost interchangeable. In what has become a classic formulation, Freire wrote:

> Through dialogue, the teacher of the students and the students of the teacher cease to exist and a new term emerges: teacher–student with students–teachers.[41]

Educators must therefore help develop processes whereby they and educatees learn together, co-investigating the object of knowledge:

> educator and learners all become learners assuming the same attitude as cognitive subjects discovering knowledge through one another and through the objects they try to know. It is not a situation where one knows and the others do not; it is rather the search, by all, at the same time to discover something by the act of knowing which cannot exhaust all the possibilities in the relation between object and subject.[42]

Freire stresses the need for reciprocal learning, arguing, with reference to peasants as learners, that,

> Of course we have a lot to learn from peasants. When I refer to peasants, my emphasis is on our need to learn from others, the need we have to learn from learners in general. I have continually insisted that we must learn from peasants because I see them as learners at a particular moment in my educational practice. We can learn a great deal from the very students we teach.[43]

Henry Giroux takes up this aspect of Freirean pedagogy, according it central importance in a process of critical, radical education:

> A radical theory of literacy and voice must remain attentive to Freire's claim that all critical educators are also learners. This is not merely a matter of learning about what students might know; it is more importantly a matter of learning how to renew a form of self-knowledge through an understanding of the community and culture that actively constitute the lives of one's students.[44]

The task of the educator is to learn the culture and community which partly constitutes the social location of the learner. The educator would therefore be, in Giroux's terms, a 'border crosser',[45] in that she or he would move across the border that demarcates one's social location in order to understand and act in solidarity with the learner(s), no longer perceived as 'Other'. The learners are also educators in this process since they play a crucial part in enabling the teacher to cross such borders.

Authority and authoritarianism

One may argue that both educators and educatees are agents in this attempt to overcome the dialectical contradiction of opposites characterising traditional education, with teacher and taught becoming 'the unity of opposites'.[46] I say 'attempt' because I do not think that this process will ever be completely overcome, especially given Freire's insistence that educator and educatee are not on an equal footing in the educational process involved. What we are presented with is not an 'education of equals'.[47] While exhorting educators to learn from learners, Freire states that,

> Obviously, we also have to underscore that while we recognize that we have to learn from our students (whether peasants, urban workers, or graduate students), this does not mean that teachers and students are the same. I don't think so. That is, there is a difference between the educator and the student. This is a general difference. This is usually also a difference of generations.[48]

In a later formulation, Freire emphasises the *directive* role of the educator, a role similar to that ascribed by Gramsci to the organic intellectuals: 'At the moment the teacher begins the dialogue, he or she knows a great deal, first in terms of knowledge and second in terms of the horizon that he or she wants to get to.'[49] This is an acknowledgement on Freire's part that the educators have a political vision and a theoretical understanding that guides their pedagogical action. This denotes a certain competence, on their part, from which their authority as educators derives.

Freire's acknowledgement of this authority on the teacher's part appeared, interestingly enough, in a 'talking book' published a year after the publication of Frank Youngman's critique of his pedagogy.[50] Youngman had argued that Freire does not admit that educators can have a theoretical understanding which is superior to that of the learners and which is an indispensable condition for the growth of critical consciousness.[51] In according the educator authority, Freire underlines the importance of this authority not degenerating into authoritarianism, the latter being the hallmark of 'banking education': 'the democratic teacher never, never transforms authority into authoritarianism'.[52] Freire reiterates the point in one of his 'talking books' in the English Language, asserting that 'Authority is necessary to the freedom of the students and my own. The teacher is absolutely necessary. What is bad, what is *not* necessary, is authoritarianism, but not authority.'[53] In one of his many exchanges with Donaldo Macedo, Freire states that 'Teachers maintain a certain level of authority through the depth and breadth of knowledge of the subject matter that they teach.'[54] For this reason, he refuses to use the term 'facilitator'.[55] Affirmation of such a difference between educator and educatee was necessary given the frequent misappropriation of the ideas contained in his earlier work, in which he had not rendered explicit the belief that educators and educatees are not on an equal footing in the learning process.

Freire has even gone so far, in his dialogue with Myles Horton, as to concede that there are moments, especially during initial meetings with learners who are accustomed to prescriptive teaching methods and therefore not used to risk-taking, when the educator must show discretion in her or his teaching style, being '50 per cent a traditional teacher and 50 per cent a democratic teacher'.[56] This may be taken as the recognition by Freire of the fact, often pointed out with regard to his advocacy of a dialogical education, that such adult learners would not be disposed to partake of transformed social relations of education overnight.[57] Indeed, as Gaber-Katz and Watson indicate,[58] they can offer resistance to processes of a dialogical education. Elements of the 'old' pedagogy can, when absolutely necessary, be incorporated into the new one, the main proviso being that the prevailing spirit in the teaching process would be democratic.

Class suicide

When dealing with the issue of educators as agents of change, or, to use Giroux's terminology, 'transformative intellectuals',[59] Freire places the emphasis not only on a democratic teaching style but also on something akin to an 'organic relationship', in the Gramscian sense of the term, between educators and the class or group of people they are dealing with, using such words as 'growing' and 'in communion' with the group.[60] According to the Freirean conception of the relationship between educator and educatee, differences between educators and learners have to be mitigated as far as possible. Freire is no doubt aware that educators can bring into the teaching situation a 'cultural capital' which is at odds with that of the learners and that this can constitute a powerful force of domestication.[61] As such, borrowing a memorable phrase from Amilcar Cabral, Freire writes/speaks about the possibility of intellectuals – and one can include educators among them – committing 'class suicide' to integrate themselves with the masses,[62] 'immersing themselves in the culture, history, aspirations, doubts, anxieties and fears of the popular classes'.[63] As I indicate later, I consider the notion of 'class suicide' somewhat problematic.

Agents of Change

Having provided an account of Freire's views regarding the role of educators as transformative agents, I will now attempt to identify whether there exists in Freire's writings a specific social category with whom the agency for social transformation lies.

Unlike in Gramsci, much of the focus in Freire's early work deals with the *campesinos* in Brazil and Chile. His work concerning the former Portuguese colonies in Africa also deals with peasants.

This indicates that the agency for change in Freire does not lie specifically with the industrial working class, a view not in keeping with the classical Marxist position whereby this class is viewed as the 'universal class' with a historic mission to accomplish. J.C. Walker,[64] referring to Freire's early work, states that, like Mao, Freire finds greater revolutionary potential in the peasantry than in the urban proletariat. However, much depends on the context. Walker quotes a passage by Freire to this effect:

> large sections of the oppressed form an urban proletariat, especially in the more industrialised centres of the country. Although these sectors are occasionally restive they lack revolutionary consciousness and consider themselves privileged. Manipulation with its series of deceits and fertile promises usually finds fertile soil here.[65]

The emphasis shifts somewhat in Freire's later works, where he engages in dialogical exchanges with prominent US or US-based critical pedagogues.[66] In these works, we discover references to the plight of a variety of oppressed groups whose cause is advanced by social movements. Viewing his work in its entirety, I would argue that Freire's oppressed vary from context to context. For instance, when referring to his later work as Education Secretary in São Paulo, he identifies the oppressed as women, who constitute the majority of non-literate persons in the city and who face a double workload. They also include in-migrants from the impoverished north-east, who end up as auxiliary workers in the area of civil construction.[67] Most of the social categories mentioned throughout Freire's works are class categories. Nevertheless, in his 'talking books', the emphasis on different groups, such as gays/ lesbians, blacks, ethnic minorities and women seems to confirm Giroux's view that, 'With the notion of difference as the guiding thread, Freire rejects the idea that there is a universalised form of oppression.'[68] In a 1991 conference session on his work in São Paulo, Freire confirmed the above view, arguing that one cannot reduce everything – that is, all forms of oppression – to the class struggle. This is not to say that he minimises the importance of class: 'Perestroika did not have the power to suppress that.'[69]

The emphasis on social movements in Freire's later books and his work in São Paulo[70] indicates that, for him, they constitute the larger context within which transformative educational initiatives can be effectively carried out. In a 'talking book' with Ira Shor he advocates that educators striving for change 'expose themselves to the greater dynamism, the greater mobility' found 'inside social movements'.[71] He reiterates this view in a taped conversation with Antonio Faundez:

> I can say without fear of being mistaken that in the seventies in Brazil and elsewhere we began to see clearly the growing development and importance of these social movements, some of them linked with the church and some not: the struggle of environmentalists in Europe, Japan and the United States, resulting in their direct intervention in recent elections in France and Germany; the struggle of organised women, of blacks, of homosexuals, all of them emerging as a force and expression of power.[72]

Sites of Practice and Content

Having underlined the sense of agency present in Freire's work and having outlined issues related to it, I will now focus on the type of adult education that Freire proposes. In the section on Gramsci, I discussed this issue in terms of sites of practice, social relations and content. As the issue of social relations in Freire's work has already been explored in the section dealing with agency and the role of educators, I will confine myself here to questions of sites and content.

Sites of practice

Like Gramsci, Freire engages in a 'war of position', and therefore his chosen sites of educational practice are various. Although he is strongly associated with adult literacy work in non-formal settings, I would argue on the basis of his later formulations that Freire favours working both within and outside the system. In his view, no space should be left unexplored in what should be a lifelong effort for social transformation. In contrast to Myles Horton, for instance, who would have no truck with formal social institutions, Freire argues that,

> I think politically, every time we can occupy some position inside of the subsystem, we should do so. But as much as possible, we should try

to establish good relationships with the experience of people outside the subsystem in order to help what we are trying to do inside.[73]

The notion of having one foot in the system (he refers to schooling as a subsystem of a larger system, education) and another outside seems to have been the guiding philosophy throughout Freire's life as an adult educator. In his 1985 interview with Donaldo Macedo, he states:

> I have been trying to think and teach by keeping one foot inside the system and the other foot outside. Of course, I cannot be totally outside the system if the system continues to exist. I would be totally outside only if the system itself were transformed. But it is not transformed because, in truth, it goes on transforming itself. Thus, to have an effect, I cannot live on the margins of the system. I have to be in it.[74]

This notion of being 'in and outside' the system is reflected in Freire's work as Education Secretary in São Paulo, where he worked 'within' the system ('being tactically inside and strategically outside'),[75] in concert with agencies operating 'outside' the system – the social movements.

Content

Paulo Freire's work is erroneously associated with adult literacy programmes. It is true that his work in the north-east of Brazil, as well as in Chile, dealt with literacy. The need to become literate was essential in such contexts in order to prevent the oppressed peasants from remaining at the periphery of political life. Even so, I would submit that adult literacy, though it served an important purpose in Brazil, in that it extended the voting population, was used by Freire only as a vehicle for the more important process of political conscientisation. It is for this reason that attempts at 'co-opting' the 'Freire method' for the purpose of spreading literacy without its political ingredients, constitute a travesty of Freirean pedagogy.[76] An example of such co-optation was provided in the course of the Brazilian literacy campaign, MOBRAL. The organisers claimed to have used Freire's methods,[77] and this despite the fact that the programme was sponsored by the military regime that kept Freire in exile for sixteen years.[78]

Freire's concern is with the attainment of political literacy, the means of reading the world.[79] As such, praxis, the process whereby people are enabled to detach themselves from their world of action to reflect upon it and begin to view it in a different, more critical light, can be applied in contexts where the participants are 'literate' in the conventional sense of the term. It can constitute an effective approach to reconsider critically 'taken for granted' aspects of one's 'reality', and therefore to convert one's 'common sense' to 'good sense', elements of the latter being contained in the former.

What constitutes the focus of reflection in a Freirean approach to learning characterised by praxis? In his early work, Freire uses the concept of praxis in a manner reminiscent of the early Marx. The area on which the adult learner is to reflect is her/his cultural surroundings. In *Pedagogy in Process*, however, the concept is used in a way that recalls the first volume of *Capital*.[80] In Letter 11 to Guinea-Bissau, Freire underlines the need to relate education to production, a view that recalls his literacy work in relation to the agrarian reform in Chile. Freire states:

> the new man and the new woman toward which this society aspires cannot be created except by participation in productive labour that serves the common good. It is this labour that is the source of knowledge about the new creation, through which it unfolds and to which it refers.[81]

One must not decontextualise such ideas, of course. They were expressed in the context of a struggle for development in a newly liberated former Portuguese colony. It also happens to be one of the world's most impoverished nations, whose economy is basically an agrarian one. Freire's notion of praxis, as advocated in this context, is reminiscent of a number of well-known theories of education and production that have emerged from the Third World. Examples would be those propounded by Mao in his attempt to destroy the long-standing Confucian dichotomy between manual and intellectual work,[82] and those of Nyerere, who proposed, among other things, the idea of school farms as part of his proposed process of education for self-reliance.[83]

Unlike Gramsci, Freire does not focus, in his writings on culture, on both sides of the conventional and problematic 'high' and 'low' divide. There seems to be no attempt, at least judging from his works in English, to explore the possibilities for critical appropriation of aspects of the dominant culture, with a view to incorporating them in a transformative adult education programme. The only exception in this regard would be the dominant language, which Freire feels ought to be learnt in a problematising manner, so that subordinated groups would not remain at the periphery of political life:

> Finally, teachers have to say to students, Look, in spite of being beautiful, this way you speak also includes the question of *power*. Because of the political problem of power, you need to learn how to command the dominant language, in order for you to survive in the struggle to transform society.[84]

Otherwise, the emphasis throughout is on elements of the 'popular culture', which he regards as capable of constituting the bases for a transformative adult education programme. Like Gramsci, Freire is wary of romanticising this culture and acknowledges the presence within it of such potentially disempowering elements as superstition, magic and traditional religious beliefs.[85]

> In order for the oppressed to unite, they must first cut the umbilical cord of magic and myth which binds them to the world of oppression; the unity which links them to each other must be of a different nature.

As with Gramsci, the popular is not to be celebrated uncritically but is to be the subject of constant interrogation. This was not always the case, even in those publications of Freire in which elements of the popular are manifested. Examples of the codifications are found in an early work, *Education for Critical Consciousness*.[86] Here, 'Man' is not only the subject of Freire's theorising but is also depicted as being at the centre of the universe. 'He' is depicted as being in a constant quest to dominate nature (perpetrating violence in the form of hunting down birds and animals). In settings which separate the 'public' from the 'private' spheres of life, 'Man', for the most part, occupies the former.[87] Such codifications smack of one important aspect of popular culture in Latin America – *machismo*. Of course one notices a difference between Freire's earlier and later works in this regard. His later work is guided by a more inclusive vision of social change. This issue will be taken up, in some detail, in Chapter 5.

Conclusion

Paulo Freire posits a process of adult education centring around the concept of praxis, an educational process through which the adult learner is encouraged, through critical 'authentic' dialogue, to unveil some of the social contradictions in existence within one's community and beyond. Praxis constitutes the means by which learners engage in an ongoing process of critical literacy, a process that entails their reading 'the word and the world'. The process of education that Freire advocates is a democratic one, which also has a collective learning dimension. His is a pedagogy in which the learners' voices are valorised and are engaged with critically throughout the learning process. It is a directive pedagogical approach which does not deny the teacher authority, provided that this authority, deriving from the teacher's competence, does not degenerate into authoritarianism.

Freire's approach foregrounds the political nature of all educational activity, stressing throughout the strong relationship that exists in all contexts between education and power. My use of the word 'approach' is deliberate. Some prefer to use the term 'method' in this context, which I am wary of since this might convey the false impression that all Freire's pedagogy involves is a set of techniques. To reduce Freire's work simply to a method – the cause of much liberal misappropriation and dilution[88] – and thereby divest it of its radical political thrust is tantamount to adulterating his work. Although, as I shall indicate in the concluding chapter, Freire's approach can find fertile ground in a variety of contexts, it does not comprise a set of techniques which can be transferred from one context to another at will, without any regard whatsoever for the process of 'cultural invasion' that this would entail. It is an approach which requires sensitivity towards the issues of oppression that emerge from the socio-cultural context in question. In this regard, we must heed Freire's warning: 'experiments cannot be transplanted; they must be reinvented'.[89]

Notes

1. A shorter version of this chapter appears as a section in Mayo, 1994a. This chapter also contains material from Mayo, 1991a; 1993a; 1995c.

2. McLaren, 1994.

3. Freire, 1976: 70.

4. Giroux, 1985: xii; 1988: 108.

5. Freire, 1970: 58.

6. Goulet, 1973: 11.

7. Jarvis, 1987b: 90.

8. Freire, 1970: 58.

9. Mayo, 1991a.

10. Freire, 1985: 80.

11. Freire, in Horton and Freire, 1990: 104.

12. Horton and Freire, 1990: 224.

13. Hammond, 1991: 93.

14. Taped interview with Maria Zuniga of CISAS (Centre for Information and Advisory Services in Health), Managua – Zuniga, 1993: 36.

15. Norris, 1992: 18.

16. Giroux, 1988: 113.

17. Freire, 1985: 131.

18. Freire, 1970: 163.

19. Giroux, 1988: 113.

20. Boff and Boff, 1986: 70.

21. Freire, 1985: 137.

22. Cf. Retamal, 1981; Elias, 1994; Cooper, 1995; Lange-Christensen, 1996.

23. Youngman, 1986.

24. Torres, 1982: 77.

25. Freire, 1985: 178, 179.

26. As Carnoy and Torres (1987) indicate, the term 'popular education' is widespread in Latin America. It is best described as a kind of non-formal education which focuses 'on those who live in poverty, especially the rural campesinos, as the source of social transformation' – La Belle, 1986: 33. One of the most prominent writers on the subject, Garcia Huidobro, argues that it is very social-class and politically oriented and 'intended to lead to a more egalitarian and classless society' – La Belle, 1986: 181, 182. It is associated with the New Left in Latin America.

27. Bruss and Macedo, 1985: 9.

28. Freire, 1970: 119.

29. Jarvis, 1987b: 90.

30. Zachariah, 1986: 28.

31. Zachariah, 1986: 36.

32. Freire, 1993: 110.

33. Freire, 1993: 111.

34. Freire, in Zachariah, 1986: 36.

35. Freire, 1993: 110

36. Freire, 1993: 108.

37. Freire, 1970: 19.

38. Torres, 1990a: 8.
39. Torres, 1990a: 8.
40. Goulet, 1973: 11.
41. Freire, 1970: 67.
42. Freire, 1976: 115.
43. Freire, 1985: 177.
44. Giroux, 1987: 22.
45. Giroux, 1992.
46. Allman, 1994: 153.
47. See Jarvis, 1985 regarding 'education of equals'.
48. Freire, 1985: 177.
49. Freire, in Shor and Freire, 1987: 103.
50. Youngman, 1986.
51. Youngman, 1986: 179.
52. Freire, in Shor and Freire, 1987: 91.
53. Freire, in Horton and Freire, 1990: 181.
54. Freire, in Freire and Macedo, 1995: 378.
55. Cf. Freire and Macedo, 1995.
56. Freire, in Horton and Freire, 1990: 160.
57. Cf. Mayo, 1991a, 1993a.
58. Gaber-Katz and Watson, 1991.
59. Giroux, 1988.
60. Freire, 1971: 61; Freire in Freire and Faundez, 1989: 56.
61. Cf. Torres, 1990b: 280.
62. Freire, 1978: 104.
63. Freire, in Freire and Faundez, 1989: 56.
64. Walker, 1980.
65. Freire, in Walker, 1980: 137, 138.
66. Freire, 1985 (includes a dialogue with the translator, Donaldo Macedo); Shor and Freire, 1987; Freire and Macedo, 1987; Horton and Freire, 1990; Freire and Macedo, 1993, 1995.
67. Freire, in Viezzer, 1990: 6.
68. Giroux, 1988: 109.
69. Freire, 1991.
70. The Workers' Party (PT), with which Freire was affiliated, has a tradition of strong links with grassroots movements and trade unions – Ireland, 1987.
71. Freire, in Shor and Freire, 1987: 39.
72. Freire, in Freire and Faundez 1989: 66.
73. Freire, in Horton and Freire, 1990: 203.
74. Freire, 1985: 178.
75. Freire, 1991.
76. Cf. Kidd and Kumar, 1981.
77. Bhola, 1984: 130.

78. I am indebted to my former teacher, Carlos Alberto Torres, for having highlighted this point in a class I took with him at the University of Alberta in May 1987.

79. Cf. Freire and Macedo, 1987.

80. Youngman, 1986: 163.

81. Freire, 1978: 105.

82. Cf. Chu, 1980.

83. Cf. Nyerere, 1979.

84. Freire, in Shor and Freire, 1987: 73.

85. Freire, 1970: 175.

86. Freire, 1973.

87. Reproduced from Mayo, 1993a: 17.

88. On this issue, see Aronowitz, 1993; Macedo, 1994; Allman, 1996; Freire, 1997a: 303–6.

89. Freire, 1978: 9.

CHAPTER 4

Gramsci and Freire:
A Comparative Analysis

In the previous chapters, I have attempted to bring out those features in the work of Antonio Gramsci and Paulo Freire which can provide some of the underpinnings for a theory of radical adult education. In this chapter, I attempt a 'side by side' comparative analysis of their ideas relevant to adult education, in order to establish a framework for a proposed synthesis of their work. By contextualising the two writers' works and providing a critical exposition of their ideas, I hope to highlight both the convergences and the contrasts.[1]

Biographical and Contextual Comparison

Before engaging in a comparative analysis of the two writers' ideas relevant to adult education, it is important to locate them biographically and contextually. The periods in which they wrote were separated by more than twenty years. Gramsci delivered his first public addresses in 1916 and was still at work on the *Quaderni del Carcere* (*Prison Notebooks*) in 1936, the penultimate year of his life.[2] Freire, for his part, is believed to have first expressed his thought on the philosophy of education in 1959.[3] Despite the gap in time, there are biographical similarities. As we have seen, neither was of humble origin; both, however, fell on hard times during their childhood, Gramsci's father having been imprisoned for embezzlement and the Freire family having suffered from the effects of the Depression. These experiences had an adverse effect on the initial schooling of each, and exposed both, at an early stage in their lives, to the concrete, material realities of poverty and, in Gramsci's case, work.[4] Furthermore, the formative experiences of both writers occurred in areas characterised by a general impoverishment and industrial underdevelopment, namely Sardinia and Recife, both eventually becoming socially and politically active in industrial metropolitan centres (Turin and São Paulo).

Both Gramsci and Freire were politically and/or pedagogically active in historical situations characterised by an intense class struggle and the mobilisation of popular forces. Turin, the city where Gramsci was active, was 'the Italian Petrograd'.[5] Its highly militant proletariat was involved in a series of insurrections. Galvanised by the news of the October Revolution in Russia, many working-class leaders believed that a similar event was about to take place in Turin. A similar situation existed in Latin America, where the staging of a successful revolution in the region (the Cuban Revolution) generated enthusiasm which served as a catalyst for the advancement of popular forces.[6] This is true of Brazil in the late 1950s and early 1960s. Trade unions, peasant leagues and worker organisations, as well as radical religious movements,[7] asserted their presence when the country was governed by the populist administration of João Goulart, who sought to establish a power base among the peasants. Goulart sought to empower the agrarian population by sponsoring a literacy programme in the impoverished north-east, coordinated by Freire, which would have enabled them to vote.[8] In both instances, however, the entire process of mass popular mobilisation was brought to an abrupt end by right-wing takeovers. In the case of Italy, it was Mussolini's 'march' on Rome in 1922, which led to the Fascist seizure of power and Gramsci's eventual arrest. In the case of Brazil, it was the military coup which toppled the Goulart government and eventually led to Freire's banishment from his homeland.

This biographical and historical detail may help to explain some of the choices of focus in Gramsci's and Freire's writings. Gramsci focused his attention, for the most part, on Western capitalist society, which he regarded as characterised by the presence of an advanced working class and a well-developed civil society.[9] This is the situation he discovered in Turin, where he became active as journalist and political activist, having been attracted to the city by a university scholarship. Perhaps one reason why Gramsci focused, for revolutionary purposes, primarily on the urban industrial proletariat is that, in his own words, 'The Turin proletariat, by a whole series of actions, had shown that they had reached a high level of maturity and capacity.'[10] It was very militant and enjoyed a tradition of organisation. It made its presence strongly felt in a situation which led many to believe that a revolution was imminent. In contrast, Gramsci regarded the South as 'an area of extreme social disintegration'.[11] He must have seen less revolutionary potential in the peasants, since he argues that they had 'no cohesion among themselves.'[12]

Freire, for his part, devoted his attention, at least in the better-known works, to areas inhabited by peasants who were either landless or were experiencing the first stages of their country's post-revolutionary or post-independence period, and marginal urban dwellers with a recent peasant past, living on the periphery of the cities.[13] Once again, this focus is no doubt influenced by the particular context in which Freire worked. He worked first in the north-east of Brazil; following his banishment and a short stay in Bolivia, he went to Chile where he worked with peasants in the context of the agrarian reform. This presents an interesting contextual contrast with Gramsci's work, although Freire, in his later 'talking books',[14] and perhaps drawing on his later experiences in the USA and Europe, focuses on quite different contexts, including industrially developed ones. This renders the comparison with Gramsci more direct.

One context Gramsci and Freire had in common was that their initiatives were being carried out in situations characterised by economic and social transformation. Piedmont was going through a process of rapid industrialisation – a change in the mode of production was taking place. In Chile, under the Christian Democrat government of Eduardo Frei, an attempt was being made to change the social relations of agrarian production. Aleksandr R. Luria[15] has concluded, following research in Central Asia, that consciousness changes when there is a transformation in the basic forms of social life.[16] The consideration that emerges and seems pertinent also to Gramsci's context is that radical adult education initiatives intended to alter the level of consciousness and aimed at social transformation are most likely to prove effective in a situation characterised by a change in the mode of production. It is relevant that, in Freire's case, the context is an adult literacy programme; for Luria considers literacy acquisition also to be capable of effecting changes in people's consciousness.[17]

It is not helpful to distinguish between the two contexts in simple terms such as 'first' and 'third' worlds or 'developed' and 'underdeveloped' countries. With the exception of the former Portuguese colonies in Africa, the contexts of Gramsci's and Freire's writings are much more complex than such divisions would suggest. The biographical parallels drawn earlier indicate the co-existence of industrially developed regions alongside industrially underdeveloped ones, a situation which is, after all, pervasive in the capitalist mode of production.

Gramsci's Italy and Freire's Brazil were both characterised by a state of internal dependency or, to use Gramsci's term, 'internal colonialism'. In Brazil, a national indigenous bourgeoisie, located in the south-east, has historically been engaged in an alliance with the rural landowning oligarchy in the north-east. As a result of the alliance, the bourgeoisie established its control over the rest of the country and 'the expansion of industry in the South-east of Brazil was premised both politically and economically, upon the stagnation of the North-east.'[18] As Timothy Ireland explains, the pact which constituted the basis of the alliance guaranteed the perpetuation of pre-established forms of land ownership. Land, therefore, remained in the possession of the rural oligarchies, and it is this situation which fostered semi-feudal relations.[19] Southern Brazil had no interest in the industrial development of the north-east and sought to stave off any competition from that region. 'It was interested, however, in securing a domestic "colonial" consumer market for its manufactured goods.'[20] Likewise, by virtue of an alliance with the landowners in the rural Italian South, a situation for which Gramsci held the southern intelligentsia to be partly responsible,[21] the industrial bourgeoisie in the North exercised economic and political control over the rest of the Italian peninsula.[22] In Gramsci's words, 'the North concretely was an "octopus" which enriched itself at the expense of the South, and … its economic–industrial increment was in direct proportion to the impoverishment of the economy and agriculture of the South.'[23]

Parallels

The politics of education

Having contextualised Gramsci's and Freire's work, I will now set about comparing their ideas, starting with an exposition of what I regard as parallel views. Both stress the political nature of adult education. In Chapter 2, I have shown how for Gramsci every relationship of hegemony is essentially an educational relationship.[24] Hegemony, the key concept in Gramsci's social theory, was employed with a view to describing how the domination of one class over another is achieved by a combination of political and ideological means.[25] And, of course, for Freire, educating is an eminently political act: 'it is impossible to deny, except intentionally or by innocence, the political aspect of education.'[26]

Because of Gramsci's political involvement and leadership, his writings reflect a concern with tactics and strategies intended to enable the working class to gain access to power. They are supported by a revolutionary theory which is, for the most part, explicit, though at times cryptic (e.g. the *Quaderni*). Despite the fact that a lot of his writings are scattered and some are fragmentary, a Gramscian theory of revolutionary strategy can be put together.

It has often been argued[27] that Freire's ideas are not supported by an explicit revolutionary theory. I have already indicated, however, that Freire's writings are underpinned by the coexistence of Christian and Marxist ideals[28] – very much the kind of coexistence that informs Liberation Theology, which constitutes the basis of a very important politico-religious social movement. This movement played a very important role in the Nicaraguan revolution and can spread itself not only across but also beyond the Latin American context. Its vision is a revolutionary one which emphasises an ongoing struggle against all forms of oppression and social injustice with a view to realising the Kingdom of God on earth.[29] The respective ideas of the two writers are therefore informed by an overarching vision of social transformation – a transformation into a society devoid of all forms of structural and symbolic violence.

Coercive power

When discussing relations of hegemony and counter-hegemony, it would be unwise to ignore the element of coercion. In his English-language writings, Freire provides examples of different forms of coercion. He refers to different instances when most extreme forms of coercion occur, most notably during the struggle for independence in Guinea-Bissau.[30] In a videotaped interview with Roby Kidd and Alan Thomas,[31] Freire refers to the violence in Guinea-Bissau and provides an account of the treatment he faced after the 1964 coup in Brazil. Other instances of repression are found throughout his work – for instance, in the introduction to *Letters to Cristina*, where he describes the emotional scars left on a woman who had been tortured and beaten in prison for having worked in a clandestine movement that opposed the *coup d'état*. She relived this pain when describing her ordeal to Freire and his family during a visit, with her husband, to their house in Geneva.[32] Freire, in one of the book's long footnotes, goes on to provide details of the kind of torture meted out in Brazilian prisons and the instruments used for this purpose.[33]

Gramsci, writing under conditions of severe Fascist repression, attaches due importance to the coercive aspect of domination,[34] considering it part of the dual nature of Machiavelli's Centaur – half animal, half human.[35] In my view, Gramsci employed the Centaur metaphor to indicate that hegemony incorporated, rather than complemented, the concept of rule by force and power. Thus, when focusing on transformative cultural activity, one must constantly bear in mind the presence of coercive forces that complement or constitute an integral part of the work of consent-inducing institutions and agents (education and law both have their consent inducing and repressive elements). The degree of coercion and the limits it imposes on possibilities for social change differ from context to context, as I shall show in the concluding chapter.

Civil society

For Gramsci, the institutions that play an important part in exercising an educational, hegemonic relationship are those that constitute 'civil society'. It is these institutions that provide the terrain on which the contestation for power takes place. They are conceived of as an outer ditch that helps defend the state, which, in Gramsci's view, cannot be conquered by a frontal attack, a 'war of manoeuvre'. On the contrary, it is necessary to engage in a 'war of position', an ideological war waged in and across the entire complex of civil society.[36] Adult education constitutes an important sphere of 'civil society' and is therefore a site of struggle. It can serve to consolidate as well as challenge the existing hegemony, in the latter case serving as a site of counter-hegemonic struggle. It can serve as one of the means whereby, in Gramsci's view, a revolutionary group aspiring to power must convince, both directly and indirectly, other groups and social sectors that it possesses a *Weltanschauung* which provides a viable and better proposition than the prevailing one. In short, it plays an important role in the 'intense labour of criticism'[37] that Gramsci regards as being crucial prior to the conquest of the state.

Using a theoretically less expansive mode of analysis, but one which focuses directly on pedagogy, Freire also sees action within the complex of civil society as serving either to consolidate existing power relations or to transform them. Traditional pedagogical methods, characterised by a 'top to bottom' communicative approach – a case of what he calls 'banking education' – constitute an example of such 'prescriptive' social practices; in his view, 'one of the basic elements of the relationship between oppressor and oppressed is prescription.'[38]

Banking education, therefore, fosters undemocratic social relations and the inculcation of what one may regard as hegemonic ideas that support prevailing structures of power and processes of domination. For Freire, however, the transformative 'cultural action' of non-formal adult education agencies, notably popular education groups/cultural circles, constitute some of the means whereby the climate for social transformation is created.

In sum, both Gramsci and Freire see educational activity in the area of civil society as essential to transforming existing power relations. In Gramsci's terms, it serves to challenge the existing hegemony.

Agency

The foregoing indicates that both Gramsci and Freire accord an important role to agency in the context of revolutionary activity for social transformation. The two explicitly repudiate evolutionary economic determinist theories of social change. Freire sees them as being conducive to a 'liberating fatalism',[39] while Gramsci regards them as theories of 'grace and predestination'.[40] The emphasis on voluntarism and on the cultural and spiritual basis of revolutionary activity is very strong in the writings of the young Gramsci.[41] This emphasis is also to be found in Freire's early writings.[42] This particular aspect of the two writers' work is generally regarded to have been the product of Hegelian influences. In Gramsci's case, however, it would be more appropriate to speak in terms of 'neo-Hegelianism', the kind of idealist philosophy derived from Croce.[43] In Freire's case, the Hegelianism may have been partly derived via the writings of such Christian authors as Chardin, Mounier and Niebuhr.[44] In later writings, however, this idealist position becomes somewhat modified as both Gramsci and Freire begin to place greater emphasis on the role of economic conditions in processes of social change. In the former's case, this is evidenced by the development of the factory council theory and Gramsci's advocacy of the councils' role in the education of workers.[45] In Freire's case, it can be seen in the 1978 book *Pedagogy in Process*, where popular education is analysed against the background of the social relations of production.[46]

Intellectuals

The importance of the role of human agency within the context of social transformation is rendered more pronounced in Gramsci's theory concerning intellectuals. Gramsci's 'organic' intellectuals are either the thinking and organising functionaries of a dominant class attempting to maintain its hegemony, or, alternatively, those of a 'subaltern' class striving to create an alternative hegemony. For Gramsci believes that intellectuals are not 'free floating', or 'socially unattached', in the Mannheimian sense of the terms, but are rather very much tied to a social group.[47]

Gramsci's study on intellectuals was, of course, motivated by his concern for the proletariat, the class to which he was committed as activist and ideologue, and its ability to develop its own thinking and organising functionaries. Adult educators who help empower members of this class would fit the category of 'organic' intellectuals in the Gramscian sense.[48] After all, Gramsci considered the task of these intellectuals, with respect to the masses, to be an 'educative' one.[49] Gramsci believed that, in so far as the working class is concerned, it would be possible to assimilate traditional intellectuals, but that it would be more desirable for this class to produce its own organic intellectuals.

Gramsci must have pinned great hopes on those proletarian workers who functioned as adult educators in the factories. These were, for him, the true organic intellectuals. They included both educators in the area of technical education and educators focusing on socio-political subjects.[50] Moreover, he constantly emphasised, in his journalistic and other early writings (cf. *Scritti Giovanili*), the need for the proletariat to establish adult education centres very much on the lines of the *Proletkult* and the group surrounding *Clarté*.[51] They were regarded as groups or movements which enable working class people to come into contact with intellectuals whose economic interests were not different from theirs.[52]

There are indirect connections between Gramsci and Freire concerning intellectuals. For example, a lot of educators operating in Christian Base Communities in Brazil, where the pedagogical influence of Freire is so strong, refer to themselves as 'organic intellectuals'. Also, Freire appears to draw on Gramsci's theory of intellectuals when offering advice to the revolutionary leaders of Guinea-Bissau regarding adult basic education for the masses.[53] Drawing also on Amilcar Cabral, Freire writes about the need to create a 'new type of intellectual' and ponders the possibility of some of these intellectuals experiencing 'their easter' and of committing 'class suicide' to integrate themselves with the peasant masses.[54] Despite the change in terminology, the views expressed by Freire with regard to the development of a 'new type of intellectual' in Guinea-Bissau appear to be a direct borrowing from Gramsci.[55] I would submit that Freire's advice is in line with the idea of forming intellectuals in such a way that they become organic to the class they serve. He suggests that students from the Lycée, the country's potential intellectuals, be encouraged to participate fully in programmes of popular education designed for the rural masses. He advocates a process whereby these students would teach and work with the peasants, in a manner reminiscent of the *brigadistas* in the Cuban literacy campaign[56] and which anticipated the literacy workers, also called *brigadistas*, of the Nicaraguan *Cruzada*.[57]

One might argue that Freire regarded all educators engaged in his kind of pedagogy as organic intellectuals. He stressed, throughout his writings, the bond that should exist between them and the oppressed on whose behalf they carry out their activities and with whom they teach and learn. The emphasis on commitment'[58] and 'growing with' the group[59] underlines this view.

Gramsci no doubt emphasised the strong relationship which had to exist between the 'organic intellectuals' of the working/peasant classes and the masses. He regarded it as incumbent on these intellectuals to *direct* the masses, tutoring that which is 'positive' about their 'common sense' with a view to transforming it into 'good sense'. Common sense is, according to Gramsci, 'a conception which, even in the brain of one individual, is fragmentary, incoherent and inconsequential.'[60] As Hoare and Nowell Smith put it, common sense constitutes 'the incoherent set of generally held assumptions and beliefs common to any given society'.[61] Good sense is 'practical empirical common sense'[62] – that is to say, common sense devoid of its contradictory, wayward elements and rendered into a systematic and coherent view.

Gramsci acknowledges a certain superiority on the part of intellectuals, in their educational role with respect to the masses. This smacks of vanguardism. In my view, however, the Italian theorist attempts to provide a theoretical solution to the problem by advocating a reciprocal relationship between intellectual and masses:

> The process of development is tied to a dialectic between the intellectuals and the masses. The intellectual stratum develops both quantitatively and qualitatively, but every leap forward towards a new breadth and complexity of the intellectual stratum is tied to an analogous movement on the part of the mass of the 'simple', who raise themselves to higher levels of culture and at the same time extend their circle of influence toward the stratum of the specialised intellectuals, producing outstanding individuals and groups of greater or lesser importance.[63]

It should be reiterated that this relationship had to be characterised by a situation of reciprocity with an interchangeability of roles between 'teacher' and 'pupil'.[64] The issue of reciprocity is also to be found in Freire's work where the emphasis is, for the most part, on the creation of horizontal social relations between educator and educatees. These relations are characterised by dialogue through which mutual learning between educator and educatees takes place.[65] In his early work, the directive relationship between educators and learners is not stressed. The emphasis on directiveness is, however, evident in later work, including the conversational book with Ira Shor, where Freire states unequivocally that, when the educator begins the dialogue, they (i.e. educator and educatee) are not on equal terms and that the teacher operates in a *directive* capacity.[66] Admittedly, the conception of what the teacher knows is much more diffuse in Freire than in Gramsci. Like Gramsci, Freire argues that the adult educator and learners are not on equal terms, as far as knowledge is concerned. What is common is that there exists a recognition that it is possible, if not indispensable, for intellectuals/educators to possess a theoretical understanding which is 'superior' to that of the learners.[67] Freire argues that this directiveness should not be brought about at the expense of a reciprocal, dialogical relationship between educator and learners. This point calls to mind Gramsci's insistence on the need for a reciprocal relationship between intellectual and masses.

From 'object' to 'subject'

The insistence by both authors on the development of such a relationship is in keeping with the image of human beings they project: that of 'subject'. This role is to be fulfilled in several spheres of life including the cultural circle and the workplace. One area in which Gramsci projects the image of human beings as subject is undoubtedly that of workers' education. Gramsci's factory council theory should, in my view, be recognised as constituting a very significant contribution to the ongoing debate on adult education for industrial democracy. Gramsci argued vehemently that the trade union, traditionally an important agent of adult education, could not organise the proletariat. He argued that the union is a form of capitalist society and not a potential successor to it. It appeared to Gramsci to be a reformist institution whose leaders believe 'in the perpetuity and fundamental perfections of the institutions of the democratic state', which could be modified here and there 'but in fundamentals must be respected'.[68]

Such reformist institutions could not, in Gramsci's view, promote the image of human beings as *subject*. In his view, the working class needed a vehicle which would enable workers to transcend their interests as wage earners since these interests are determined by the capitalist wage relation. This vehicle was to be a social movement intended to engender worker control. It was the factory council movement that was to provide the means whereby the proletariat could 'educate itself, gather experience and acquire a responsible awareness of the duties incumbent upon classes that hold the power of the state'.[69] This movement was therefore intended to transform the workplace, an important site of social practice, into a site of adult learning.

The councils were to serve as the agency whereby workers would experience the entire production process and not be a 'partial operation' in it. In a process inspired by Marx's notion of a 'polytechnical education', knowledge of the entire production process was to be imparted. This knowledge was to be combined with other knowledge, provided by organic intellectuals acting as adult educators, in the areas of economics, administration and social skills. Such an all-encompassing knowledge was meant to give workers the kind of mental control necessary to engage in self-management and ownership. In a later piece, written and published in *L'Ordine Nuovo* in 1921, Gramsci argued for the transformation of trade unions through a fusion with the factory councils: 'fusion must take place naturally, spontaneously, and the unions must base themselves firmly upon the councils, becoming the means for their centralization.'[70] A new trade organisation would thus come into being which would strengthen the means whereby workers would be transformed from object, selling their labour as a commodity, to subject, controlling the entire workplace in a radically democratic manner. The issue of control is a crucial one in Gramsci, as it is in Freire.

The transformation of human beings from object to subject is of central concern to Paulo Freire. In his proposed process of cultural action, the learners participate in the unveiling of their own reality in the creation of their own knowledge. The horizontal social relations of education, which are encouraged, are intended

to project the image of the learners as both educatees and educators. They 'teach' the educators who relearn their knowledge
through dialogical interaction with the learners and the other circle
members. Ideally, both educators and educatees modify their views
through the constant group interactions taking place. When taped,
their conversations often become the subject of their reading
texts,[71] a situation which renders them subject in that it confirms
them as authors of their own knowledge. Furthermore, instead of
being passive recipients of knowledge, they are allowed to reclaim
a voice which an entire prescriptive social system appears to have
denied them. Furthermore, the pedagogy of which they partake is
one based on *the question*,[72] a pedagogical process which Freire
considers indispensable for the kind of problem-posing education
that he advocates.

This approach would, ideally, enable the learner to acquire the
decision-making skills necessary for her or him to become an active
participant, a 'critically conscious' agent,[73] in the life of the community. The sense of participation, on which any theory of the
subject is contingent, is emphasised by Freire in those sections of
his English-language publications where he writes about the application of his methods in the context of agricultural production:

> 'When all this land belonged to one latifundio' said another man in
> the same conversation, 'there was no reason to read and write. We
> weren't responsible for anything. The boss gave the orders and we
> obeyed. Why read and write? Now it's a different story.'[74]

The passage relates to Freire's experience in the literacy programme that was carried out in the context of the Chilean agrarian reform, a case of carrying out transformative adult education
activities in the context of a change in the mode of production –
the sort of situation Luria studied empirically. With the latifundium
system having been done away with, it did become 'a different
story' for the peasants. These words were spoken during the *asentam-
iento*, the period of settlement intended to precede the one in which
lands were to be assigned to peasants. Freire's participatory adult
literacy education was being used as a vehicle for the peasants to
acquire the skills to run their own lands eventually. In Gramsci,
we discover a theory of the subject in a proposed process of adult
education for a participatory industrial democracy. In Freire, such

a theory of the subject is contained in similar educational propos-
als for a participatory agrarian democracy. The concern in both
contexts is with the struggle for popular power and therefore with
the fashioning of a radical democracy in the field of work.

Praxis

Central to the process of learning advocated by the two authors
is the concept of praxis.[75] I would submit that it is the key concept
in their writings that are of relevance to adult education. The
concept is indeed central to Gramsci's thought. The term 'philosophy of praxis' appears in the *Quaderni* both as a euphemism for
Marxism, to circumvent the prison censor, and as a term which
refers to what he regards as the central tenet of Marxism. This is
the forging of a strong relationship between theory and practice,
consciousness and action.[76]

Praxis, as we have seen, also lies at the heart of Freire's
approach,[77] which often entails a process of 'codification and
decodification' whereby elements related to the social reality of
the adult learner are objectified in such a way that they can be
perceived in a partly detached and more critical manner. The
concept, entailing an ongoing process of transformative action and
reflection, is a recurring one in Freire's writings. Even the discussion on exile, in Freire's 1989 conversational book with Antonio
Faundez, deals with this issue. Having been forcibly and tempo-
rarily detached from the world of their daily practical activity, the
two writers claim to have reflected more critically upon it. They
claim to have developed insights which, they felt, made them view
their respective country and culture in a different light.[78] This is
also a situation which invites parallels with Gramsci's predicament, imprisonment arguably having provided, despite the terri-
ble physical and emotional hardship, the space wherein profound
critical reflection on his world of action took place.

It is often argued that praxis, on its own, does not bring about
social change. It has been a standard critique of Freire that the
kind of praxis he advocates, at least in his earlier and most popular
work, is 'intellectual praxis'. This is a kind of praxis that is capable
of transforming the learners' consciousness but would not, however, lead them to engage in social action to transform their situ-

ation of oppression.[79] If linked with social action, however, the educational process would involve 'revolutionary praxis', which is akin to what Marx calls, in the third of his *Theses on Feuerbach*, 'revolutionising practice'.[80] It is the kind of 'praxis' which not only changes the people's consciousness but, being carried out in relation to a strong social movement, contributes to social and political action.[81] This was very much the case with the consciousness-raising activities, inspired by Freire's educational thought,[82] which took place in Nicaragua prior to the overthrow of Somoza.

Adult education and social movements

Gramsci's bitter final experiences with the factory council movement must have led him to appreciate the importance of carrying out counter-hegemonic activities not in isolation but in relation to a strong movement or alliance of movements. Reflecting, in his prison years, on the demise of the movement, Gramsci formulated the concept of the *historical bloc*, which implies engagement in a concerted counter-hegemonic effort on all fronts. It is an effort which entails the support of numerous other social groups or movements fighting for social justice. He advocated efforts, and I would include here adult education initiatives, which had to be carried out in the context of an alliance between the industrial working class and the peasants,[83] an alliance created in a spirit of 'national popular' unity.

Freire, too, argues in favour of carrying out transformative action not in isolation but in relation to strong social movements or an alliance of movements. In his later writings, Freire maintained that adult education cannot 'transform society by itself'.[84] As with Gramsci, we are presented with ideas that are matched by a practical commitment on their proponent's part.

Freire's ideas and work are often seen against the background of radical religious movements in Latin America (e.g. Ação Popular), most particularly the Liberation Theology movement, which, in the case of Nicaragua, played an important role, as part of a convergence of forces, in the process of political change.[85] And, as I pointed out in the biographical sketch, Freire's work as Education Secretary involved the administration of educational programmes, including popular education ones, in concert with mass organisations/movements.[86] After all, the party to which he belonged has a history of links with grassroots movements and trade unions.[87]

Language

There is a belief in Freire in the virtues of dialects, their 'unwritten grammar' and their 'unrecognised beauty'.[88] This belief notwithstanding, he stresses the importance of a language which serves as a source of unity and organisation for the oppressed. He advocates the use of 'national popular' languages, or media of expression, in literacy campaigns. Writing about Guinea-Bissau, Freire states that the use of the coloniser's language, Portuguese, instead of the more popular Creole, was the main reason for the disastrous outcome of the literacy programme in the former Portuguese colony. Nevertheless, he underlines the importance of the oppressed learning the standard language, as a means of survival in the struggle for power.[89] Freire, then, argues that teachers committed to the working class should teach this language. They should do so, however, with one proviso, namely that the language's political ingredients be discussed in the process. In short, the language should be problematised by the radical adult educator – certainly no mean task.

Like Freire, Gramsci, for his part, stressed the use of language for 'national popular' unity in Italy, where several different dialects are spoken. He expressed such views at a time when 80 per cent of Italians still spoke dialect for most purposes.[90] Unlike Freire, however, he says little about the need for problematisation. Like Freire, though, he feels that mastery of the common standard version of the national language was necessary if the working class was not to remain at the periphery of political life.[91] Furthermore, also like Freire, Gramsci does this without underplaying the need for teachers to understand peasant speech.[92]

Differences

Having outlined the main points of similarity between Gramsci and Freire with regard to adult education, I shall now move on to a consideration of the crucial areas in which the work of the two thinkers diverges.

Political affiliation is a major point of differentiation between Gramsci's biographical context and Freire's – something that is reflected in the nature of their respective writings. Freire's active engagement with party politics occurred at a late stage in his life, soon after his return from exile, when he joined the Workers' Party. His pedagogical ideas, therefore, cannot be seen against a backdrop of years of intense activity on behalf of a party or organisation embracing a specific ideology. In contrast, Gramsci's involvement in party politics started during his university years in Turin. Gramsci was involved with the Italian Socialist Party (PSI) between 1913 and 1921, and the Italian Communist Party (PCI), of which he was general secretary from the year when it was launched, 1921, to 1926, the year of his arrest.

Perhaps the most fundamental difference revealed in their writings is simply the range of analysis. Gramsci's range is all-embracing, ranging from economics, education, industrial relations and art to social and political theory. In his most popular work, Freire does not reveal a similar breadth of analysis, though this changes somewhat in his later conversational books. Characteristic of Freire's work is a sustained analysis of the pedagogical dynamics involved in educational situations – of which one finds very little in Gramsci. There is nothing in Gramsci's writings that approximates to the elaborate process devised by Freire whereby the central concept of praxis is translated into a pedagogical, consciousness-raising method. Such differences are indicative of the fact that Gramsci writes from the vantage point of political analyst-cum-strategist while Freire writes, for the most part, from the perspective of pedagogue and educationist.

Literacy

In Freire's case, the processes involved relate mainly to adult basic education. One may argue, however, that there emerges from his writing on and around this subject a theory of knowledge and of transformative educational practice which may be applicable to a variety of educational contexts. The focus on adult literacy in Freire's better-known work, however, reflects once again his involvement with the oppressed masses of Latin America. Nevertheless, it ought again to be stressed that, for Freire, literacy education was merely the vehicle for a process of political conscientisation and was therefore not an end in itself.[93] Freire mainly focuses on literacy education in his English-language publications prior to 1985; whereas Gramsci almost completely neglects this aspect of adult education in his writings, except for those pieces where he talks about standard languages and dialect. This is understandable, considering that his focus was on the industrial North, where the illiteracy rate was very low.[94] It should be remembered, however, that the rate of illiteracy in the southern Italian regions was very high, and Gramsci himself was a southerner. Given such considerations, it is surprising that he should overlook the issue of illiteracy. One explanation may be that Gramsci intended to address the issue in 'The Southern Question',[95] which was left incomplete following his arrest. Or perhaps Gramsci viewed the issue of the emancipation of the southern peasants within the framework of an alliance of classes, a historical bloc, under the leadership of the industrial proletariat.[96]

Given the primary role he assigned to the proletariat, Gramsci must have regarded as of more immediate importance an adult education process capable of instilling in its members the essential qualities of sound organisation, good leadership and cultural awareness. This could explain why he focused almost exclusively on a process of adult education for the northern industrial proletariat, rather than on one related to the peasants' needs. In Gramsci's view, the onus of preparation for leadership fell on this class. In contrast, Freire's focus is on the peasant class, where he finds greater potential for social transformation than in the urban proletariat. He does this, one must add, without idealising the former as some kind of 'universal class' with a historic mission to accomplish.[97]

'Universal class' or 'polyphony of voices'?

Gramsci's theory of social transformation gravitates around the conception of a 'universal class', the working class. The reference to the directive role of the industrial working class in the 'general revolutionary action,'[98] in the unfinished piece on 'The Southern Question' (see Chapter 2) is indicative of this. His is an essentialist view that is considered problematic by a number of writers, notably Ernesto Laclau and Chantal Mouffe. Though centring their theory of radical democracy on Gramsci's concept of hegemony, these two advocates of a 'post-Marxist' position stress the open, unsutured nature of the social. In their view, social conflict is decentred and no single group is predestined to subsume the varying struggles, the 'polyphony of voices', under a unified discourse.[99] This explains their rejection of the idea that the working class is predestined to exercise a leadership role. As Chantal Mouffe argues:

> What is specific to the present situation is the proliferation of democratic struggles. The struggle for equality is no longer limited to the political and economic arenas. Many new rights are being defined and demanded: those of women, of homosexuals, of various regional and ethnic minorities.[100]

Other authors, however, affirm the primacy of class in the struggle for social transformation. Norman Geras is one who holds this position. There are many points in Laclau and Mouffe's work which Geras refutes. These include the notion of the decentred nature of the social, and the related sense of social indeterminacy, which, according to Geras, can 'support any kind of politics'.[101] He also takes issue with them for their denial that 'the abolition of capitalist relations of production'[102] is the most important target for the purposes of bringing about an emancipatory social transformation. Ellen Meiksins Wood,[103] too, scathingly critiques their tendency, and that of other adherents to 'New True Socialism', to deny priority in the quest for socialism to the economic sphere and therefore to the working class. One of the points she makes in her critique of Laclau and Mouffe's position is that it is precisely in the economic sphere, and against the working class, that the New Right, one of the dominant hegemonic forces in Western society, staged its offensive.[104] A similar critique of the kind of position taken by writers like Laclau and Mouffe is forthcoming from Michael Apple, who argues that 'we can multiply forms of domination to such an extent that there are no meaningful organisations to combat oppression left'. He adds that, in moving beyond class reductionism to demonstrate how racial/gender/sexual and other forms of domination operate we tend to forget 'the massive structuring forces that do exist'.[105]

In my view, Freire's frequent passing references, in his 'talking books', to diverse social movements can be taken as a recognition, on his part, of the diversity of the struggles occurring in various parts of the world. There seems to be no universal class in Freire's theory. The term 'oppressed', as used by Freire, is not group specific and critics like Frank Youngman[106] have criticised his work on these grounds, arguing that the term is used vaguely and loosely. In so doing, they fail to recognise the diversity of the groups of persons struggling under oppressive conditions, each one of whom would be termed 'oppressed'. In effect, Freire's 'oppressed' vary from context to context. They range from the *campesinos* or African peasant class to the many underprivileged groups in industrialised Western societies, including women, gays/ lesbians, blacks and ethnic minorities. I would submit, therefore, that, in contrast to Gramsci, Freire provides a notion of oppression that recognises the existence of a 'polyphony of voices', to use Laclau and Mouffe's term. Unlike Gramsci, therefore, Freire provides us with a theory of social change that is non-essentialist. This is a view that he reaffirmed at the 1991 AERA Conference, using words to the effect that one cannot relegate everything to the class struggle.[107] This is not to say, however, that he does not acknowledge the importance of class when dealing with social differentiation.

Cultural production

There is also a difference between Gramsci and Freire in so far as cultural analysis is concerned. In Freire's better-known works, one notices an almost exclusive concentration on elements of 'popular culture'. He regarded these elements as the basis for a transformative process of adult education. Nevertheless, there seems to be no attempt in Freire to extend the range of analysis beyond that of 'popular culture' to develop a systematic critique of 'highbrow culture'. As essentially a pedagogue rather than a committed and influential political ideologue, it seems he was primarily concerned in his writings with that specific area of which he had direct vocational experience.

The situation with Gramsci was different. Unlike Freire, he operated in a city which had all the makings of a typically West-

ern European metropolis, including a well-developed 'civil society'
and a tradition of industrial organisation. Also, his working life
was different from that of Freire. Gramsci worked as a journalist;
he therefore dealt with cultural affairs – a lot of his writings on
theatre, literature and the figurative arts are, in fact, reviews for
newspapers. This particular occupation placed him in an ideal
position from which to observe, at close quarters, the many cultural productions that made up the Italian artistic scene. Gramsci
focuses on both aspects of the 'high' and 'low' divide. He does
this as part of a constant search for a synthesis between the
potentially emancipatory aspects of both with a view to establishing the basis for a proletarian culture.

For Gramsci, a critical appropriation of the dominant, established culture is central to the emergence of a new 'subaltern',
and proletarian, culture. Writing on 'Problems of Marxism',
Gramsci argues that:

> The philosophy of praxis presupposes all this cultural past: Renais-
> sance and Reformation, German philosophy and the French Revolu-
> tion, Calvinism and English classical economics, secular liberalism and
> this historicism which is the root of the whole modern conception of
> life. The philosophy of praxis is the crowning point of this entire
> movement of intellectual and moral reformation, made dialectical in
> the contrast between popular culture and high culture.[108]

This quotation is central to Entwistle's (1979) representation of
Gramsci's view of the development of proletarian culture.
Gramsci's position, in this respect, is quite interesting in view of
the contemporary debate over what should form the curriculum
in the USA. Writers such as Alan Bloom and E.D. Hirsch argue
for a cultural literacy which involves the reading of the 'great
books', a position which has been the subject of much critique by
writers on the left, notably Henry Giroux, himself inspired by
both Gramsci and Freire. The 'great books', Gramsci seems to be
saying, need to be learnt but through a process of critical appropriation, which might also involve reading them against the grain.
Furthermore, central to Gramsci's conception of culture and education is the notion that the popular also matters, as it contains,
as part of its 'common sense', emancipatory potential which is

worth developing. I shall return to this point in the two chapters that follow.

A sense of history

The idea of appropriating that which emerges from the past is reinforced when one considers the importance Gramsci attached to the development among the proletariat of a sense of history. Gramsci considered history to be of crucial importance for the education of the working class, since it enabled members of this class to 'be themselves and know themselves consciously.'[109] The chain metaphor referred to in Chapter 2 underlines his conviction in this regard.[110] This is a linear and evolutionary conception of history in keeping with the Marxist tradition, which recognises progress throughout the ages. This view is at odds with certain current postmodern positions, where the emphasis is placed on discontinuity and where it is argued that, rather than bringing about progress, the Enlightenment tradition allowed the perpetration of the Holocaust and the setting up of the Gulag.

A similar stress on the importance of history, with respect to the education of the oppressed, is nowhere to be found in Freire's English-language publications. Gramsci must have felt that the information to be derived from such a subject would render the discourses and opinions of adult learners informed ones. Such information also includes 'facts':

> previously, the pupils at least acquired a certain 'baggage' or equipment (according to taste) of concrete facts. Now that the teacher must be specifically a philosopher and aesthete, the pupil does not bother with concrete facts and fills his head with formulae and words which usually mean nothing to him, and which are forgotten at once.[111]

Banking education

The above quotation deals with the education of children. Nevertheless, what Gramsci says there appears relevant also to adult education. The idea of acquiring 'baggage' is relevant not only to the area of workers' cultural preparation but also to that of technical education. For Gramsci, this constituted an essential component of workers' education which the trade union and factory council together had to provide.[112] Freire would regard the transmission of such facts as an essential feature of the process of 'banking education'. It is a process whereby the pupil is regarded, in Goulet's words,[113] as a passive recipient of knowledge, or, in a metaphor used by Freire, as an empty receptacle to be filled.[114] In a much-cited piece from *Pedagogy of the Oppressed*, Freire delineates, somewhat mechanistically, the roles of teacher and student under conditions of 'banking education'.[115]

Gramsci, for his part, provides a less mechanistic account, though not a developed one, of learning under such conditions. In a position which strikes me as being opposed to that conventionally associated with Freire, Gramsci argues that there cannot be a passive learner, a 'mechanical' recipient of abstract knowledge. Gramsci argues that knowledge is assimilated according to the learner's consciousness which 'reflects the sector of civil society in which the child participates' and the social and cultural relations to which the learner is exposed.[116] At issue here is the manner in which meaning is circulated, mediated and assimilated. I would argue that this can be taken to apply not only to children but also to adults, who, given their greater life experience, can perform the task of assimilation even better as their consciousness reflects a much broader set of cultural and social relations.

Conclusion: Towards a Synthesis

The foregoing exposition of some of the differences between Gramsci's and Freire's ideas relevant to adult education leads me to argue that each of the two theorists stresses some aspects that the other either overlooks or underplays. One can therefore write in terms of their providing complementary views. I have already indicated that there are indeed similarities between the two authors on a number of issues. Among these similarities, one discovers an emphasis on the political nature of educational activity and on the role that institutions of civil society play in processes of social transformation.

I have also emphasised the sense of agency to be found in their works, coupled with their advocacy of the need to project educational programmes in which human beings are transformed from

'object' to 'subject'. This is a binary opposition, strongly emphasised in Freire, which is being refuted by certain postmodernist
writers and often overlooked by others who are quick to give the
Brazilian's work a postmodernist coating. There is also a focus on
committed adult educators who themselves have to undergo a
transformation to work with subaltern social groups, becoming
organic intellectuals in the Gramscian sense or 'experiencing their
Easter' in the sense advocated by Freire. There is also the stress
on praxis as the heart of liberating education and on the need to
carry out such pedagogical work in the context of a larger movement or alliance of movements striving for social change.

I have shown that there are also differences. I have indicated
that Gramsci's focus is on the requirements of a particular social
group which plays a leadership role in the process of social transformation, as opposed to Freire's non-reductionist view of the
struggle for democracy and the creation of a socially just society.
There are also differences in the range of social analysis provided,
with Gramsci presenting us with a much wider spectrum, given
that his project was all encompassing. The dynamics involved in
teacher–learner encounters are accorded much wider treatment
in Freire's work than in Gramsci's, which is understandable given
that a substantial part of the Brazilian's focus is on pedagogy.

Gramsci provides a complex, though undeveloped, view of how
ideas are taken up in settings where education takes place. This
view is close to certain poststructuralist theories regarding the
multiplicity of readings of texts.[117] Gramsci's view stands in contrast
to Freire's early, somewhat mechanistic description of what goes
on in a situation of 'banking education'. And yet, though the
distinction between oppressor and oppressed is clear cut in this
situation, one must not forget Freire's early exposition of the
concept of 'oppressor consciousness'[118] which indicates that people
can easily be perpetrators as well as victims of oppression, a point
he reiterates elsewhere, notably in one of his very last works.[119] It
is worth noting that Kathleen Weiler has raised this point as a
criticism of Freire's ideas in general, arguing that the dichotomy
between oppressor and oppressed is a false one.[120]

The notion of 'oppressor consciousness' and the light it sheds
on the way an apparently subordinated group is implicated in
oppression relate to the process of contradictory consciousness that

characterises relations of hegemony/counterhegemony, in the Gramscian sense. It is a situation that brings to mind Foucault's dictum that, in resisting power, one is not external to it. We are all implicated in relations of power. In fact, one of the major contributions of Gramsci's hegemony theory is that it places emphasis on the way power is ubiquitous and manifests itself even in the most intimate social relations.[121] It is a position which underlines the diffuse nature of power, a notion which once again brings to mind Foucault. Existing hegemonic arrangements are said to be supported by a number of beliefs and practices in a variety of settings, ranging from the home to adult education. All individuals are thus conceived of as 'sites of power' but not all individuals possess the same amount of power.

Often the different levels of power exerted by persons in different sites can render them incoherent beings. Freire provides the example of the socially oppressed father and son who would not allow their socially oppressed wife and mother respectively to learn to read.[122] It is the 'search for coherence', based on the recognition that we are 'incomplete beings,'[123] that would characterise a process of transformative education on Freirean lines. Using Gramscian terminology, I would argue that this incoherence would be part and parcel of the contradictory nature of our 'common sense'. The 'search for coherence', therefore, would involve the means of transforming 'common sense' to 'good sense'.

This suggests an important point of contact between the ideas of Antonio Gramsci and Paulo Freire. For the most part, the relationship between the two is best conceived of as one of complementarity. There are a number of similarities, as I have shown, but we come across several instances when one thinker provides insightful material that the other overlooks. Together, the similarities and complementary aspects could provide the foundation for a possible synthesis of their ideas relevant to adult education. An attempt at an initial synthesis will be made in Chapter 6. However, I shall first underline what I consider to be some of the limitations in both Gramsci and Freire as regards their incorporation into a theory of transformative adult education relevant to the present time.

Notes

1. An earlier version of this chapter appeared as Mayo, 1994c.
2. Hoare and Nowell Smith, in Gramsci 1971b: xxx–xxxi; Festa, 1976: 14.
3. Shaull, 1970: 11.
4. Shaull, 1970: 11; Fiori, 1970: 15, 25.
5. Adamson, 1980: 50.
6. Torres, 1982.
7. De Kadt, 1970; Jarvis 1987a; Elias, 1994.
8. Ireland, 1987: 16; Torres, 1990a: 40.
9. The term 'civil society' is not being used here in the sense intended by Marx – i.e. the realm of economic relations (Bobbio, 1987: 147) – but in Gramsci's sense of the entire complex of ideological institutions.
10. Gramsci, 1957: 40.
11. Gramsci, 1957: 42.
12. Gramsci, 1957: 42.
13. Torres, 1982: 88.
14. Cf. Shor and Freire, 1987; Horton and Freire, 1990.
15. Luria, 1976.
16. Cf. Youngman, 1986: 84–6.
17. Youngman, 1986: 84–6.
18. Ireland, 1987: 12.
19. Ireland, 1987: 12.
20. Ireland, 1987: 13.
21. Nairn, 1982: 174.
22. Ireland, 1987: 9.
23. Gramsci, in Ireland, 1987: 11.
24. Torres, 1985: 4793.
25. Abercrombie et al., 1984: 99.
26. Freire, 1976: 70.
27. E.g. Youngman, 1986.
28. Cf. Elias, 1994: 47–60.
29. Giroux, 1988: 113.
30. Freire, 1978.
31. See *Guns and Pencils*, videotape, OISE, University of Toronto.
32. Freire, 1996: 8, 9.
33. Freire, 1996: 205–7.
34. Anderson (1976) has indicated, in his discussion on the 'antinomies' in Gramsci's work, different formulations relating the concept of hegemony to force and consent. This has led to different interpretations as to whether hegemony includes force or not. This is not to say, however, that Gramsci intended his analysis to indicate that, in capitalist society, one rules through consent rather than through force and consent.

35. Gramsci, 1971b: 170. Alden takes issue with Entwistle (1979) on this matter, arguing that the latter believed 'that the ruling position of the capitalist class in Western societies is not based on political and economic power or force, but solely on "hegemony"' using 'hegemony' in the sense of ruling through consent – see Alden, 1981, 92. Alden goes on to say that 'Entwistle neglects to explain the considerable evidence in the prison notebooks that suggests he meant his doctrine of hegemony to complement, not to replace the Marxist and Leninist conception of class domination and class struggle through power and force.' – see Alden, 1981: 92.

36. Gramsci, 1971b: 238.

37. Gramsci, 1977: 12.

38. Freire, 1970: 31.

39. Freire, 1985: 179.

40. Gramsci, 1957: 75.

41. Morrow, 1987: 2.

42. Youngman, 1986: 162, 163.

43. Broccoli, 1972: 49; Morrow, 1987: 2.

44. Youngman, 1986: 159.

45. Morrow, 1987: 2.

46. Youngman, 1986: 63. Gramsci progressed from this particular phase to elaborate a theory of revolution within the context of party strategy. His involvement as secretary general of the PCI must have been a determining factor in this regard. As for Freire, one wonders whether his involvement latterly with the Workers' Party (PT), which led to his becoming Education Secretary in the municipal government of São Paulo (see Freire, 1993; Torres, 1993, 1994b), had a similar effect on his writings and on the development of his future pedagogical and social theory. In later years, his political party and administrative involvement apparently caused his early sense of voluntarism to mellow. One gathers this from his various emphases, made at the 1991 AERA Conference, on the difficulties involved in bringing about social change – see Freire, 1971.

47. Gramsci, 1971b: 5.

48. For a sustained analysis of the relevance of Gramsci's concept of organic intellectual to adult education, see Hommen, 1986. There is a growing literature on Gramsci's theory of intellectuals, which he conceived as an important component of the study embarked on in prison. For a recently published discussion, wherein Gramsci's ideas are taken up in the context of a larger debate concerning the role of intellectuals in contemporary society, see Barney, 1994.

49. Merrington, 1977: 168.

50. Cf. Entwistle, 1979.

51. Broccoli, 1972: 49.

52. Broccoli, 1972: 49, 51.

53. This point confirms Gramsci's influence on Freire.

54. Freire, 1978: 104.

55. Freire, 1978: 143.

56. Bhola, 1984: 97, 98; Leiner, 1986: 177, 178; M. Mayo, 1997: 67, 68.

57. Arnove, 1986: 32, 33; 1994: 17, 27.

58. Freire, 1970: 61.

59. Freire, 1971: 61.

60. Gramsci, 1971b: 419.

61. Hoare and Nowell Smith, in Gramsci, 1971b: 323.

62. Hoare and Nowell Smith, in Gramsci, 1971b: 323.

63. Gramsci, 1971b: 334, 335.

64. Gramsci, 1971b: 350.

65. Freire, 1970: 67.

66. Freire, in Shor and Freire, 1987: 103.

67. I am here referring to Frank Youngman's critique of Freire's peda-gogy. Youngman's critique appeared a year in advance of the Shor–Freire conversational book. Until then, Freire did not emphasise the directiveness referred to in the text. As such, I consider justified Youngman's observa-tion that Freire is 'ambivalent about saying outright that educators can have a theoretical understanding superior to that of the learners' – Youngman, 1986: 179.

68. Gramsci, 1977: 76.

69. Gramsci, in Merrington, 1977: 158.

70. Gramsci, 1978: 21.

71. Freire, 1973.

72. Freire, in Bruss and Macedo, 1985: 9.

73. Allman, 1988.

74. Freire, 1985: 60.

75. See Allman and Wallis, 1990 on this concept.

76. Hoare and Nowell Smith, in Gramsci, 1971b: xiii.

77. Some prefer to use the term 'method' in this context. See Chapter 3, concluding section and note 88 for references.

78. Cf. Freire and Faundez, 1989.

79. La Belle, 1986: 181.

80. Marx, in Tucker 1978: 144.

81. La Belle, 1986: 181.

82. Arnove, 1986: 8.

83. Gramsci favoured an encounter (*incontro*) between the workers' movement and the Catholic masses – Amendola, 1978. He argued that some kind of *modus vivendi* with the Catholic Church has to be found – Lojacono, 1977: 22. The Communist faction at the Livorno Congress accused the Socialists of failing to reach an agreement with the Catholic-inspired Partito Popolare of Don Luigi Sturzo which would have stemmed the tide of Fascism – Lojacono, 1977: 25.

84. Freire, in Shor and Freire, 1987: 37.

85. See Mayo, 1993a and final chapter in this volume.
86. Cf. Freire, 1991.
87. Ireland, 1987.
88. Shor and Freire, 1987: 72.
89. Freire, in Shor and Freire, 1987: 73.
90. Gramsci, 1985: 43.
91. Gramsci, 1971b: 325.
92. Entwistle, 1979: 25.
93. Mayo, 1991; 1993.
94. In Gramsci, 1988: 53.
95. Cf. Gramsci, 1964: 797–819.
96. Gramsci, 1957: 30; cf. Gramsci, 1964: 799.
97. Freire, in Walker, 1980: 137, 138.
98. Gramsci, 1957: 30; Gramsci, 1964: 799.
99. Laclau and Mouffe, 1985: 192.
100. Mouffe, 1988: 100.
101. Geras, 1987: 77.
102. Geras, 1987: 44.
103. Meiksins Wood, 1986.
104. This section on Norman Geras and Ellen Wood has been reproduced from a footnote in Mayo, 1994a.
105. Apple, 1991: 28, 29.
106. Youngman, 1986.
107. Freire, 1991.
108. Gramsci, 1971b: 395.
109. Gramsci, 1971b: 37.
110. Cf. Gramsci in Broccoli, 1972: 32.
111. Gramsci, 1971b: 36.
112. Entwistle, 1979: 147.
113. Goulet, 1973: 11.
114. Freire, 1970: 58.
115. Freire, 1970: 59.
116. Gramsci, 1971b: 35.
117. Cf. Apple, 1992: 10.
118. Freire, 1970.
119. Freire, 1997a: 311, 312.
120. Weiler, 1991; 1994.
121. Holub, 1992: 197.
122. Freire, 1997a: 312.
123. Freire, 1997a: 312.

CHAPTER 5

Some of the Limitations in Gramsci and Freire for a Contemporary Project

Thus far, I have attempted to provide the groundwork for a synthesis of those ideas of Gramsci and Freire which are relevant to adult education. I would argue, however, that in order for a synthesis of their ideas to be relevant to some of the most pressing concerns of this day and age, it is necessary to underline certain absences in their work. These absences need to be addressed at some length to render their work useful for projects of contemporary relevance. This is what I set out to do in this chapter.[1]

Gramsci: Class and Other Forms of Social Difference

It can be argued, given the role of leadership Gramsci ascribes to the industrial working class in the revolutionary process, that his vision of social transformation is, in Laclau and Mouffe's terms,[2] 'essentialist', or, more precisely, 'class essentialist'. And even in so far as class is concerned, it focuses primarily on the transformative role of just one of the two main 'subaltern' classes in Italy: the industrial proletariat rather than the peasant class.

Peasants and adult literacy

The peasant class is by no means overlooked in Gramsci's writings, and furthermore constitutes the subject of an unfinished study. Indeed, Gramsci's love of Sardinia is reflected in several of his writings, especially his letters. Nevertheless, he does not romanticise life on the island; indeed he brings out its brutal aspects.[3] Yet little that relates to the image of the peasant in Gramsci's cultural writings is of relevance to the creation of a proletarian culture. Gramsci attaches too much importance to the written word in his promotion of popular culture (e.g. his discussions of the serial novel).[4] Little consideration seems to be accorded to the rich oral traditions that have always been a feature of cultural production in the Southern Italian regions, where access to cultural products involving the medium of the written word was limited in view of the high rates of illiteracy prevalent there.[5] As David Forgacs points out, citing the 1911 census, illiteracy among persons over six years of age in Piedmont, where the industrial proletariat was concentrated, was down to 11 per cent.[6] In the South, the percentage was higher. Forgacs indicates that the figure for Sardinia was 58 per cent,[7] though Hoare and Nowell Smith put it much higher at 90 per cent;[8] while that for Calabria was 70 per cent.

The industrial working class and cultural formation

The limited references to the issue of adult literacy in Gramsci's writings and his constant focus on cultural activities that emphasise the written word indicate that the educational requirements of the industrial proletariat were uppermost in his mind. He saw the peasant class's role as secondary in importance to that of the Northern industrial working class. It is to the industrial proletariat, 'the universal class' in the classical Marxist sense, that Gramsci devoted his attention for revolutionary purposes. This is reflected in his cultural and educational concerns. The emphasis he places on the setting up of cultural associations where workers can indulge in free, 'disinterested' discussions suggests that the people he had in mind were the literate workers of the North. However, irrespective of how literate workers are, one assumes that there has to be some process of mediation which enables them to be able to appropriate critically those elements in the 'canon' – those works which form part of the established 'cultural heritage' – of relevance to them in their quest for developing a counter-hegemony. What role, if any, do the organic intellectuals play in this process of mediation and how do they go about it? What kind of provision ought to be made for those adults who lack the necessary background to be able critically to appropriate this culture? These are the questions that have to be addressed by those who are exploring ways of developing forms of cultural production commensurate with the aspirations of a subaltern group.

With regard to the problem of creating a synthesis between the established and the popular forms of cultural production, Gramsci has seemingly limited himself to indicating what should be done and where exploration should be carried out. He has not indicated how to go about it. This is also a feature of other areas in his work. Thus his work in this area is best described as being of a tentative and groping nature.

Other forms of marginalisation

So far we have dealt only with issues relating to social class in Gramsci's work. However, in discussing the relevance of his work to the development of a contemporary democratisation project, one has to deal with other issues of difference that have been brought to the forefront of sociological and cultural, including adult educational,[9] debate in recent times. Of course, it would be ironic to accuse Gramsci of some 'politics of absence' and yet fail to recognise that his voice is also that of a marginalised person, given his location as a disabled, Southern islander, one whose mixed feelings regarding Sardinian popular life has also to be seen in the light of the traditional prejudice with which Sardinians regarded and dealt with disabled people – his shocking description of the disabled youth chained within a hovel is highly indicative in this regard.[10] There was considerable prejudice regarding hunchbacks, like himself, who were believed to have been possessed by evil spirits.[11] It would be grossly unfair therefore to infer that Gramsci was not conscious of social difference in his projects, given his own experience, as well as his empathy for those whom he felt were more excluded than him.[12]

Gender relations

This having been said, one needs to register absences in his writings for the purpose of underlining their relevance and inspiration for a contemporary project. When dealing with the factory

council movement, conceived of as a movement of worker education for greater, and ultimately complete, worker control, Gramsci
provides little, if any, indication regarding how traditionally un-
equal power relations between male and female workers can be
improved through a process of education for industrial democracy. And one can argue that gender considerations are not
integrated into Gramsci's analysis of oppression even though he
wrote some isolated pieces on the issue.[13] Gramsci dealt with the
issue of gender in some of his writings, notably the piece on 'Americanism and Fordism'[14] and his review of Henrik Ibsen's *The Doll's
House*.[15] One of Gramsci's first public speeches in Turin was on
the emancipation of women, a speech which was inspired by
Ibsen's play.[16] Gender considerations, however, do not form part
of the analyses in those aspects in his work that are relevant to
adult education. This is very much a reflection of the time in
which he wrote. As Holub argues:

> I do not expect Gramsci to think or act differently from the way he
> does when it comes to women. If, in spite of a few decades of intensive
> feminist discourses and practices, many contemporary men often dis-
> play little feminist consciousness in the practices of their daily lives,
> despite all theoretical claims to the contrary, ... I find it difficult to
> insist on feminist practices when it comes to a thinker and a man such
> as Gramsci whose experiences were not confronted, the way ours now
> are, with a series of continuous radical, complex and extensive femi-
> nist discourses.[17]

Eurocentrism and regionalism

The same can be said of Eurocentrism, an obvious feature of
Gramsci's cultural writings. It has been a feature of a great deal
of Marxist writing, including Marx's own work. As David W.
Livingstone argues: 'Marx as well as subsequent orthodox Marxists and most critical Western Marxist intellectuals have operated
from a Eurocentric world view which has regarded European
civilisation as the dynamic core of global life.'[18]

An obvious example of a Eurocentric approach to knowledge
is provided by Gramsci's controversial piece on education, in which
most of the discussion regarding content centres around the Western
classical writings, even though, as argued in Chapter 2, this piece

has to be read carefully before one argues that Gramsci is simply advocating a reversal to the classical, conservative curriculum. Echoing Holub, one should not expect anything different from him, given the era in which he wrote and given the fact that, even today, despite the experience of the civil rights movement and the pressures posed by anti-racist writers, activists and movements, as well as the multi-racial nature of most Western societies (which could not have been the case in Italy in Gramsci's time), Euro-centrism remains pervasive in Western institutions.

Although one might not have expected Gramsci to act differently with regard to the issues of regionalism and Eurocentrism, given the historical period in which he lived, there is a particular form of regionalism[19] that is endemic to Italian society and to which Gramsci himself would have been exposed, namely the Northern prejudice against the South. Gramsci indeed rebels against this in his writings and inveighs against those from the North and other parts of the Italian mainland who would attribute situations of poverty and material hardship, deriving from an unjust and ex-ploitative social system, to genetic inferiority.[20] He must have been confronted by the issue of whether Southern workers, with a recent peasant past, could gain acceptance in a workers' environment located in the North of Italy. To what extent did the traditional North–South form of regional prejudice rear its ugly head in the Turin factories? What role should the factory councils, as adult education agencies, play in combating the form of prejudice gen-erated by this particular type of regionalism? These are pertinent questions in view of the concerns that are constantly expressed within the trade union movement worldwide with respect to the prevalence of patriarchal, racist and homophobic attitudes.

Sexual regulation and production

On the issue of homophobia, it may be argued that, in the piece on 'Americanism and Fordism', Gramsci shows a fine understanding of the connection between sexual regulation and the demands of industrial production.[21] The problem with Gramsci's views, though, is his justification of this connection, his legitimation of certain forms of sexual discipline, and his failure to distinguish between different sexualities and their social and cultural effects.[22]

The alleged high incidence of sexual, homophobic and racial harassment at the workplace makes an ongoing struggle against these and other forms of oppression a task that I consider of primordial importance for movements and organisations seeking social change. I would argue that these issues will have to be dealt with in adult education programmes connected with such movements and organisations, including trade unions, which have often been criticised in this respect.[23] They will also have to be dealt with by adult educators whose intention it is to provide a democratic adult education experience and yet who are employed in community colleges and other established institutions where the emphasis is placed on training for work, probably as part and parcel of a new vocationalism. It is, after all, not uncommon to find educators inspired by radically democratic ideals who work within institutions that are more geared towards consolidating the status quo than challenging it. Educators of this kind would be operating 'in and against' the system,[24] or, once again, as Freire often puts it, in a situation of being tactically inside and strategically outside the system. I shall return to this point.

In both situations, I would argue that, unless consideration is given to differential social locations, there will be severe limits to the extent to which adult educators, acting as organic intellectuals, can help mitigate potential barriers between themselves and the learners. Of course, they might be 'organic' to them in terms of class, though there could be barriers also in this regard, since commitment to the working class does not necessarily mean that one lives like members of this class. They could, however, be estranged from them, or at best from a number of them, in terms of gender, race, ethnicity or sexual orientation. Failure to account for such differential location can lead to elements of domestication emerging from an ostensibly emancipatory practice.

Freire and Social Difference

Freire, for his part, only in his later years took on board issues concerning social difference. He refers in the 'talking books', in the interviews with Donaldo Macedo[25] and in one of his last books,[26] to the situation of women, gays/lesbians, ethnic minorities, blacks, and so forth. There may be various reasons for this. One may argue that Freire represents a voice from the so-called 'majority world', and such voices have traditionally been marginalised within the context of Eurocentric regimes of truth. However, he also happened to live in an era when the issue of difference was affirmed in the radical sections of cultural discourse.

Race and gender

In Freire's earlier work, from the early 1970s to the early 1990s, as I have indicated, despite constant references to social movements there was no sustained discussion on gender, race and sexuality issues. These issues and movements are mentioned only in passing.[27] This is especially true of the 'talking books' in English. I argued that, despite his many references to class in his early work (thirty-eight, according to Freire himself),[28] even this particular aspect of social differentiation is not analysed in a sustained way. And even when referring to the oppressed in the impoverished north-east, Freire does not differentiate in terms of race, despite the fact that blacks and indigenous people suffered considerable oppression during the period. One wonders whether, in his literacy work in this area of Brazil, when he used the dominant Portuguese language, account was taken of the different literacies engaged in by members of different tribes. It is tempting to argue that this is a limitation in Freire similar to the one concerning peasants and literacy in the work of Antonio Gramsci. Freire argued latterly, with respect to his early work, and particularly *Pedagogy of the Oppressed*, that:

> In the various dialogues I have had with Donaldo Macedo we have addressed these issues [concerning social difference] in more detail that need not be repeated here. Still, even though I may run the risk of repeating myself, I would like to reiterate that when I wrote the *Pedagogy of the Oppressed*, I tried to understand and analyze the phenomenon of oppression with respect to its social, existential, and individual tendencies. In doing so, I did not focus specifically on oppression marked by specificities such as color, gender, race, and so forth. I was more preoccupied then with the oppressed as a social class. But this, in my view, does not at all mean that I was ignoring the many forms of racial oppression that I have denounced always and struggled against even

as a child. My mother used to tell me that when I was a child, I would react aggressively against any manifestation of racial discrimination. Throughout my life, I have worked against forms of racial oppression, which is in keeping with my desire and need to maintain coherence in my political posture. I could not write in defense of the oppressed while being a racist, just as I could not be a machista either.[29]

As I have argued elsewhere, with particular reference to the talking books in English, a sustained analysis of particular forms of oppression is not available, even when the situation clearly lent itself to it.[30] A case in point is Freire's transcribed conversation with Myles Horton.[31] It is a well-known fact that Myles Horton was a social activist and educator whose work in the 1950s was closely connected with the civil rights movement.[32] The citizenship schools, coordinated through Highlander Folk Highschool, the centre he founded, constituted one of the means whereby African-Americans attained the basic level of literacy required of them so that they could become eligible to vote. Yet despite Horton's close connection with the civil rights movement, the issue of racism is not explored in any depth[33] in his book with Freire. References to African-American educators like Bernice Robinson are made only in the context of demonstrating how one can be effective as a pedagogue working with underprivileged groups. Such a sustained analysis of racism would have presented Freire-inspired adult educators with a wonderful opportunity to examine closely the application of Freire's ideas within the context of a social movement. After all, Freire has argued that these movements can be important agents of social change.[34]

As I and others have argued elsewhere, gender is another area which, until latterly, Freire had not dealt with in a sustained way and as part of an integrated analysis. His early work has been the subject of much critique by feminists, who have pointed to the invisibility of women and their experiences in his project of liberation. Some, like Kathleen Weiler, sought to fuse his ideas with those representing different strands within feminism.[35] bell hooks, one of Freire's admirers who has engaged with some of his ideas in her earlier work,[36] refers to the 'phallocentric paradigm of liberation'[37] which informs Freire's work. She regards this phallocentrism as the 'blind spot in the vision of men who have profound insight', and includes Freire, together with Memmi and

Fanon, among such people.[38] Attention was drawn[39] in the previous chapter to the patriarchal[39] settings of some of the codifications illustrated in one of the early works.[40] Freire, while acknowledging that he was not 'acutely aware' of gender issues when writing his most celebrated work, argued a point which Renate Holub[41] makes with respect to Gramsci, namely 'that the knowledge base with respect to gender oppression we have today, thanks to the great and comprehensve works of feminists, was not available to me then nor was it available to many women.'[42]

Feeling the pain

One place where Freire deals with gender in a sustained way is in a published conversation with his long-time friend, translator and co-author, Donaldo P. Macedo.[43] A number of interesting issues are raised in this dialogue, not least of which is Freire's statement 'I am too a woman,'[44] which was intended to express his solidarity with women in their struggle for liberation from patriarchal, *machista* oppression. In my view, 'to be a woman' one has to feel the pain and share the knowledge of gender oppression. Can men feel this pain and share this knowledge, in their solidarity with women? Is there not a limit to the amount of 'border crossing'[45] possible in this regard? In this respect, even a discussion on racism with Horton, a white male, would not reflect any of the pain suffered by victims of racial oppression. Of course, one may argue that, in his struggles in support of better working conditions for miners in Wilder, and later for racial justice, Horton did place himself on the line. He risked his life with respect to the first struggle. Here, one need only consider the fate suffered by other people involved, notably Barney Graham, the miners' leader, who was eventually killed in the most brutal manner. Horton was even arrested in Wilder and charged with gathering and disseminating information.[46] At the time of the 'citizenship schools', Horton also suffered the stigma of being branded a 'communist infiltrator', with all the connotations of being 'un-American' and a 'menace to Constitutional government'[47] that it carried. Needless to say, the work carried out for the purpose of achieving inter-racial progress did invite repression – drawing 'fire from Southern white racists.'[48] One can perhaps speak of pain here.

The pain I was referring to earlier, however, is the everyday pain suffered by disenfranchised people as a result of their social location. And here one must therefore note the social difference between Horton and the people he supported, a difference he himself acknowledged.

> Horton realized Highlander could help lay the groundwork for the struggle, but they couldn't take much part in it. They were white and the struggle was Black. Even more important, the leadership was now Black. The people were leading themselves.[49]

Horton understood the race barriers that existed, in the citizenship programme, between whites at Highlander, including himself, and blacks. As Adams stresses,

> Horton never entered a Citizenship School classroom as a teacher, and, as the idea spread, he discouraged other well-meaning whites from doing so too. He felt the presence of any white stranger in the classroom altered, even stopped the naturalness of learning. Citizenship schools were run by Blacks from the start.[50]

Given such an awareness, Horton would have recognised the limits being imposed on a discussion on racism. These limits would, I am sure, have made him wary of the danger of 'speaking on behalf of' someone else. This is not to say that, in an exchange like the one between Horton and Freire, the issue of racism should be avoided. On the contrary, I feel that it should be taken up, especially if, as in Horton's case, the experiences of the citizenship schools lend themselves to such a discussion. I would argue that, in these situations, the limits of the discussion should be acknowledged and underlined, limits which Horton acknowledged with respect to his engagement in anti-racist struggle in the 1950s and early 1960s.

The pain and knowledge resulting from a first-hand and ongoing experience of oppression can have a direct bearing on the conversation and on the nature of engagement with Freire with regard to specific forms of oppression. For in all his conversation books in the English language, a style of writing for which he seemed to have developed a predilection, Freire did not engage, in a publication of this kind, with either a woman or a person of colour, a point I have registered elsewhere.[51] In this respect, bell hooks'[52] open invitation for him to engage in a 'talking book' with her ('my great wish') provided a golden opportunity. This engagement, had it taken place, would have served as a source for further examination of the suitability of his radical pedagogical ideas for an adult education project intended to confront racism, patriarchy and other forms of oppression.[53]

It has to be said, however, that Freire's later work explicitly demonstrates his recognition of the intersections between various forms of oppression that occur in our everyday life. He stresses the multiplicity of subjectivities involved in structural and systemic forms of oppression. He underlines the importance of *coherence* in people and societies claiming to be progressive, as well as his commitment to a politics characterised by 'unity in diversity'.[54] He writes about the need for human beings to engage in an ongoing search for coherence, a never-ending learning process:

> The high level of incoherence that such societies exhibit within their populations tends to contribute to this mismatch. On the one hand, there is the passionate democratic discourse of those who mysteriously recognize their roles as teachers of world democracy and guardians of human rights and, on the other, there are evil racist practices that aggressively contradict democratic ideals. The struggle against racism, sexism, and class discrimination is an undeniable demand in a democratic society and indispensable for its development.[55]

> No doubt racist, sexist and elitist teachers who speak about democracy and call themselves progressives must become truly committed to freedom, must undergo their own Easter. They must die to their old selves as sexists, racists, and elitists and be reborn as true progressives, enlisted in the struggle for the reinvention of the world.[56]

Class suicide, habitus and marginality

While Freire's later work rendered explicit the intersections between various forms of oppression, the earlier work attached a lot of importance to social class. In *Pedagogy in Process*,[57] Freire echoes Amilcar Cabral in referring to the concept of 'class suicide' when dealing with the issue of differential location between educator and educatee. Yet 'class suicide' strikes me as being very difficult to accomplish, especially when there are so many factors, like one's habitus (values, norms, taste for culture, 'master patterns' of thinking and speaking, relationship to language and culture, etc.), one's educational background, the nature of one's everyday work (especially cerebral work), possibly even one's acquired coherent and systematic view of the world (Gramsci's notion of 'good sense'), that can distinguish the adult educator from the working-class participants with whom he or she is working. Writing in a piece in which he dwells on Gramsci's and Freire's influence on the Warwick School of Social Work, Peter Leonard states:

> As intellectual defectors we faced, but never fully escaped from, the dangers inherent in traditional bourgeois intellectual activity – élitism, the cult of the expert, the belief in the superiority of mental over manual labor.[58]

As for habitus, bourgeois-formed educators will probably find it extremely difficult to break away from it. Habitus is considered by Bourdieu and Passeron to entail 'irreversible' processes of learning which condition 'the level of reception and degree of assimilation of the messages produced and diffused by the culture industry, and, more generally, of any intellectual or semi-intellectual message'.[59] While the French sociologists seem to be too deterministic in this regard, they do stress an aspect of our class location as educators which provides a formidable barrier in the way of committing class suicide.

On the other hand, I feel that a position of marginality with respect to the system can possibly help draw the educator closer to the learner. Working in a position of marginality seems to be or have been the case with a number of adult educators.[60] The case of Raymond Williams stands out in this respect. Referring to the Oxford University Delegacy for Extra-Mural Study, which worked in collaboration with the WEA (Workers' Education Association) and with whom Raymond Williams was employed for several years, McIlroy states:

> In 1946 tutors did not enjoy the same tenure, facilities, or opportunities for promotion as internal lecturers. But by 1961 assimilation was advanced, although it was only in 1960 that Williams secured a form of promotion. This reflected and reinforced the marginality of university adult education. Critics felt that this work 'is not of university quality'. It was noted that 'extra-mural tutors, many of whom work at places remote from the university, have little effective contact with their

internal colleagues and are not in fact regarded as of equivalent status'. At Oxford, Frank Jessup recalled staff tutors in the post-war period as being connected with the university but not of it, 'irregulars skirmishing on the periphery.'[61]

In these situations, there could be a mutual feeling of marginality between educator and educatee which can help draw them closer. One must acknowledge, however, that there would still be differences in the degree of marginality experienced by the two. There would still be differences in the degree of marginality experienced by different types of adult educators. That is, barriers would persist.

War of Position: Contestation and Cooptation

Freire-inspired pedagogy can be taken up as a strategy for transformation even by progressive educators working within the state system, attempting, in Freire's words, to be 'tactically inside and strategically outside' the system. Of course, the task, here, does present its problems, with the threat of cooption being ever present. After all, people who seek to strengthen the system often accommodate elements of the oppositional discourse, leaving out some important, threatening ingredient, as part of their own 'war of position'. This having been said, those working 'in and against' the system should be wary of the tensions created by gender, race and other differences, between educators and educatees, tensions which can undermine their proposed liberatory practice.[62]

These tensions can be encountered in most situations but most particularly when operating within the system, since the educators involved would not have the freedom to choose where and with whom they are going to carry out their adult education work. A male teacher can be assigned a class entirely made up of females. A white teacher can be assigned a class of black students. A strong sensitivity to such tensions is therefore warranted, if one is to work effectively 'in and against' the system. Weiler is instructive on this issue, as it affects teaching both within and outside the system:

Without naming these sources of tension, it is difficult to address or build upon them to challenge existing structures of power and subjectivities. Without recognizing more clearly the implicit power and limitations of the position of teacher, calls for a collective liberation or for opposition to oppression slide over the surface tensions that may emerge among teachers and students as subjects with conflicting interests and histories and with different kinds of knowledge and power.[63]

In much of Freire's work, this issue is not taken up. This comment appeared in the context of a critique of Freire on these grounds. Weiler argues that his dichotomy of 'oppressor' and 'oppressed' is somewhat simplistic and that it reveals a failure, on his part, to indicate the multiplicity of subjectivities involved in the learning process. A person can, after all, be oppressed in one situation and an oppressor in another. I have indicated earlier in this chapter that Freire, in his most recently published work, demonstrated sensitivity to this issue, given his discussions around multiple and layered identitities. And what is more, his notion of the 'oppressor within', clearly manifest in his early work, indicates awareness of such potential tensions.

This having been said, I feel that radical adult education theory would have to address this issue in a substantive and far from token manner. It would therefore have to go beyond the work of Gramsci and Freire to take into account other writings. This would include the writings of Weiler herself[64] and a host of other writers in the areas of feminist and anti-racist education, including those who draw on either Gramsci's or Freire's work.[65] It would include, to a certain extent, the work of major exponents in the area of critical pedagogy for whom Freire and, to a certain extent, Gramsci are constant sources of reference.[66]

Information Technology

There is another issue that should be touched upon briefly in this chapter. It concerns the ever-increasing role of information technology, itself a product of capitalism which can serve as an instrument of domination but which can nevertheless be critically appropriated in the interest of subaltern groups. Gramsci's emphasis on journalism,[67] and the creation of such periodicals of working-class culture as the *Proletkult* in Russia, *Clarté* in France and *L'Ordine*

Nuovo in Italy, raise the critical issue of working-class access to the media, mainly newspapers, which featured among the most important sources of communication at the time.

Times have changed since Gramsci's period of writing. Much more sophisticated communication technologies are now in place, although they were already beginning to emerge then. In Gramsci's time, radio and cinema were the emerging forms. Alas, they are given little consideration in the *Quaderni*. As Forgacs and Nowell Smith point out:

> His concept of culture became richer and fuller, but it retained un-criticized residues of its original bias towards the written word as the core of cultural formation in individuals and in society. It is significant that the emerging forms of radio and cinema receive minimal attention in the Notebooks.[68]

Gramsci's lack of attention to these emerging forms of technology must be registered when embarking on a project involving the incorporation of his ideas. Given that the radio was an emerging form, it might have been expected that he would give consideration to the possibilities it offered for the future dissemination of information. After all, this was a person whose exploration of different forms of adult education for workers was wide enough to include the setting up of a correspondence school for the PCI, a school for which he was also entrusted with the task of preparing materials.[69]

Similarly, I would regard Freire's lack of analysis of contemporary forms of information technology as a limitation. For example, how can they best be utilised in the context of adult education strategies for social transformation? One would expect more from Freire than from Gramsci on this issue, given the contemporary historical context in which the former lived. Perhaps it could be argued that part of the 'war of position' for a movement or organisation striving for social transformation in this day and age lies in adult educational experiences intended to provide people with greater and critical access to information technologies.[70] Access to such technologies would constitute one of the means for greater international mobilisation of resources[71] to counter the ever-growing threat to democracy posed by the increasing internationalisation of capital.

Conclusion

In this chapter, I have argued that there are pressing concerns today which need to be addressed if one is to propose guidelines for the creation of projects intended to contribute towards the generation of greater social justice. I have shown how these concerns are often obscured by Gramsci and Freire, even though, with respect to issues concerning social difference, the latter sought to address them in his later work. I have indicated how this later work by Freire underlines the multilayered and often contradictory identities we possess and the need for us to engage in an ongoing struggle for greater coherence. Echoing hooks' views regarding Freire,[72] I would argue that these limitations should not obscure Gramsci's and Freire's great insights into the workings of power, and the liberatory potential contained in their work. In order to take on board their several valid ideas, however, it is necessary to engage critically with their work. One important aspect of this critical engagement would, in my view, be that of constantly registering and politicising the absent discourses in their writings. In this respect, adult education theorists would do well to supplement and sharpen the insights of these two figures – themselves victims of marginalisation – with those deriving from writings and practices in such relevant fields as feminisms, anti-racism, cultural studies and critical pedagogy. Here I would particularly stress the work of those who themselves draw on the influences of either (e.g. Stuart Hall, bell hooks) or both (e.g. Giroux, Shor) of the two theorists analysed in this book.

It is necessary to be sensitized to and address these limitations to avoid engaging in a totalising discourse when confronting oppression. Westwood, citing Bauman, argues that we must constantly be made aware that roads which have often been regarded as the uncontroversially appropriate ones to take can indeed be slippery.[73] Strategies pursued and theories relied on need to be constantly re-examined in a process of ongoing critique. No matter how insightful and resourceful they are, the works of Gramsci and Freire, like those of other advocates of social change, are not immune to this process.

Many of the themes broached in this chapter will re-emerge in the following one, where I attempt to outline a possible synthesis, drawing on Gramsci's and Freire's insights and supplementing them with those of other writers and pedagogues. I shall also attempt to draw on insights deriving from the new forms of social struggle that are developing in this period.

Notes

1. An earlier version of this chapter was published as Mayo, 1994b.
2. Laclau and Mouffe, 1985.
3. Cf. Germino, 1990: 1–24.
4. Forgacs and Nowell Smith, in Gramsci, 1985: 345.
5. Forgacs and Nowell Smith, in Gramsci, 1985: 344.
6. Forgacs, in Gramsci, 1988: 53.
7. Forgacs, in Gramsci, 1988: 53.
8. Hoare and Nowell Smith, in Gramsci, 1971b: xviii.
9. See, for instance, Thompson, 1983, 1988; Rockhill, 1987; Taking Liberties Collective, 1989; Miles, 1989, 1997, 1998; Westwood, 1991a; Ball, 1992; Blundell, 1992; Hart, 1992; Schedler, 1993, 1996; Brookfield, 1993; Hill, 1996; Darmanin, 1997.
10. Gramsci, 1996: 674; Germino, 1990: 3.
11. Germino, 1990: 2.
12. Germino, 1990: 3.
13. For a discussion on Gramsci and feminism, see the conclusion to Holub, 1992: 191–203, in which she focuses on two key women in his life, Julia and Tatania Schucht.
14. Gramsci, 1971b.
15. Gramsci, 1985: 70–73.
16. Hoare and Nowell Smith, in Gramsci, 1971b: xxxi.
17. Holub, 1992: 195.
18. Livingstone, 1995: 64.
19. Cf. Apitzsch, 1993.
20. Germino, 1990: 11.
21. Gramsci, 1971b.
22. Holub 1992: 198.
23. Cf. Taking Liberties Collective, 1989: 124.
24. London–Edinburgh Weekend Return Group, 1979.
25. See Freire and Macedo, 1993; Freire and Macedo, 1995.
26. Once again, the reader is referred to the last chapter of Freire et al., 1997, a paper in which Freire responds to a number of writers.
27. Mayo, 1993a: 18.
28. Freire and Macedo, 1993.
29. Freire, 1997a: 309.

30. Cf. Mayo, 1992: 80.
31. Horton and Freire, 1990.
32. Cf. Adams, 1972; Peters and Bell, 1987; Horton and Freire, 1990.
33. Mayo, 1992: 80.
34. Mayo, 1992: 80.
35. Weiler, 1991.
36. hooks, 1988.
37. hooks, 1993: 148; hooks, 1994: 49.
38. hooks, 1993: 148; hooks, 1994: 49.
39. Cf. Taylor, 1993; Mayo, 1993b.
40. Freire, 1973.
41. Holub, 1992.
42. Freire, in Freire and Macedo, 1993: 173.
43. Freire and Macedo, 1993.
44. Freire and Macedo, 1993: 175.
45. Adopted from Giroux, 1992.
46. Adams, 1972: 104.
47. Adams, 1972: 113.
48. Adams, 1972: 112.
49. Adams, 1972; 114.
50. Adams, 1972; 112.
51. Mayo, 1991b: 82.
52. hooks, 1993: 154.
53. Mayo, 1991b: 82.
54. Freire, 1997a: 310.
55. Freire, 1996; 175.
56. Freire, 1996: 163.
57. Freire, 1978.
58. Leonard, 1993: 166.
59. Bourdieu and Passéron, 1990: 43, 44.
60. Because of the often non-formal nature of adult education and the engagement of volunteers in this sector, adult educators are often regarded as of inferior status to the other educators in the formal educational system, the latter often being regarded as professionals for having gone through a period of professional preparation.
61. McIlroy, 1993a: 275.
62. Mayo, 1993a: 18, 19.
63. Weiler, 1991: 454, 455.
64. Weiler, 1991, 1994.
65. E.g. bell hooks, 1988, 1993.
66. See, for instance, Aronowitz and Giroux, 1991; Giroux, 1992; Shor, 1992; McLaren and Da Silva, 1993.
67. Gramsci, 1971b; Gramsci, 1985.
68. Forgacs and Nowell Smith, in Gramsci, 1985: 13.

69. Buttigieg, 1992: 83.

70. Baldacchino, 1997.

71. Holub concludes her study on Gramsci by stressing the point of international collaboration within the context of feminist struggles, 'which the rapid dissemination of information technology more powerfully enables as each day passes' – Holub, 1992: 203.

72. hooks, 1993: 148.

73. Westwood, 1993: 336.

CHAPTER 6

A Gramscian–Freirean Synthesis and Beyond

The argument in Chapter 4 indicates that there are points of convergence and difference in Gramsci and Freire with respect to the issue of adult education, and that a synthesis of their ideas is possible. I argued that each of the two theorists stresses aspects which the other either overlooks or underplays. Thus there is a complementarity aspect to their contrasting ideas when they are juxtaposed. Gramsci's more extensive analysis, in terms of power relations in the wider society and in terms of cultural analysis in its broader context, complements Freire's remarkable insights into the power dynamics that lie at the heart of pedagogical encounters. Whereas Gramsci provides a systematic and wide-ranging analysis of the dominant culture, Freire focuses, for the most part, on popular culture. One of the key points I shall be making here is that insights for the purposes of developing a theory of radical adult education can be derived from a synthesis of Gramsci's ideas concerning the dominant culture and Freire's ideas on the popular.[1]

A Gramscian–Freirean synthesis would be based on a consideration of issues in adult education relating to both process and content. In stressing the differences that exist between the two theorists in this regard, I am not playing down the fact that each in his own way contributes to theory in both areas. There are insights by Freire that can contribute to the macro-level analysis normally associated with Gramsci, in the same way that Gramsci addresses issues pertinent to the Freirean analysis of learning processes.

Commitment

One point that emerges from Gramsci's and Freire's views regarding adult education is that radical initiatives in this area, intended to transform existing dominative power relations within society, require a strong commitment on the part of organisers and educators alike. Such commitment is implied in Gramsci's notion of the 'organic intellectual', which suggests conscious alignment with a particular political movement. In Gramsci's case, the commitment is to the class which undertakes the task of transforming society. According to my understanding of Gramsci's usage of the term and its application within the context of his revolutionary vision, those who performed counter-hegemonic work within the ambit of *L'Ordine Nuovo*'s sphere of influence would be the prime exemplars of such commitment. These would include technical educators and organisers within the factory council movement, educators in the various *Vita Morale* clubs, and those who occupied the position of educators within the 'prison school' at Ustica.

As shown in the previous chapter, popular educators in Latin America, especially in Nicaragua and El Salvador, demonstrate the extent of such commitment by placing their lives on the line for the cause of social transformation. Another example would be centres of radical adult education like Highlander, whose founder, Myles Horton, dwells at length on this issue in his conversational book with Paulo Freire.[2]

Forms of oppression

Like all education, adult education is not neutral and is very much tied to hegemonic interests within a given society. This is certainly the case with conventional, mainstream adult education. A transformative and emancipatory adult education would, in my view, be born out of recognition of this point and inspired by theoretical perspectives that highlight the strong relationship that exists between knowledge, culture and power, and aim to render the kind of knowledge provided by mainstream institutions and the manner of its dissemination problematic. Nevertheless, it would be erroneous to deny agency for change to those working within mainstream institutions.

However, it would not do to underestimate the dynamism of those in a position of dominance, who seek to consolidate the dominant power bases. These people also adapt and change in reaction to counter-hegemonic challenges in societal politics generally and in education in particular. Mainstream institutions can also be conceived of as sites of struggle, where domination is never complete. Transformative adult education initiatives, developed on Gramscian–Freirean lines, should therefore be sustained by a theory that is couched in a 'language of possibility', to adopt the Blochian terminology rendered so popular in critical pedagogical circles by Henry Giroux[3] and Roger I. Simon.[4] Such initiatives would emphasise a strong commitment to the emancipation of subaltern groups from hegemonic domination. For, as I have shown, while Gramsci focuses for the most part on the issue of class domination, Freire's notion of oppression extends beyond class considerations, which, as he himself acknowledges,[5] were the main concern of his earlier works. (Even when he deals with class, Freire does not provide the sort of grounded analysis that would have been useful for effective counter-hegemonic thinking and practice, opting instead simply to provide 'references'.[6]) He also moves beyond a consideration of the revolutionary role of the industrial working class to a wider recognition of social difference and oppression, although it should be added that he fails to go beyond universalised forms of oppression.[7]

In combining the insights of Gramsci and Freire on this matter, I would argue that, irrespective of whether they focus on single-issue or multiple-issue politics, radical adult education initiatives would be rooted in a commitment to confronting oppression in its different forms. Therefore adult education initiatives directed towards the emancipation of a particular social group from oppression should be carried out in a manner that does not perpetuate the domestication and subordination of another:

> Any system of representation which signifies (by silence or by positive branding) some group as less than fully human has to be transformed on the road – a long and winding road – of socialist construction.[8]

Workers' organisations have often been taken to task for the perpetuation of gender oppression in the name of worker advancement,[9] which in reality means the advancement of white male workers. In this respect, one can learn a great deal from the writings of Audre Lorde, bell hooks[10] and a host of other black feminists, who have underlined the failure of certain white feminist writers to acknowledge the forms of oppression experienced by women of different race. As Wendy Ball states:

> there has often been a failure by feminists to respect differences between women of racial origin and of social class. Anti-racist, anti-sexist struggles in education need a theoretical framework which acknowledges the interrelationship of racial, gender and class-based sources of oppression. In turn, this will have implications for the model of political change pursued.[11]

Equally pertinent are certain criticisms levelled at Freire and other central male figures in critical pedagogy, and at academics theorising about, say, class oppression.[12]

Alliances

The issue of alliances is central: it is important for the radical adult educator to link his or her work with that of other cultural workers striving for social change within the broad process of 'cultural politics'.[13] I would also argue, learning from Gramsci's own experience, that there are moments in history when links must be established with intellectuals/cultural workers who may not be committed to the same radical project but who share a concern for the creation or preservation of a democratic environment, a concern which would be manifest through ideas and action that resonate with what Laclau and Mouffe[14] call 'the democratic imaginary'. Renate Holub indicates how Gramsci managed to engage in a communicative process with Piero Gobetti, a liberal intellectual, whom he invited to direct the literary and drama sections of *L'Ordine Nuovo*.[15] Such a communicative process was possible because of the latter's commitment to a democratic environment, the possibilities for which were undermined by Mussolini's Fascist regime. The same applies to the links which the *Ordine Nuovo* group are said to have established with certain intellectuals associated with the Futurist movement, especially its ideologue, the poet Filippo Marinetti. These relations were eventually stalled when several young futurists turned 'reactionary'.[16]

The left intelligentsia will engage in dialogues and even forge alliances with individual bourgeois intellectuals, particularly with anti-fascist intellectuals of the liberal bourgeoisie when politically expedient and appropriate, while it will simultaneously participate in cultural processes that both engage and further the intellectual potential among the working class.[17]

The situation described above arguably finds a parallel in the experience of several Latin American popular educators during the periods of totalitarian rule that various states in the region experienced during the 1960s and 1970s. It is also a situation that radical adult educators will have to deal with in liberal, bourgeois democracies, especially in those cases where the educators are operating within a system[18] that is generally non-conducive to radical activities. Often the programme organisers will have to make do with facilities available within the system, including teaching personnel. As a result, radical adult educators will have to team up with others of different orientation and political persuasion. It is important, however, that within these contexts a dialogue[19] takes place with these non-radical educators.

Agency

The above emphasis on cultural politics testifies to the two writers' view that cultural activity plays an important role in the consolidation or transformation of power relations in a given society, especially in Western capitalist social formations. Both writers have shown that dominant groups exercise their power in society not merely through coercion but also, and perhaps more importantly, through consent.

The cultural terrain of contestation

As shown in Chapter 4, coercion is given importance in the thinking of Gramsci and Freire. Both were, after all, victims of some of its worst forms. However, it is arguably in their analysis of the consensual basis of power that Gramsci and Freire have been particularly instructive. Mainstream cultural and educational activities help generate consent through the promotion of legitimating ideologies and social relations. Both Gramsci and Freire conceive of the terrain of such cultural activity as a site of struggle. There is therefore a strong sense of agency in their work, wherein radical cultural and educational initiatives are accorded importance in the struggle for change.

Transformative adult education plays its part in this context. It can constitute a vehicle whereby dominant ideologies can be unveiled and dismantled. The realm of everyday experience, characterised by 'taken for granted' notions, becomes part of the focus in a process of transformative adult education. In an age characterised by the intensifying globalisation of capital, these notions would include the prevalent ideology of consumerism[20] and the marketplace, whereby even some of the most basic services are turned from a public good to a 'consumption good'. This 'everyday experience' is evoked through a dialogical process that entails the means of 'extraordinarily re-experiencing the ordinary'.[21] It is not celebrated uncritically but rather interrogated. A white male proletarian voice might contain racist and sexist elements, which it needs to shed if it is to realise its potential of contributing to the creation of a democratic environment:

> it is not enough for teachers merely to affirm uncritically their students' histories, experiences and stories. To take student voices at face value is to run the risk of idealizing and romanticizing them. The contradictory and complex histories and stories that give meaning to the lives of students are never innocent, and it is important that they be recognized for their contradictions as well as for their possibilities. Of course, it is crucial that critical educators provide the pedagogical conditions for students to give voice to how their past and present experiences place them within existing relations of domination and resistance.[22]

Prefiguring democratic social relations

'Common sense' would thus have to be converted into 'good sense', and this conversion can come about not merely through a climate which allows learners to 'give voice' but, most importantly, through a climate which allows for the interrogation of such voices and the recognition of the contradictions that lie therein. Furthermore, radical adult education, with its emphasis on voice(s) and their interrogation, democratic social relations of education and praxis, constitutes prefigurative work. It prefigures transformed democratic social relations in the wider society. This was true of Gramsci's factory councils, with their emphasis on radically democratic social relations of work, power sharing (including ownership of the work-place itself) and education. It is equally true of Freire's cultural circles, with the emphasis on dialogue, a critical interrogation of experience, the unveiling of social contradictions and the promulgation of democratic social relations of education characterised by teacher authority but not authoritarianism.[23] Both theorists provide an emancipatory education approach that confronts the kind of social relations traditionally prevalent in capitalist environments.

I emphasise the word *traditionally* since it is necessary to stress that elements of a radical adult education, such as those indicated above, can be partly appropriated by management to provide the process of extracting surplus labour with a democratic façade. This is all part of the dynamic nature of hegemony; part and parcel of the 'war of position' engaged in by the organic intellectuals of transnational capital, who 'constantly struggle to change minds and expand markets'.[24]

Appropriation of Freire's work is common. In Brazil, his work was amazingly coopted by the same regime that banished him from his homeland. His work is often also the target of liberal appropriation, with his method extricated from its underpinning political philosophy, a process underlined by a number of writers,[25] not least Freire himself.[26] Worker-management teams are a classic example of present-day capitalist appropriation of partici-patory educational experiences (see the concluding chapter for further discussion of this alliance). Participation that entails power sharing, as advocated in Gramsci's factory council theory, and that finds its common expression in such ventures as cooperatives, must be distinguished from the form of participation that allows managment to retain its prerogative over capital accumulation.[27]

Social Movements

It is relevant to enquire at this stage when the sense of agency accorded to adult education initiatives is likely to be strong. What we learn from Gramsci's reflections on the isolation of the Turin factory insurgents and from Freire[28] when he engages with Liberation Theology[29] and the new social movements,[30] is above all that radical adult education initiatives are unlikely to prove effective when carried out on their own. They must operate in relation to a social movement, itself often conceived of as a site of social revolutionary learning,[31] or an alliance of such movements. Gramsci's notion of the historical bloc, signifying an alliance of social groups, becomes particularly significant in this age characterised by the globalisation of capital.

Social movements and global capital

I return now to the question posed in the previous chapter and in my work elsewhere.[32] Given the increasing mobility that characterises the latest stage of the globalisation of capital, is it possible for social movements, especially those with an international character, to serve as the vehicle whereby, in Gramsci's terms, a historical bloc can transcend its 'national-popular' character[33] to become an alliance across national boundaries? This is not to minimise the role that indigenous movements, such as the revitalisation movements of conscientisation and sarvodaya,[34] can still play in this process. For, as Leslie Sklair[35] argues, many forms of resistance to global capitalism can only be effective when they disrupt the smooth accumulation of capital locally, or, I would add, within a restricted sphere of influence. Yet Sklair also argues that such movements need to 'find ways of globalising these disruptions'.[36]

New social movements with a strong international character, like the women's and environmental movements, are perhaps more likely to make headway in this respect. Nevertheless, it would be a mistake to romanticise such movements and present them as a *deus ex machina* in an age when global capital holds sway. Sklair warns in the conclusion to his study: 'No social movement appears even remotely likely to overthrow the three fundamental institutional supports of global capitalism that have been identified, namely the TNCs [transnational *corporations*], the transnational capitalist class and the culture-ideology of consumerism.'[37] He nonetheless affirms and illustrates some of the resistances effected by social movements in each of the three spheres. Furthermore, these movements need constantly to enhance their spheres of influence by engaging in alliances at local, regional, continental and global levels, possibly by gaining access to and making effective use of electronic networking.[38]

An alliance can develop out of a recognition of the different forms of oppression that exist and thus of the need to create a radically democratic society characterised by an equitable distribution of power on class, gender, race and ethnicity lines. A workers' education programme, developed along Gramscian–Freirean lines, must deal with issues such as sexual harassment at the workplace and the underrepresentation of women in trade-union hierarchies, as well as draw on non-Eurocentric sources of learning.[39] With a view to creating a radically democratic society, the different social movements would engage in solidarity, thereby creating something akin to a 'historical bloc'.

Class matters

Economic restructuring in what is fashionably termed the 'post-Fordist' era has led to a burgeoning peripheral labour market, consisting primarily of women (working part-time in the home), ethnic minorities and blacks, all of whom suffer from unstable conditions of work. We are witnessing a situation in which the labour market continues to be segmented on an international scale by increasingly mobile capital, a process that exacerbates racism and, in doing so, weakens working-class solidarity. This scenario is one of several reasons why class politics should not be too readily dismissed as a thing of the past. For all their shortcomings and often myopic vision, working-class organisations such as trade unions still have an important role to play, provided they undergo a process of rethinking and reorientation similar to that called for by Gramsci when advocating a strong relationship between unions and the factory council movement.[40] Part of this rethinking process consists of understanding the way class constantly intersects with issues of race, gender and ethnicity, and other forms of oppression. These organisations also have to be transformed so that they are able to 'reconnect with the general interest', to use the words of John McIlroy, written in relation to Raymond Williams.[41]

The recognition by working-class organisations of multiple forms of oppression will expose them to the pressures and ideas emanating from the various social movements fighting for social justice. This will involve broadening their agendas to confront the issues of racism, Eurocentrism, patriarchy, ageism and homophobia, which continue to fragment a potentially strong popular force. A programme of adult education for workplace democracy, such as that analysed in my Malta case study,[42] would, for instance, seek to contribute to the democratisation of the social relations of production in both domestic and public spheres. Opening up to the social movements would also entail major organisational restructuring to ensure greater social representation. And adult education programmes carried out within and across such organisations should reflect this. These programmes would ensure greater social representation as regards project planners, teaching personnel and adult learners. Furthermore, the curriculum devised – preferably through a process of negotiation – should incorporate as broad a range of social agendas as possible.

Moreover, the analyses of issues should be integrated, thereby reflecting the intersections of class, race, age, gender, sexuality and ethnicity. The issue of racism toward immigrant workers and other ethnic groups becomes ever more urgent in an age of continual global reorganisation of capital across national boundaries.[43] It is common knowledge that in this age we have been witnessing the bifurcation of the labour market on racial and gendered lines.[44]

Transformative adult education can play its part in drawing connections between the various struggles with which different movements are engaged. What is being advocated here is the development of programmes that do not serve to promote one voice at the expense of other voices but that are inclusive of different voices and stress the multiplicity of subjectivities involved in processes of structural and systemic oppression. This applies equally to workers' education programmes inspired by Gramsci's factory council theory as to Freire-inspired programmes. Codification and decodification strategies would serve as the means of interrogating popular experiences to explore how one is implicated in, as well as suffering from, processes of structural oppression – how, for example, one suffers gender and racial oppression while occupying a subaltern position in the class structure.

This would also involve, in Gayatri Spivak's terms, a process of unlearning one's privilege.[45] Programmes developed along these lines would hopefully draw the support of different movements and make a contribution, however small, towards bringing these movements closer. The relationship between radical adult education and social movements would be reciprocal in this context. A lot of the impetus to the work carried out by radical adult education is provided by the social movements, by virtue of their various demands and the issues they raise. These issues will, in turn, become part of both the programme's hidden and its overt curricula. Radical adult education will, for its part, help prepare citizens for such movements by increasing their awareness not only of the issues with which they are directly concerned but also of issues affecting others, in the interest of generating greater solidarity.

In and against the system

Radical adult education initiatives as well as radical adult educators need to be sustained by a social movement or movements. Each movement should develop enough strength to sustain counter-hegemonic efforts, including radical adult education ones, in as wide a range of institutions of 'civil society' as is possible. This follows the example of Gramsci's notion of counter-hegemonic educational work within and across different sections of civil society (journalism, cultural clubs, workplace, prisons containing political detainees, etc.), which is reflected in his keen interest in a variety of adult learning agencies, including the popular libraries.[46] It is in keeping with the notion of a 'war of position', entailing an engagement in critique and counter-hegemonic activity on all fronts, and indeed with Freire's exhortation to have 'one foot inside and another outside' the system.[47] It acknowledges the potential of different sites of social practice to become sites of counter-hegemonic, and therefore transformative, learning. Major focus would, of course, be placed on autonomous agencies like non-governmental organisations, and, in this respect, there exists a strong tradition in Europe and North America (for instance, High-lander in the southern USA, the Coady Institute in Antigonish, and the Jesuit Centre in Toronto) of agencies seeking transformation from outside the system.[48]

Social movements can play a role in bringing about counter-hegemonic activity even within the system. They are necessary in order to put pressure on state agencies in capitalist societies to serve the interests, including adult educational interests, of particular target groups. This is something that the state agencies appear loath to do, to judge by the totalising discourse that camouflages the class content,[49] and other contents, reflected in the state's policy-making: 'Centrally, state agencies attempt to give unitary and unifying expression to what are in reality multifaceted and differential historical experiences of groups within society, denying their particularity.'[50]

In this respect, social movements need to sustain progressive social organisations applying for state funds or funds from larger entities such as the European Union, a point to which I shall return in the concluding chapter. Yet these movements also need to sustain progressive adult educators working within the state system,[51] carrying out their day-to-day work within the context of a long-term strategy for social transformation. Committed adult educators working in state institutions can become mediating influences in the process of cultural transmission. After all, no matter how reproductive (in the sense of reproducing the social conditions that sustain certain social arrangements) a state programme may be at face value, this reproduction is never complete. This is a point which Giroux makes forcefully in his critique of neo-Marxist accounts of education.[52] These committed educators would reinterpret mandates in the light of their own radical agendas, and therefore be 'in and against the state'.[53] However, the pressures on such adult educators would be great, including resistance by learners to innovative approaches. The educators could easily become demoralised, considering that they operate within a hierarchical, prescriptive system which imposes restrictions on the degree of freedom they may wish to create and encourage adult learners to explore.

There is, after all (to make free with a famous phrase by Audre Lorde) a limit to the extent to which one can use the master's tools to bring down the master's house. Social movements can help sustain morale in the face of the frustration experienced by adult educators. They can provide spaces, within organisations that subscribe to the movement, for discussions and reflection involving adult educators and other cultural workers. In short, they can provide a sphere of autonomy outside official state apparatuses. In the absence of such support, isolation, burn-out and a paralysing sense of helplessness could result, in response to which the educator would fall back on traditional 'coping strategies', which serve a reproductive rather than a transformative function.

Adult Educators

I have so far discussed some of the issues relating to the work of adult educators in the context of social movements. However, other issues relating to the role of the adult educator need to be discussed. Gramsci's views concerning organic intellectuals and Freire's views regarding value-committed educators can be combined to project an image of the adult educator, working in the context of a radical adult education programme, as a person who, equipped with a theoretical understanding of the adult learners' predicament, engages in a *directive* form of adult education. It is directive in the sense that it is inspired by a utopian vision of a society characterised by greater social justice.

The sense of authority she or he possesses, as a result of competence in the area being explored, does not degenerate into authoritarianism.[54] On the contrary, every effort is made to promulgate democratic social relations and to render the learners the 'subject' of the learning process. The culture of the learner makes its presence felt through a dialogical teaching process. The educator's task is to facilitate the means whereby this culture is examined critically by the learners themselves, so that the 'common sense' is converted to 'good sense'. Freire's codification/decodification process, which can be applied not only to literacy education but also to forms of knowledge pertaining to other aspects of social life, can constitute an appropriate vehicle for the conversion of 'common sense' to 'good sense'.

Unlearning and relearning

In a dialogical process, it is not only the learners who begin to appreciate what they 'know' in a more critical light, but also the adult educator, who constantly modifies his or her theoretical understanding through contact with the adult learners. This is akin to Gramsci's notion of intellectuals testing their theories through a dialectical engagement with the masses. Whatever knowledge the adult educator possesses at the outset of the learning process is relearned, and possibly unlearned, through dialogical contact with the learners.[55] Gramsci's ideas concerning the instruction–education nexus[56] need to be combined with those in Freire concerning dialogue to produce a view of adult education which does not preclude the possibility that a certain amount of 'teaching' occurs when absolutely necessary.[57] I would argue that this has to be done for a variety of reasons. In the first place, the adult educator has to deal with the possible 'fear of freedom', to use Freire's words, which may render any attempt at creativity – the hallmark of a participatory and democratic education process – a journey into the unknown. Such a 'fear of freedom' can make learners resist attempts at a democratic learning process and thus the pressure increases on the educator to adopt traditional 'tried and tested methods' of teaching.[58]

Another important consideration is that of rendering the discussion an informed one. One should not overlook, in this context, the process, highlighted by interactionists, whereby *negotiation of meaning* between educator and educatees takes place. As intimated in Chapter 3, a conflict of intention may arise here, inasmuch as the former conceives of his/her work as a component of a liberatory, democratic project, while the adult learners seek to obtain from the learning process the means of 'making it' in the system. This may render the educator's efforts to provide an emancipatory dimension to learning a long and arduous process, one which calls for constant negotiation and renegotiation between her/him and the learners. Furthermore, the teacher would occasionally have to accede to learners' demands for traditional teaching, for which there may be a strong case. For what they are demanding is, in my view, that sense of rigour and disciplined learning which Gramsci advocates in his piece 'On Education'. As Gramsci indicated, this is what the subaltern classes require in order to defy the odds when engaging in counter-hegemonic action. I would argue, from my previous experience as coordinator of a state-sponsored literacy programme in Malta, that a lot of adult learners demand this seriousness and would consider any initial attempts at 'dialogue facilitation' as a sheer waste of time.

I would argue that they too bring with them this sense of seriousness. As Paul Ransome points out, in a chapter dealing with Gramsci's views on education and the role of intellectuals, 'if an individual or group of individuals is largely preoccupied with the business of earning a living, then the time available for intellectual development and subsequently for participation in democratic practices will be more limited.'[59] This is very much the case with the adult learners attending the literacy programme I was involved in. It takes discipline on their part to utilise the little free time they have to participate in the programme, not least in a situation where people are increasingly taking up a second, part-time job in order to keep up with the increasing cost of living. They therefore expect to find such discipline in the programme too, and who can blame them? After all, for them, this represents a strategy for survival in a world governed by the ideology of competitive individualism. I reiterate the point made in the Introduction: one has first to survive in order to be in a position to transform.

The need for rigour and discipline has to be satisfied if the educational experience is to be truly meaningful. What is being called for is rigour within the context of a critical education agenda: that is to say, an education which not only enables one to survive but, more importantly, has a transformative edge. Rigour in such a context involves efforts to appropriate what is necessary to enable one to question/challenge hegemonic and, I would add, even certain forms of counter-hegemonic discourse (for example, one may come across a counter-hegemonic class discourse devoid of race/gender considerations). The important aspect of this approach, which renders it different from forms of 'banking education', is that, in being rigorous, one is still being critical. In generating respect for rigour, the educator creates the conditions whereby he or she can be challenged. This demands considerable effort and application on the part of the learner, the kind of effort Gramsci calls for in his much discussed piece on the 'Common School', and indeed which Freire has also stressed in his writings and talks, including an exchange with community workers in the course of a 1991 conference.[60] Furthermore, I would argue, echoing Bourdieu, that a dialogical teacher risks losing his or her authority when moving outside the 'cultural arbitrary' of education[61] (the popular and conventional notion of what a teacher should do and stand for – 'pedagogic action' as 'symbolic violence', in Bourdieu and Passeron's terms),[62] which is generally determined by the dominant class. The committed educators must therefore deal constantly with the tension arising from this situation. He or she must tread carefully so as not to undermine the spirit of democracy that, in principle, characterises the social relations of education within the learning group. Tact and discretion, born out of mutual trust and respect between educator and educatees, is called for here.

Cultural capital and habitus

The image of the adult educator that emerges from the combined insights of Gramsci and Freire is that of a person committed to the learners' cause. Implicit in Gramsci's concept of the organic intellectual and Freire's insistence that the adult educator commits, in Cabral's terms, 'class suicide',[63] is their awareness that the process of emancipation can be severely undermined – indeed, can degenerate into mere domestication – if the educator invokes a 'cultural capital' that is at odds with that of the learners.[64] By 'cultural capital', I mean a cultural value system and 'grammar of taste' that reflects a particular social location. For instance, a male teacher might bring into the classroom a set of cultural referents that do not resonate with the female learners' own experiences as women, a point which has been well documented in the literatures of both the sociology of education and adult education.[65]

Similarly, the educator can draw on bourgeois cultural referents which do not resonate with the distinctly working-class culture of the learners. This, as we have seen, is a situation Gramsci criticised with respect to the popular universities.[66] Similar examples could be given with respect to the issues of race and sexual orientation. One of the effects of such 'cultural capital' is that the experiences and culture(s) of those learners who are located differently are not valorised. The tensions produced must be confronted and worked through in order to minimise the extent to which domesticating forces are able to emerge from an ostensibly liberatory practice. This entails the educator seeking every means possible to break any barrier that might exist between her/him and the learners in the interest of creating truly democratic and transformative social relations of education.[67] This is no easy task, involving, as it must, a process of sensitisation to the particular class, race or gender concerns of the learning group.[68] 'Suicide' is, as I indicated in the previous chapter, somewhat unlikely given that it is extremely difficult for traditionally formed 'bourgeois' educators to break out of their habitus.

While the French sociologists are arguably too deterministic in this regard, they do stress an aspect of our class location as educators which provides a formidable barrier to committing class suicide. I would argue that the best one can hope for in this regard is a recognition on the educator's part of the gender, race and class differences that set her or him apart from the learners. This entails a process of unlearning one's privilege. Such recognition would constitute an important step towards minimising the elements of domestication that may emerge from her/his position of social privilege. Part of the struggle for social transformation in this regard is coming to terms with the tension that arises between domestication and liberation as a result of different social locations.[69] For example, tension could arise in a situation where educator and educatee are of the same gender but not of the same race or sexual orientation.

Cultural Production

The discussion concerning a Gramscian–Freirean synthesis has hitherto centred mainly around the issue of process. I shall now focus on content, and more specifically on questions of culture. Gramsci and Freire both attach importance to popular culture in their writings. While Freire uses the popular as the basis of his conscientisation process, Gramsci, for his part, engages in little sustained analysis of this particular form of culture in his writings. Nevertheless, there exists in Gramsci a systematic and wide-ranging analysis of the dominant culture. For the purposes of developing a theory of radical adult education, I propose a productive synthesis of Gramsci's ideas on the dominant culture and Freire's ideas concerning the popular.

Cultural studies

I advocate a cultural studies programme which is inclusive and which focuses on cultural products from both the established legitimate culture (popularly referred to as 'high culture') and the popular. Each can be critically appropriated for the subordinate group's ends. Popular forms of cultural production, ranging from oral activities such as popular narratives and ballads to forms of mass popular culture such as rock music and videos, can be the subject of critical interrogation. The same applies to forms of so-called 'high culture' – for example, a Shakespeare text – some of which, of course, have their roots in the popular. Gramsci[70] devoted attention to these latter kinds of work, writing reviews of plays that form part of the established canon (e.g. Shakespeare's *Macbeth*, Ibsen's *The Doll's House* and numerous works by Luigi Pirandello). With respect to Shakespeare's plays, the conventional view, given the audience they drew when first performed, is that they constituted a form of popular culture. According to this view, common folk (the 'groundlings' who jeered and cheered in 'the pit') constituted a substantial part of the audience.[71] This leads to a questioning of the dichotomy of the 'popular' and 'high'. Raymond Williams argues that popular Elizabethan drama had within it 'all that is creative in the national life'.[72] Shakespeare's work was part of a popular drama which, according to Williams,[73] was protected by the court against the commercial middle classes. Eventually, this support was gradually withdrawn as the court became alienated from 'decisive elements in the national life',[74] as a result of which the drama grew increasingly class-oriented, appealing to a narrow audience. In Shakespeare's case, the tradition that ranks his works as 'high culture' dates not from Shakespeare's time but arguably from a much later date. Given the focus on royalty and, occasionally, pageantry in Shakespeare's plays, they may well have contributed to the mystique surrounding this feature of British society that was given fresh impetus in the second half of the nineteenth century.[75]

To problematise the dichotomy between the highbrow and the popular is to indicate the paths that can be explored by subaltern groups to enable them critically to appropriate works for their own end. It is worth reiterating here the point made by Gramsci regarding the manner in which information and knowledge are assimilated in the classroom. For him, it is foolish to conceive of the pupil, under traditional conditions of learning, as a 'mechanical receiver' of abstract notions. Rather, knowledge is assimilated according to the learner's consciousness, which reflects the 'sector of civil society' wherein the learner is located.[76] This anticipates recent works on the manner in which meaning is socially circulated and created. It is often argued that meaning does not lie solely within texts. Michael Apple, for instance, writes:

> As poststructuralist theories would have it, meaning is 'the product of a system of differences into which the text is articulated'. Thus, there is not 'one text' but many. Any text is open to multiple readings. This puts into doubt any claim that one can determine the meanings and politics of a text 'by a straightforward encounter with the text itself'.... Meanings, then, can be and are multiple and contradictory, and we must always be willing to 'read' our own readings of a text.[77]

Educators play an important role in mediating the material at hand; learners 'bring their own classed, raced, and gendered biographies with them as well', and are therefore 'active constructors of the meanings of the education they encounter',[78] a point which echoes Gramsci. Recognition of the multiplicity of meanings emerging out of texts – and I am here using the term 'text' in its wider sense, to include all sorts of cultural products – can lead to critical appropriation for transformative ends. This cannot occur under conditions of 'banking education', where learners are treated as though they are empty receptacles to be filled, even though in reality they are not. 'Banking education' denies learners a forum wherein the various meanings, which they construct from what is 'being taught', can be brought into the open for these meanings to circulate freely, be critically interrogated and, ultimately, be renegotiated and reconstructed.

Because of the multiplicity of meanings to which they lend themselves, works can be read 'against the grain'. And just as Roger I. Simon has indicated how one can go beyond the racist text to discover the emancipatory possibilities of a multiplicity of readings of it[79] (his accounts of the Yiddish interpretation of Shylock and Achebe's insurgent reading of *Heart of Darkness*[80] are quite revealing in this respect), so can learners within a radical adult education circle generate discussions around a work in which they are encouraged to give voice to the different meanings deriving from their particular locations within regimes of power/knowledge.

Once again, this voice should not be celebrated uncritically, given that it can incorporate negative aspects of 'common sense'. Also, in reading a text against the grain, one is not denying the politics of the text itself – hence Simon's chapter title, 'Beyond the Racist Text'. A racist text remains a racist text despite the provision of anti-racist readings of it. As such, while reading a work against the grain in the interest of critical appropriation, it would be appropriate, in adult education circles, to do so in a manner that highlights, where necessary, the author's/painter's complicity or otherwise with respect to the existence of structures of domination.

Critical interrogation and appropriation would be the hallmark of such a cultural studies programme carried out in the 'public sphere'[81] and therefore no longer solely within the hallowed walls of the academy. It may be argued that, in so doing, one would be taking Cultural Studies, an area over which Gramsci's writings have exerted considerable influence,[82] back to one of its old sites, that of *adult education*. This is where it began in Britain.[83] David Scholle argues:

It is often forgotten that British cultural studies arose as a project for adult education and that much of its focus was on pedagogical issues ... cultural studies began as a specific educational project – as a way of helping people to understand the pressures upon them.

The relationship between the British Cultural Studies tradition and adult education is eloquently stressed by the cultural theorist and former adult educator, Raymond Williams:

we are beginning, I am afraid, to see encyclopedia articles dating the birth of Cultural Studies from this or that book in the late fifties. Don't believe a word of it. That shift of perspective about the teaching of arts and literature and their relation to history and to contemporary society began in Adult Education, it didn't happen anywhere else. It was when it was taken across by people with that experience to the Universities that it was suddenly recognised as a subject. It is in these and other similar ways that the contribution of the process itself to social change itself, and specifically to learning, has happened.[84]

An inclusive programme

I would argue that such a proposed Cultural Studies programme should be inclusive. It should encompass elements of the popular and 'high culture', and include oral, visual and written cultural products; it should be neither ethnocentric nor androcentric. In this respect, it would differ from the approach adopted by Williams and other figures related to the Extra-Mural Delegacy at Oxford. Such a programme should be one in which what is taught is not fixed but open to negotiation and renegotiation – a 'cultural borderland'[85] in constant flux where 'subordinated cultures push against and permeate the alleged unproblematic and homogeneous borders of dominant cultural forms and practices'.[86]

One has to go beyond Gramsci to avoid Eurocentrism and beyond both Gramsci and Freire to avoid patriarchal bias. This applies not only to Cultural Studies (including a workers' Cultural Studies programme *per se*) but to any other programme developed with transformative ends in view – for example, a workers' education programme (it can also incorporate a cultural studies component) intended to contribute to industrial democracy.[87]

The issues of critical appropriation and interrogation apply to all dealings with the dominant language. Gramsci's and Freire's insights show us that this is one aspect of the dominant culture which needs to be learnt if subordinate groups are not to remain at the periphery of political life.[88] For the purposes of a theory of radical adult education, however, I would reiterate Freire's insistence that the dominant language should be taught by radical adult educators in a problematising manner. Educators and educatees must explore together the manner in which the language being learnt is tied to the process of hegemony, and therefore that of power/knowledge, either on a worldwide scale (for example, the roles of the English, Spanish, Portuguese and French languages in colonial and post-colonial countries) or within national boundaries (e.g. 'standard' language as opposed to dialects).

History

Gramsci insisted on the need for working-class people to engage in the study of history, arguing that, if this class is to assume its role in the perennial struggle for liberation from oppression, it

must know by whom it was preceded.[89] It also needs to gain knowledge of preceding social forms, institutionalised practices and
beliefs, and the historical contexts that gave rise to the invention
of the traditions to which these forms, practices and beliefs belong.
Following Hobsbawm,[90] one would want to enquire when exactly
these traditions came into play, with a view to dispelling myths
regarding the extent of their continuity. Furthermore, one would
want to know what function these 'invented traditions' play with
respect to such perceived needs as social cohesion, the legitimisa-
tion of relations of authority and socialisation?[91] The implication
is that historical enquiry would constitute a feature of an adult
education programme conceived on Gramscian lines.

Recuperating collective histories

This emphasis on macro-level history is not to be found in Freire's
writings. In his examples from popular education we gain the
impression that the emphasis in the *cultural circle* is on the present.
I would argue, however, that a critical analysis of a codified situation as part of the process of conscientisation would be incomplete
unless it is analysed and placed in its historical context. After all,
the process involves a critical engagement with historically accumu-
lated concepts and practices.[92] This would involve moving between
present and past with a view to contributing towards a transformed future. In this respect, I take up the idea, conveyed by
Peter McLaren and Tomaz Tadeuz da Silva,[93] regarding the relevance of Freirean pedagogy to the issue of recuperating collective
histories. This process is becoming ever more widespread in a
variety of fields. It is, for instance, evident in women's cultural
work, especially in films like *Fried Green Tomatoes*, commemorative
events like anniversaries of the *Montreal Massacre*,[94] and in literature.[95]

This application of Freirean pedagogy is also widespread in
Latin American research, 'excavating the substratum of collective
memory as it is embedded in popular cultural practice',[96] in life-
history projects (given prominence in adult educational research[97]),
and in adult education initiatives involving the elderly. This is one
way in which ideas from Freire and Gramsci can be drawn upon
in the context of using history for adult educational purposes.

McLaren and da Silva[98] point to Freire's insistence on the

'importance of affirming the stories that students tell – stories that
are based on their own experiences.' I would argue that, in Fou-
cauldian terms, this entails the affirmation of areas of 'subjugated
knowledge', for the purpose not of 'colonisation' but of collective
emancipation. This view of history, rooted as it is in the realm of
the popular, which complements a more macro-level conception
derived from Gramsci, strikes me as particularly relevant to the
project under discussion. Even Freire's codification/decodification
processes offer the radical adult educator an excellent means of
engaging in moments of transformative collective histories, referred
to by Walter Benjamin as 'redemptive remembrance'.

Roger I. Simon describes this particular kind of remembrance
as 'the practice in which certain images and stories of a collective
past are brought together with a person's feelings and comprehen-
sion of their embodied presence in time and space'.[99] Simon himself shows the effectiveness of codifications, in the form of visual
images, as a means of creating a *dialogue with the past*.[100] An image
he reproduces is a powerful illustration of the plight of Italian
immigrant workers in present-day Germany. One has the Star of
David, in the colours of the Italian *tricolore*, superimposed on his
shirt. This illustration, by the German artist Klaus Staeck, evokes
the Holocaust to highlight 'present day struggles which call to
mind long collective histories characterised by racial discrimination'.[101] The result is that history is conceived of 'not as a con-
straint on the present but rather as "source or precondition of
power" that can illuminate our project of emancipation'.[102] It re-
discovers the past, which has turned the present into 'now time',
with a view to creating that kind of society which is 'not yet'.[103]
Codifications can therefore be used not simply to facilitate processes
whereby the present is viewed critically, to obtain greater awareness of the contradictions underlying it, but also as a means of
engendering the dialectical process, involving the juxtaposition of
and critical reflection upon past and present. This dialectical process
can open up possibilities for transformation.[104]

Practical examples

On a practical level, one obvious 'redemptive' historical exercise,
within the context of an adult education programme, would con-

sist of the adult learners being encouraged to engage in reminiscences concerning their schooling experiences. In this respect, the adult learners can be encouraged to bring photographs and items relevant to their schooldays (e.g. school annuals). Their accounts of their own schooling experiences can be interrogated by the 'directive' adult educator for the purposes of underlining connections between the kind of schooling organisation and pedagogy described and power structures in the larger society. Descriptions by the learners can also be interrogated for the purpose of highlighting and politicising absences, notably in terms of race, class, gender, sexual orientation and disability. Such an analysis of one's educational past will help throw critical light on current educational practices and suggest options for a transformed educational future. Furthermore, it can establish the critical frame of mind necessary for the learners to partake of a different, potentially transformative adult education programme.

A combination of Gramsci's and Freire's ideas in this area would also entail a process whereby collective experiences of the learning group are evoked, discussed, interrogated and linked to macro-level issues derived from relevant historical research, which would include different, insurgent perspectives on historical events. In the case of a workers' programme, this could involve their providing visual and other forms of documentation from their own as well as their families' past, including photographs and memorabilia. Ideally these would relate to the kind of work in which family members, possibly elderly family members, were engaged. In the group discussion, the various life/work experiences would be compared. Through discrete, though timely, interventions by the educator, these experiences would be linked to aspects of the macro-level historical discussion concerning the working class, which I would argue should constitute an important component of the learning project. Such a discussion would aim to foster understanding of the changing modes of capitalist exploitation throughout the ages, and the degree of gender, racial and ethnic segmentation involved in the labour process; it would also indicate the 'gains' made by labour organisations and other social movements during these periods and the threat to these from the 'New Right'. Emphasis on these gains would hopefully instil the sense of agency required for further transformative action in the world of work.

Of course, the situation of the adult learning process depends, to a large extent, on the context in which this process takes place. In my home country, Malta, one might consider the recent tendency to erect and unveil war memorials in various towns and villages. Radical adult educators working within such communities can utilise this situation to engage in discussion concerning the country's historical and economic connections with war – the 'fortress economy'; this can take in the plight of the Maltese under British colonialism, the perpetuation of colonial attitudes even during the post-independence period, and the need to 'decolonise the mind'. The subject could be broadened in scope by, for instance, juxtaposing to images of these war memorials and certain images pertaining to the present, such as scenes from neo-Nazi demonstrations in Germany. The connection between the two sets of images would be elicited through careful prompting and questioning; the discussion could then be opened up to incorporate the issue of race. This in turn might lead to consideration of the way the Maltese, as a people, are also implicated in racism. As a consequence, the group members would begin to see the Maltese not only as an oppressed people, owing to a long history of colonialism, but also as oppressors, thereby attesting to the multiplicity of subjectivities involved in processes of oppression worldwide.

Conclusion

I have attempted in this chapter to create a framework for radical adult education on the basis of ideas expressed by Antonio Gramsci and Paulo Freire. Bearing in mind both the complementary aspects of their work and the limitations of their ideas for a contemporary project, I explored elements that might constitute the basis for a theory of transformative adult education. The areas I have explored are commitment, agency, social movements, the role of adult educators, issues concerning cultural production, and the role of history in transformative adult education. These are just some themes around which a Gramscian–Freirean synthesis might cohere. The exercise has by no means been exhaustive; there is ample scope for further work and new ideas. Elsewhere, Paula

Allman and I have explored other ideas, gleaned from Gramsci and Freire, for the purpose of exploring socially committed adult education strategies in an age characterised by the intensification of capitalist globalisation.[105]

Of course, the degree of effectiveness of the concepts discussed in this chapter largely depends on the nature of the specific context in which they are intended to be developed. In the concluding chapter, I attempt to explore some of the limits and possibilities for transformative adult education along Gramscian–Freirean lines.

Notes

1. An abridged version of this chapter was published as Mayo, 1996.
2. Horton and Freire, 1990.
3. Giroux, 1988.
4. Simon, 1992.
5. Freire, in Freire and Macedo, 1993: 172. In this interview, Freire states, with respect to this issue: 'When I wrote *Pedagogy of the Oppressed* I was so influenced by Marx's class analysis, and given the incredible cruel class oppression that characterized my developing years in Northeast Brazil, my major preoccupation was, therefore, class oppression. It is ironic that some Marxists even criticised me for not paying enough attention to social class analysis. In *Pedagogy of the Oppressed*, if my memory serves me correctly, I made approximately thirty-three references to social class analysis.'.
6. Cf. Macedo in Freire and Macedo, 1993: 172.
7. Cf. Macedo in Freire and Macedo, 1993: 172.
8. Corrigan, Ramsay and Sayer, 1980: 22.
9. See, for example, Taking Liberties Collective, 1989.
10. Lorde, 1984; hooks, 1981; Stefanos, 1997.
11. Ball, 1992: 8.
12. See Weiler, 1991; Ellsworth, 1989; Gore, 1992; Lynch and O'Neill, 1994.
13. Cf. Simon, 1992: 39.
14. Laclau and Mouffe, 1985.
15. Holub, 1992.
16. Gramsci, 1985: 54.
17. Holub, 1992: 156.
18. See Mayo, 1995b, 1997a.
19. Holub, 1992: 162.
20. Sklair, 1995.

21. Shor, 1987: 93.

22. Aronowitz and Giroux, 1991: 130, 131. I am indebted to Brookfield (1993: 73) for drawing my attention to this quotation.

23. Horton and Freire, 1990; Shor and Freire, 1987.

24. Said, 1994: 4.

25. Aronowitz, 1993; Macedo, 1994; Allman, 1994, 1996; Mayo, 1995c.

26. Freire, 1997a: 303, 304.

27. The last few paragraphs are taken from Mayo, 1996: 151, 152.

28. Cf. Adamson, 1980.

29. Freire, 1985.

30. E.g. Shor and Freire, 1987; Freire and Faundez, 1989; see Findlay, 1994.

31. Welton, 1993.

32. Mayo, 1994b, 1994c.

33. Gramsci, 1971b: 130.

34. Zachariah, 1986.

35. Sklair, 1995.

36. Sklair, 1995: 507.

37. Sklair, 1995: 507.

38. Cf. Hall, 1993.

39. For a discussion of this theme backed by illustrative interview material, see my case study of a Maltese workers' education programe – Mayo, 1997b.

40. Gramsci, 1978: 21.

41. McIlroy, 1993b: 277.

42. Mayo, 1995a, 1997b.

43. Foley, 1994.

44. Ross and Trachte, 1990.

45. Spivak, in Giroux, 1992: 27.

46. Gramsci, 1995: 154, 155.

47. Freire, 1991.

48. Cf. Sharp, Hartwig and O'Leary, 1989.

49. Torres, 1991a: 31.

50. Corrigan and Sayer, 1985: 4.

51. Freire, in Horton and Freire, 1990: 203.

52. Giroux, 1981, 1983.

53. Cf. London–Edinburgh Weekend Return Group, 1979: 80. For an extensive discussion on the possible application of Gramscian and Freirean ideas to the issue of working 'in and against the state', see Leonard, 1993 and Mayo, 1997b.

54. Shor and Freire, 1987: 103; Horton and Freire, 1990: 181.

55. Freire, 1985: 177; Shor and Freire, 1987.

56. Gramsci, 1971b: 36.

57. Freire, in Horton and Freire, 1990: 160.

58. Cf. Arnove, 1986: 24, 25; Baldacchino, 1990: 53, 54; Gaber-Katz and Watson, 1991.

59. Ransome, 1992: 195.

60. The conference in question, 'Challenging Education, Creating Alliances: An Institute in Honour of Paulo Freire's 70th Birthday', took place at the New School for Social Research Curriculum and Pedagogy Collaborative, Greenwich Village, New York in December 1991. See Clover, 1991: 1. Freire is on record as having said 'Learning is not a vacation on a beach; it is very difficult, even for me' – Clover, 1991: 1. See also the discussion by Ira Shor and Paulo Freire centring around the question, 'Is there Structure and Rigor in Liberating Education?', in Shor and Freire, 1987: 75–96.

61. Blackledge and Hunt, 1985: 165.

62. Bourdieu and Passéron, 1990: 5.

63. Freire, 1978; Freire and Faundez, 1989.

64. Cf. Torres, 1990b.

65. See, for example, Thompson, 1983; Taking Liberties Collective, 1989.

66. Broccoli, 1972.

67. Mayo, 1993a: 180.

68. Educators, I believe, are in a position to acquire such sensitisation, so far as class is concerned, given that they are situated in a contradictory class location.

69. Mayo, 1993a: 19.

70. Gramsci, 1985.

71. It should be stressed that this is the conventional view. Controversy surrounds the question of what the Globe and similar theatres actually looked like. The evidence for this conventional view is based on a drawing of the Swan by the Dutch traveller, Johannes de Witt, to which drawing he attached a written description (Harwood, 1984: 115). I should like to express my gratitude to Ivan Callus, a friend and English Literature scholar, for a highly stimulating discussion of some of the issues raised in this section. While I have profited immensely from his insightful comments, any flaws in my argument are entirely my responsibility.

72. Williams, 1961: 277.

73. Williams, 1961: 278.

74. Williams, 1961: 278.

75. For a discussion of the invention of tradition with respect to the British Monarchy, see Cannadine, 1983.

76. Gramsci, 1971b: 35.

77. Apple, 1992: 10.

78. Apple, 1992: 10.

79. Simon, 1992.

80. Achebe, 1975.

81. Cf. Giroux et al., 1988.

82. Cf. Turner, 1990: 210–214; Morrow, 1991: 38–59.

83. Scholle, 1991: 124, 125.

84. Williams, in McIlroy and Westwood, 1993: 260. The article is in *Adult Education and Social Change: Lectures and Reminiscences in Honour of Tony McLean*, WEA Southern District, 1983: 9–24.

85. Giroux, 1992: 169.

86. Giroux, 1992: 169.

87. Mayo, 1995a.

88. Cf. Gramsci, 1971b: 325; Shor and Freire, 1987: 73.

89. Cf. Entwistle, 1979: 41.

90. Hobsbawm, 1983.

91. Cf. Hobsbawm and Ranger, 1983: 9.

92. I am indebted to Professor David W. Livingstone for the suggestion and formulation of this point. See also Mayo, 1996: 156.

93. McLaren and Da Silva, 1993.

94. I refer to the slaying, by a 25-year-old man, of fourteen women undergoing a course in engineering at the University of Montreal's School of Engineering (École Polytechnique). The killings took place on 6 December 1989, after which the man shot himself. In a note found on his body, he stated that the murders were a political act and he blamed feminism for ruining his life. See Rosenberg, 1992: 32.

95. I would include here feminist literature centring on memory and confession. Cf. Haug, 1987; Schenke, 1992: 58.

96. Hoechsmann, 1993: 55. Hoechsmann makes this statement in a review of Rowe and Schelling's *Memory and Modernity: Popular Culture in Latin America* (Verso, London, 1992).

97. The European Society for Research on the Education of Adults (ESREA) devotes an entire research network to life history.

98. McLaren and Da Silva, 1993: 74.

99. Simon, 1992: 149.

100. McLaren and Da Silva, 1993: 75.

101. Borg and Mayo, 1993: 165.

102. McLaren and Da Silva, 1993: 75.

103. McLaren and Da Silva, 1993: 77.

104. Borg and Mayo, 1993: 166.

105. Allman and Mayo, 1997.

CHAPTER 7

Conclusion: When Might it Work? Transformative Adult Education in Context

This book has focused on two of the most cited figures in the literature on transformative education: Antonio Gramsci and Paulo Freire. As well as engaging with the complexities of education, including adult education, they have provided an analysis of the manner in which processes of education and cultural production are related to issues concerning power. Educational practices intended to generate democratic possibilities must, as both Freire and Gramsci argue, be conceived of not as neutral processes but as political acts. These acts can either contribute to the consolidation of the existing hegemony, thereby serving a reproductive function, or they can be guided by an alternative transformative social vision. Of course, the position calling for pragmatism and for a critical engagement with the complexities involved in any situation of hegemony/counter-hegemony, as outlined in the Introduction, still holds.[1]

Social Transformation: Limits and Possibilities

One challenging question that arises at this concluding stage of the work is: to what extent and under what circumstances can the pedagogical ideas developed in this book, and specifically in the previous chapter, contribute to a process of social transformation? In answering this question, one has to be mindful of context. Freire has been strongly connected with the Latin American and African contexts, especially in countries characterised by sharp divisions into colonial and postcolonial periods, dictatorial and revolutionary periods, and so forth. It is not uncommon to find Gramsci's name associated with the struggles involved in both types of context, especially in Latin America and the New Left movement there.

Pre-Revolutionary Context

Can transformative pedagogical action on the lines suggested in the previous chapter be successfully carried out in a pre-revolutionary context? With regard to Freire's experiences in Brazil, I would submit that such action was successful partly due to the presence of a populist regime in an era marked by the staging of a successful revolution in the region (the Cuban Revolution), which generated enthusiasm among those striving for liberation.[2] The political climate was marked by the advance of popular forces. Trade unions, peasant leagues and worker organisations all made their presence felt. Situations such as this, during which the populist leader João Goulart sought to win the support of disenfranchised masses in a struggle against the industrial bourgeoisie and rural landowning oligarchy, are conducive to liberatory educational practices. It is therefore no coincidence that it was during this period that Freire carried out his consciousness-raising literacy programmes in the north-east. The situation of ferment echoed that in Turin with its *biennio rosso* and other moments of revolutionary activism in 'Italy's Petrograd'. Nevertheless, in a situation characterised by a power alliance between the industrial bourgeoisie and the rural landowning oligarchy,[3] in a nationally controlled dependent, productive system such as that of Brazil,[4] the extent to which such liberatory efforts can survive is limited.

The form the reaction took in Brazil – a military coup backed by the multinationals – confirms this, echoing the Fascist rise to power in Italy in the aftermath of the 'revolution that failed', to use the title of Martin Clark's book.[5] Thus, from a gradual path towards liberation, there was a sudden swing towards authoritarianism with its concomitant emphasis on domestication. Morrow and Torres, in their comprehensive work on social theory and education, provide a necessary distinction between the two situations: the Fascist rise to power signalled the defeat of the industrial working class in Italy, while the Brazilian coup terminated an attempt at populist reorganisation of Brazilian society.[6]

Spaces in situations of repression

Both Gramsci and Freire were victims of the repression that ensued in the two cases. The former became a 'martyr' of Fascism, like several others, including Giacomo Matteotti, Giovanni Amendola, Piero Gobetti and Carlo Rosselli.[7] Freire was first imprisoned and then 'invited' to leave Brazil.[8] Of course, it is not only figures like Gramsci and Freire who suffer for their engagement in transformative activities. As I indicated in Chapter 3, popular educators constantly place their lives on the line, and are frequently murdered in cold blood. And, despite the process of *concertación* (national accord) reported to have been taking place in Central America,[9] the 'culture of fear' still prevails.[10]

I would submit that the tension between 'liberation' and 'domestication', to use Freire's preferred terms, which often serve as poles of a continuum (see the discussion of Jane Thompson's view in the Introduction), prevails even during a period of extreme repression. As Foucault would say, 'where there is power there is resistance.'[11] With Gramsci, the interesting attempts to carry out meaningful education in Italy even under conditions of extreme repression, as in the case of the prison school at Ustica, were short-lived. With reference to Freire's experiences in Brazil in the early 1960s and in Chile when the Christian Democrats were in power, it seems likely that periods of popular mobilisation prior to dictatorships can be long enough to enable transformative activities to become consolidated within the popular tradition and therefore constitute an important source of popular resistance during times of repression.

There is documented evidence, for instance, that conscientising education, of the kind associated with Paulo Freire, was carried out in Chile under Pinochet, albeit clandestinely and often in connection with (or under the guise of) vocational education.[12] Both the Church and the Christian Base Communities constituted an important site of struggle and resistance during the Brazilian dictatorship, taking on overtly political tasks.[13] These communities are associated with Freirean pedagogy and consciousness-raising.

Freire himself relates how priests involved in such work read Italian, French and Spanish translations of *Pedagogy of the Oppressed*, since the book was banned in Brazil and could only be read furtively.[14]

While Freire was read secretly in Brazil, Gramsci's works were tolerated in the same country. Carlos Nelson Coutinho refers to a tacit 'division of labour' between the purely philosophical/cultural in Marxism and that which was overtly political.[15] Censorship was exercised in relation to the latter but not in relation to that which was perceived as being philosophical and sociological/cultural. Gramsci's work was introduced and taken up in such a way that it was perceived as belonging to this area.[16] His work therefore continued to be read even after the coup of 1964, and was given even more space during the relatively more 'liberal' phase of the dictatorship, when certain constitutional guarantees existed. This situation pertained until the end of 1968 when the institutional Act no. 5 virtually suppressed these guarantees.[17]

One may argue therefore that, in these instances, and especially in relation to the furtive reading of Freire's work, processes of education for liberation were serving to resist and counter despotic attempts at domestication. It would be interesting to explore the degree to which these resistance activities had, within them, residual elements from the pre-coup period. In Freire's case, the question becomes even more pertinent when considering that the pre-coup period was marked by a process, albeit a slow one, of radicalisation within the Church that gave rise to such movements as Ação Popular, very much concerned with literacy among the poor.[18] It is in the context of Ação Popular that Freire's ideas were developed.[19]

Spaces within larger movements

We have seen that the connection between the Church, especially its radical wing, and liberation is a strong one in Latin America. Freire's work continues to be seen against the background of this tradition of radicalism in the region. Indeed, it is arguably in this context that Freirean pedagogy has made one of its most effective contributions to social and political transformation. His influence was strong among the Church-inspired popular education initiatives in pre-1979 Nicaragua, referred to in Chapter 3. In this particular case, Freirean pedagogy was carried out not in isolation but in relation to a strong social movement which drew together three strands: 'Sandino's popular national revolt, Marxist class analysis and Christian Liberation Theology'.[20]

While it is unwise to generalise from one particular historical experience at the expense of the contextual specificities involved, the Nicaraguan experience seems to suggest that adult education, no matter how emancipatory in process and content, does *not*, on its own, lead to social transformation. Education is not an independent variable and, as Freire has stressed time and time again, should not be attributed powers it does not have. It appears likely to prove effective in this regard only when it is carried out in the context of a strong all-embracing social and political movement, preferably within a kind of Gramscian 'historical bloc', a concept probably developed by Gramsci in the light of the isolation of the insurgent activity by factory workers in Turin, culminating in the occupation of the factories. This important activity on the part of Turin workers did not find support from other institutions within the Italian working-class movement and was not connected with other action throughout the peninsula. With respect to the second point, Gramsci's own reflections are contained in a letter from Vienna to Alfonso Leonetti:

> In 1919–20 we made extremely serious mistakes, which ultimately we are paying for today. For fear of being called upstarts and careerists, we did not form a faction and organize this throughout Italy. We were not ready to give the Turin factory councils an autonomous directive centre, which could have exercised an immense influence throughout the country, for fear of a split in the unions and of being expelled prematurely from the Socialist Party.[21]

Freire also made an important point regarding the dangers of isolating educational activity from a broader range of transformative actions. He states that one should not 'expect' from education what it cannot do, namely 'transform society by itself'.[22] This point was not lost on the animators of the Adult Learning Project in a working-class area of Edinburgh, Scotland, who conclude their book, in which they describe and reflect on the project, with an excerpt from Freire's conversation with Ira Shor:[23] 'Liberating education in general and the single classroom in particular cannot transform society by themselves. This limit needs to be repeated so that none of us mistakes what dialogical learning means.'[24] If carried out in isolation, Freire's pedagogy would only involve 'intel-lectual praxis'. This is a kind of praxis that would probably be capable of transforming people's consciousness; but it would not enable them to engage in direct political action to change their plight.[25] If linked with social action, however, the educational process would involve 'revolutionary praxis' – the kind of praxis that took place in Nicaragua, carried out in the context of a social movement.[26] This particular experience has to be viewed in the light of the strong alliance that exists throughout Latin America between Freire-inspired popular education and the movement referred to throughout this book as Liberation Theology.

The Nicaraguan example

The Nicaraguan experience seems to have indicated that work within an all-embracing social movement proves effective in con-tributing towards social transformation. Some will argue that, in the case of Nicaragua, as of Guinea-Bissau, it took military action on the part of a guerrilla movement to bring about change. How-ever, this argument minimises the role of popular education and the related movement/s in providing a sense of liberation, and therefore creating the right climate for revolution.[27] It also mini-mises the role popular education plays within grassroots move-ments in prefiguring the kind of social relations that would char-acterise the revolutionary society. Popular education, within the context of social movements, plays its role in the 'war of position' engaged in by the subordinated groups prior to the conquest of power. It offers possibilities for counter-hegemonic action because of its flexible nature and the relative autonomy it enjoys. Carlos Alberto Torres and Daniel Schugurensky, state that,

> This autonomy is mostly enjoyed in nonformal education, and it is more evident in prerevolutionary processes. Examples of this assertion can be found in the educational work carried out by the revolutionary guerrilla movements in Cuba and Nicaragua, by the Jesuits of the Universidad Centroamericana in Nicaragua, or by the repatriated in-tellectuals of MACE and *The New Jewel* newspaper in Grenada.[28]

The same applies to the way Gramsci conceived of educational activity for the working class. This was not to be isolated from concentrated action in different sites of political struggle. Gramsci conceived of a whole complex of sites of revolutionary action, with different adult education sites complementing each other. As with Freire's 'prefigurative' educational work, the kind of adult educational activity advocated by Gramsci, to be carried out in the context of the factory council movement, was to prefigure the new socialist state, which was to be characterised by a change in social relations. It was conceived of as being part and parcel of that 'intense labour of criticism' which precedes 'every revolution'[29] or social transformation.

Industrialised contexts

A question that arises at this stage is: to what extent can the foregoing considerations apply to transformative action not only in industrially underdeveloped societies but also in industrially developed ones? Notwithstanding his influence in Latin America[30] and his Southern origins, Gramsci is widely regarded as someone whose ideas were born out of years of political activism in one of the industrial centres of Western Europe. It suffices to mention that, in Italy, the decade 1910–1920 'had seen a vertiginous expansion of the country's productive forces, above all during the war years (production of iron and steel multiplied five times during the course of the war, and firms like Fiat – whose workforce rose from 4,000 to 20,000 in that period – increased their capital tenfold).'[31] Freire, for his part, cannot be associated solely with Latin America or Africa. His action and analyses have a more global reach. In this respect, distinctions between 'first' and 'third' worlds are simplistic.

I have shown, in Chapters 2 and 6, that Gramsci's conception of a historical bloc can easily imply, in this day and age, an alliance of movements. It can therefore constitute a useful conceptual tool in the coalition-building/fragmentation debate concerning social movements. Gramsci would, however, conceive of such an alliance of popular movements as one forged by a 'national-popular' party, the 'Modern Prince'. It is precisely this kind of party which Ireland saw lacking in Brazilian popular education, where the learning activities remained largely uncoordinated efforts.[32] Would a party that embraces the various issues put forward by progressive social movements, thus promoting 'unity in diversity', constitute the 'Modern Prince' in this day and age? Would it provide the right context for the kind of transformative adult education we have been discussing? Can the Brazilian Workers' Party (PT), with its links to grassroots movements (e.g. MST) and trade unions,[33] Freire an illustrious founding member, and a proven receptiveness to Gramscian formulations and ideas,[34] be regarded as a 'Modern Prince' operating in a given national context?

The experience of operating in the context of social movements was not lost on Freire. This is evident even in some of the published dialogues, such as that with Ira Shor, which focuses mainly on the struggles for greater social justice in Western society.[35]

This book has stressed the relevance of both Freire and Gramsci for action within the context of new social movements, which are widely recognised as important agents of social change in the struggle against existing forces of domination and domestication. This view is based on the following considerations. (1) It would be erroneous to reduce Freire's ideas to adult literacy education. For Freire, adult literacy education functions, in those contexts where it is necessary, only as a vehicle for the process of political conscientisation; it is not an end in itself. His 'codification/decodification' method and broader pedagogical ideas can be applied in contexts where the participants are 'literate', in the conventional sense of the term. (2) Freire's pedagogical ideas explore the contradictions that are masked by the dominant ideology. This is a task that most social movements must face when raising awareness about the particular issues with which they are concerned. (3) Freire's pedagogy recognises the political nature of all educational activity, where the aim is to do away with undemocratic social relations and replace them with radically democratic ones. This, I would submit, is the concern of the feminist, anti-racist and lesbian/gay movements, who challenge the bases of 'legitimised' social relations in society.

Freire is more relevant than Gramsci in this regard because, as indicated in Chapter 5, his politics were less essentialist: there is no identification in his work of a single 'universal' class or group destined to play the primary role in the process of social transformation. The emphasis on 'unity in diversity' in Freire's later works, notably the exchange with Faundez,[36] and his response to a series of contributors in a recently published book, give his work relevance not just to single movements but to alliances of movements.[37] His insightful dialectical conceptualisation of the 'oppressor consciousness' in *Pedagogy of the Oppressed* and elsewhere in many respects anticipated the formulations concerning 'layered and multiple identities' that figured prominently in his later presentations, particularly in North American seminars, and in his most recent published works.

Bureaucratic control

The notion of movements immediately brings to mind the 'free spaces' existing far from the manacles of bureaucratic control. Yet in adult education worldwide, funding structures gradually tie organisations, operating within broader social movements, to bureaucracies. As indicated in the Introduction, both Gramsci and Freire have argued in favour of working critically inside as well as outside the system. Gramsci's 'war of position' for effective counter-hegemonic action and Freire's constant exhortation that we be 'tactically inside and strategically outside the system' are possibly born of the recognition that we have to deal with systems that exert bureaucratic control.

Bureaucratic control can undermine the very freedom it is intended to safeguard. This can cause a variety of problems. Social organisations engaging in progressive adult educational activities, some of which Freire inspired, are often dependent on state funding or, in the case of EU countries, on money from the European Social Fund. This dependence on the state, or 'the larger state', and its bureaucratic procedures can adversely condition the manner in which these organisations implement their project. Dependence on state funding may also lead to cooptation of the organisations concerned. This problem applies not only to organisations but also to educational workers within the state system who are inspired by Freirean ideals.[38] In my work in connection with the Adult Education Unit of Malta's Education Department I have often felt that certain ideas introduced with transformative ends in view become diluted as a result of stifling bureaucratic procedures. By the time they are brought to fruition they end up serving the status quo. In colonial and revolutionary societies, the state bureaucracy has often been an inherited one where the procedures might not be in keeping with the kind of social relations the new government is attempting to promote. In Nicaragua, for instance, there were attempts to institutionalise 'popular education'.[39] Freire was certainly aware of this situation, which would exacerbate the tension between liberation and domestication. Indeed, one of the reasons he advocated the continuation of conscientisation in the revolutionary or post-colonial phase was to constitute a force against bureaucrats, who can 'deaden the revolutionary vision'.[40]

There is, however, another side to this issue. While not denying the stifling character of bureaucratic apparatuses, I would argue that they can offer organisations an avenue for transformative education in areas not conventionally associated with such a process. For instance, in order to gain access to necessary EU funds, social organisations that organise Freire-inspired adult education programmes might be required to design projects related to 'education for the long-term unemployed', an area given priority by funding agencies in Europe. While not denying that the agenda of these organisations is partly being defined for them by an external bureaucratic body, I would argue that they would be introducing critical pedagogical perspectives in an area which traditionally has had a narrow focus – skills transmission. They would be projecting the image of learners as the *subject* in an area where they have traditionally been the *object*. Spaces for transformation might also be found in areas that are generally associated with control and lack of freedom. Yet many might consider such notions idealistic, given that the literature on adult education is full of accounts of what can happen to an organisation that is dependent on state or 'supranational'[41] state funding.[42]

Lesirge and Mace highlight the price that has to be paid to secure such funding. Referring to women's programmes in Britain, they argue that the paperwork involved in trying to make a case for funding, in a context where the 'prizes are given to training which delivers women to jobs, as fast as possible',[43] is daunting. The implication is that a lot of energy is expended which could otherwise have been put to better and more constructive use. Longer-term personal and collective change is sacrificed to short term 'outputs', while the women participants 'have to consent to their knowledge and experience being dismantled into separate pieces – a process encouraged by what John Field has called the "parcellisation" of the competency movement.'[44] Such experiences stress the need for social movements and their component organisations involved in transformative adult education to explore ways of creating internal and autonomous sources of funding to avoid cooptation. This is not to say that these organisations should not tap into state and supranational state funds where possible; however, they should ideally be supplemented by internal funding in order to provide some autonomous base.

The threat of global capital

The tension between liberation and domestication is in all contexts exacerbated nowadays by the shadow of mobile, global capitalism. Capitalism's ability to shift its terrain of operation has given it leverage over the state; this has led to a decline in the latter's relative autonomy.[45] Global capitalism can have a devastating impact on the allocation of public funds to social programmes, including adult education programmes, intended as a response by the state to popular democratic demands and struggles.[46] In Ross and Trachte's terms, the 'rhetoric of the business climate'[47] takes precedence over concerns for democracy. This immediately calls to mind the legacy of Freire's work as Education Secretary in São Paulo. The tension between the quest for better education and better working conditions and the demands of foreign mobile capital must have been felt and continue to be felt in this Brazilian city. As Ross and Trachte argue, 'Manufacturing capital has been attracted to the Third World precisely because the workforce receives low wages, has few rights and offers little threat to the interest of capital.'[48] Can the kind of democratic social relations that Freire's policies in São Paulo sought to promote be implemented in such a way that they begin to pose a serious threat to the interests of mobile capital? Can they, in the circumstances, survive 'the witholding of investment by global firms, credit denial by the International Monetary Fund and global banks, and economic and political pressures by core states'?[49]

To legitimate itself, the Brazilian state has often had to bow to pressure from social movements for greater expenditure on pro-grammes for the poor, the disenfranchised and so forth. Funds for adult education, which allowed progressive adult educators work-ing within the state system or for organisations dependent on state funding to indulge in Freirean pedagogy, were made available as a result. The danger is that, given capitalism's ability to withdraw investment and set up plant elsewhere, such funding will diminish. Once again, this would be presented as part and parcel of 'struc-tural adjustment'.

The situation in Nicaragua following the UNO electoral victory testifies to this. As elsewhere in industrially underdeveloped countries, 'structural adjustment' programmes have been intro-duced. This has led to a forfeiture of some of the gains of the Sandinista revolution.[50] Robert F. Arnove stated in 1994 that he anticipated 'major cuts in governmental spending [to be] recom-mended by the International Monetary Fund and the World Bank.'[51] Popular educator Maria Zuniga states:

> Most of the social programmes of the Sandinistas are suffering greatly today because of the change in the government, the requirements of the international lending banks and the requirements of such govern-ments as the US government in making these famous structural adjustments. And 'structural adjustment', although it sounds very good – it sounds as though you're changing structures – creates problems, since what you're really doing is taking away from people the possibility to carry on with some of the most basic functions in their lives. You're taking away from them their educational services, their health services, their day care and social services, pensions for the elderly, care for disabled people. All of these services that make life, make living, more possible for the majority of the people.[52]

The emphasis in most places, as far as funding for adult edu-cation is concerned, is on upgrading vocational skills. As Dorothy Marshall puts it:

> The message to workers is about a skills crisis rather than a job crisis. Get retrained and the jobs will come, is the message from management and various government training bodies set up by politicians eager to be seen to be addressing job creation. The reality, of course, is that alarming levels of unemployment continue, with no likelihood of abate-ment without a radical change in the global economic agenda.[53]

Vocational reorientation is considered necessary, as part of the 'global competitiveness discourse'[54] simply to maintain investment, let alone attract it. This situation makes it even more imperative for social organisations seeking state funding to design programmes in such a way that elements of popular education are provided within the context of what would be marketed as a vocational education project. It is a moot point whether target learning groups would be excluded as a result of such a process.

The foregoing are some of the factors that affect the success or otherwise of the implementation of Freirean or Freire-inspired pedagogy in different contexts. Reference has been made to revolutionary and post-colonial societies. Tension between domestication and liberation is strongly felt in these societies. It might be argued that it is these societies that provide the climate most congenial to the carrying out of transformative adult education projects. As such, it is worth examining the situation of popular education in such societies more closely. The following section therefore discusses the application/misapplication of Freire-inspired pedagogy in adult education for social transformation in revolutionary and post-colonial societies. The process in such cases is intended to be one of 'cultural revolution', which, in Freire's words, should 'occur ... in complete harmony with the revolutionary regime'.[55]

Cultural Revolution

Freirean pedagogy has been applied in revolutionary situations where Gramsci's ideas have been taken on board. As a form of popular education, Freirean pedagogy has been of relevance to education in the 'liberated zones' of countries in a state of civil war or where a struggle for liberation from colonial oppression has taken place. References to schools for adults in the liberated zones of Guinea-Bissau are numerous throughout *Pedagogy in Process*.[56] It is argued[57] that the kind of education provided in such zones is, with some modification, similar to that carried out in certain revolutionary societies. Freire was directly involved in consultations concerning the launching of programmes in revolutionary and post-colonial societies. We have seen that, while in exile working for IDAC in Geneva, he acted as advisor to the governments of a number of African countries, including Guinea-Bissau, which had been involved in bloody wars of liberation against Portugal. We have also seen that he acted as consultant to the revolutionary New Jewel government in Grenada and to the Sandinista government in Nicaragua.[58] He was also advisor to Nyerere's government on the literacy campaign in Tanzania, although his involvement with this Unesco prize-winning campaign has been described as 'peripheral'.[59]

Adult education and development

In post-independence or post-revolutionary situations, governments tend to pin their hopes for the achievement of widespread literacy on non-formal rather than formal education. The feeling is that 'we must run while others walk', to cite the slogan from Tanzania. As Tanzania's first Five-Year Development Plan stated, 'the nation cannot wait until the children have become educated for development to begin.'[60] Large segments of the population in countries conventionally classified as 'Third World', including adolescents and people in the prime of their working lives, lack formal education. Robert F. Arnove states that, in Nicaragua, only 65 per cent of the relevant age group attended primary school during the final years of rule by the Somoza dynasty.[61] The situation was similar to that obtaining in several African countries during the period of colonisation. Witness the famous treatise 'Education for Self-reliance', by former Tanzanian president Julius K. Nyerere, who writes about lack of schooling in Tanganyika, now part of Tanzania, prior to independence in 1961. Another source, registering the rapid increases in school enrolment in Nicaragua, Cuba and Grenada during revolutionary periods,[62] indicates that, in many parts of Latin America, 'dropout rates in basic education are above 50% and the average level of schooling is 4.5 years.'[63] Or consider the city of São Paulo, the context for Freire's work as Education Secretary, where the situation concerning school attendance has traditionally been desperate. In her postscript to Freire's *Pedagogy of the City*, Ana Maria Saul reports that,

Even though two million children and youths are enrolled in three school districts in elementary education in particular, approximately four hundred thousand children between the ages of seven through fourteen have not yet gone to school. To this alarming number one adds six hundred thousand preschool children who are locked out of classes due to lack of space, while 14 percent of youths and adults are illiterate.[64]

Under the foregoing circumstances, non-formal education would be a very important source of post-colonial or revolutionary educational provision. Moreover, economic constraints may prevent impoverished countries from providing adequate schooling facilities, Tanzania being a case in point. In this East African country, it was a major achievement to provide universal primary education, and secondary schooling remained beyond the reach of many. In these situations, non-formal education would constitute a cheaper alternative.

The change agenda in adult education

Schools are notoriously slow to change, even following dramatic political events such as a revolution.[65] People concerned with vocational preparation have, for years, been emphasising that schools have been slow to respond to new labour market demands; this is one of the many criticisms of the human capital theory approach to schooling.[66] The same applies to the issue of radical social change. It is an issue that Myles Horton raised with Paulo Freire in their 'talking book': 'it's quite obvious that a revolution to my knowledge has not changed any schooling system or any that I've ever known about. School systems stay pretty much like they were before.... It happened in Cuba, happened in Nicaragua.'[67]

As Nyerere once told Freire: 'Paulo, it's not easy to put into practice the things we think about.'[68] Whatever the dream is that generates political action concerning schools, such as the creation of a self-financing 'school farm' in the rural areas of Tanzania, it is never easy to bring about change, however possible it might seem. Freire himself highlighted this at a 1991 AERA meeting in Chicago with respect to his experience as Education Secretary in São Paulo.[69] Horton, for his part, pinned his hopes on working outside rather than inside the system.[70] It would appear that, because of its flexibility, non-formal education offers greater possibilities for a process of a transformative education along the lines suggested in this book. The possibilities and alternatives that non-formal education offers with regard to transformative pedagogy become greater in former colonies, where administrative structures and procedures are inherited from the colonial period and are rarely replaced quickly.

The common task facing former colonies and countries that have undergone a revolution is to alter the social relations prevalent during the dictatorial or colonial period.[71] This involves, ideally, (a) changing the prescriptive 'top to bottom' mode of communication; (b) giving due recognition to 'popular cultures' and establishing them as the starting point of the learning process; (c) increasing the level of participation on the part of a previously subordinated people; (d) allowing the people to reclaim the voice that previous governments had denied them; (e) rendering the country as self-reliant as possible. There is also the task of deciding what to retain or critically appropriate from the established culture inherited from colonial or pre-revolutionary times. Here Gramsci's writings become relevant.

These are all goals and tasks that lend themselves to transformative pedagogy inspired by Gramsci and Freire. Accounts of the educational changes that took place in a number of countries indicate that the revolutionary governments tried hard to realise the goals.[72] The possibilities for effectively engaging in transformative pedagogy under such conditions are thus considerable. The spirit that prevails in such a context is a congenial one.

The threat to revolutionary gains

The achievements attributed to the revolutionary governments in question are to be seen as part of an ongoing process of social transformation. Nevertheless, the forces favouring processes of domestication remain. This may take the form of outside pressure, partly in reaction to the threat posed to the existing overall hegemony by revolutions such as those in Cuba, Nicaragua or Grenada. Embargoes, planned or actual invasions (e.g. Grenada) and the funding, for civil war purposes, of counter-revolutionaries (e.g. the Contras) – all are graphic illustration that external threats to the processes of liberation taking place within post-revolutionary societies remain. As such, it may be argued that there are severe limits on the extent to which transformative pedagogy can be successfully carried out. There was a determination to sabotage any form of development in these countries, including educational development. An invasion such as that which took place in Grenada creates a situation not unlike that in Brazil in 1964 and that in Chile in 1973. Long-drawn-out wars, such as the 'Contra war', also place material constraints on popular education programmes and generate fear among those involved.

Such external factors undoubtedly disrupt the effective implementation of transformative popular education. On the other hand, certain situations can, paradoxically, lead to increased exposure to liberatory practices. During civil wars, like that in Nicaragua in the 1980s and in El Salvador, schools became dangerous places in which to be: education can be a target of counter-revolutionary attacks.[73] (See the interview with Julio Portillo, cited in Chapter 3, with respect to the repression against teachers in El Salvador.[74]) Non-formal education allows for greater flexibility in the use of premises.[75] Consequently, popular education has proved to be a viable alternative to schooling.[76]

However, the extent to which a sense of liberation really takes place within popular education circles in revolutionary situations is questionable. It has often been argued that revolutionary governments tend to be overzealous when implementing popular education programmes.[77] This, in my view, was certainly the case in Nicaragua, as we shall see presently. The Sandinista government, in order to maintain revolutionary momentum and to legitimise itself in the eyes of a people who had been denied education in the pre-revolutionary period, implemented a mass literacy campaign within three months of taking office. To judge from the literature,[78] it seems that this campaign had some very positive features: it brought urban and rural dwellers together in a spirit of 'national-popular' unity, to adopt Gramsci's term; it de-professionalised knowledge; it fostered a greater spirit of popular participation; it reduced the illiteracy rate; and it mobilised mass organisations. The liberatory, transformative goal was clear. An attempt was made to deploy a Freire-inspired pedagogy throughout

the campaign and its successor, the popular basic education programme. Popular educator Maria Zuniga elaborates on some of
these points:

> the educational process involved was a two way one and was not re-
> stricted to the literacy that the young person was teaching them. It
> involved the entire experience of many people coming to know one
> another and learning to respect one another. This brought about a
> change in the society. There wasn't the kind of separation whereby
> city people felt they were different from country people or country
> people felt that they were inferior to city people because they had less
> education. City and country people shared this experience and learnt
> from one another. I think that was terribly important in all the
> processes of popular education taking place in Nicaragua under the
> Sandinista government but certainly at the beginning, during the
> *Alfabetización,* the literacy crusade.[79]

This two-way reciprocal process was one which, as Marjorie
Mayo points out in her discussion of competing perspectives in
adult education, Gramsci would have endorsed in his insistence
that intellectuals have to respect and learn from workers if they
are to make a difference.[80] She refers, in this context, to a conversation between Gramsci and a young university lecturer, reproduced by Felice Platone, one of Gramsci's colleagues on the
editorial board of *L'Ordine Nuovo*. In a subtle way, Gramsci indicated his disapproval of anyone who adopted a patronising tone
when attempting to engage in worker education, after the lecturer
had indicated his intention to 'help' workers, 'instruct them' and
'educate them'.[81]

Learning and respecting workers also entails understanding their
material conditions. Revealing, in this regard, is the episode in
Pedagogy of Hope concerning the lesson in 'class knowledge' which
Freire admits to having been given by a member of the audience
for one of his talks. This 'man of about forty' stressed the difference between the lifestyle that Freire's family enjoyed and the
harsh realities of those whom Freire had been addressing. Freire
had appeared oblivious to this difference.[82]

With regard to the literacy campaigns in Nicaragua, I would
argue that transformative pedagogy under these circumstances can
unwittingly oversee a shift from liberation to domestication. Trans-

formative 'revolutionary' pedagogy was applied within the context of a crusade, the large scale of which necessitated the involvement, as literacy workers, of young students and the newly literate. One wonders whether these people were equipped to engage in Freire-inspired pedagogy.[83] Accounts of the campaign indicate that they were not.[84] The more likely result was, in effect, what has been termed 'banking education'.[85] The would-be educators were under the added burden of having to complete the programme in three months. Significant, in this respect, is the view of Fernando Cardenal, Minister of Education in the Sandinista government and Coordinator of the Literacy Crusade, who in 1985 admitted that since the Revolution Nicaraguan education has fallen far short of its aims.[86] Later, in a visit to Toronto subsequent to UNO's electoral victory, Cardenal was reported in *ICAE News* as having stated that only now was Nicaragua beginning to advance beyond 'banking education'.[87]

Maria Zuniga has interpreted this[88] to mean that the excessive dependence of the people on the Sandinistas led them constantly to expect directives from above. Now that the Sandinistas are in opposition, they can engage in greater grassroots-level work. This necessitates the kind of 'bottom-up' communicative approach which Freire advocates. The Sandinista government could not promote this successfully as it was in the contradictory position of seeking to promote participatory democratic relations from above.

Post-revolutionary societies also face the contradictory situation whereby, on the one hand, they are trying to change social relations through popular education and, on the other, they need to produce the qualified personnel necessary to enable the country to survive economically. Under these circumstances, two educational systems develop, one of which is governed by technocratic rationality and is therefore likely to encourage domesticating pedagogical practices, and the other, which, in theory at least, is likely to be more congenial to a transformative and liberating pedagogy. Carnoy and Torres argue[89] that this was very much the case with the formal and non-formal educational systems in Nicaragua. The tension between liberation and domestication in post-revolutionary societies is reflected in the coexistence of the two systems, which, according to the Gramscian conception of revolutionary politics, ought to have been combined. The factory council theory called for a situation in which technical and administrative skills were to be learnt in the context of democratic, non-hierarchical social relations of production.

There might well be moments when the relation between 'cultural revolution' and the revolutionary regime would not be a harmonious one. The notion that transformative pedagogy works best in a post-revolutionary period is further problematised in the case of Portugal. Following the so-called 'revolution of the carnations' or 'silent coup', Portugal witnessed a profusion of popular education activities.[90] The cultural and political climate that prevailed in the aftermath of the revolution was one which should have lent itself readily to the use of transformative and Freirean pedagogy, given the strong cultural and political ties that exist between the Portuguese and Brazilian contexts.[91] In the words of Melo, 'The programmes were to promote what the people had in abundance ... popular culture, the people's own store of knowledge ... in short, their own living culture.'[92]

There is an obvious connection between the foregoing ideals and the basic tenets of Freirean pedagogy. Notwithstanding this, the national director of the Freire-inspired state-sponsored programme in Portugal was suspended because of the programme's 'political implications of action or potential action against the government'.[93] In sponsoring Freire-inspired programmes, therefore, the state would be furnishing the people with a weapon that can eventually be wielded against itself.[94]

Some Concluding Remarks

In this chapter, I have looked at various contexts and situations to examine the limits they impose on and the possibilities they offer for transformative action along the lines outlined earlier. Each situation is sufficiently complex to prevent me giving a straight answer to the question I posed at the outset: namely, to what extent and under what circumstances can transformative pedagogical ideas be successful in contributing to a process of social transformation? Having said this, there is enough evidence to suggest that Gramscian–Freirean transformative pedagogy is more likely to prove effective within the context of a social movement, or an alliance of movements, than in isolation. Nevertheless, each situation is sufficiently contradictory to suggest that the tension between liberation and domestication is ever present. In situations governed by extreme repression there may be spaces which allow for resistance. Transformative pedagogy can occupy these spaces as part of a Gramscian 'war of position', thereby countering the prevailing domesticating practices with liberatory forms of resistance. In revolutionary societies seeking to promote democratic social relations to counter years of dictatorship, transformative pedagogy, though often unrestricted, can suffer as a result of the contradictions that emerge from the revolutionary situation itself. In societies that lie somewhere in between, especially those characterised by Western-style democracy, transformative pedagogy suffers fluctuating fortunes, as a result of the struggle for democratic spaces carried out by movements and the individuals or organisations that they sustain.

Globalisation and civil society

The perpetual tension between domestication and liberation in all contexts renders the struggle for transformation an ongoing process. The challenge which remains, though, is that, although specific action by organic (in Gramsci's sense) and specific intellectuals (in Foucault's sense) in particular localities and contexts is valuable, this action must somehow connect, via larger movements, with action that transcends the boundaries of nation-states to counter the constant threat posed by the intensification of globalisation. For, with respect to Gramsci's theory of power and the state, is it still useful to talk in terms of limiting oneself to engaging the locus of power in a 'war of position' across the entire complex of 'civil society', when the locus of power has to be seen in the context of larger, international forces? Writing on the impact of globalisation on adult education, Korsgaard refers to the need for transnational action.[95] He argues for the building of a global civil society:

> Increasing globalization is a two-edged sword. On the one hand it is
> quite obvious that it removes competence from the national context

and that it thus undermines the institutions which civil society and the democratic public hitherto have used for communication. On the other hand globalization opens up new possibilities for a democratic influence on essential common issues which by their nature are about the notion of the nation-state. Attempts to democratize are, therefore, forced to work for the establishment of democratic global structures, including international organs for civil society.[96]

Of course, the term 'civil society' has been used differently by different authors. In this book, I have used the term in the sense advocated by Gramsci. According to this conception, a 'global civil society' would already be in existence, irrespective of whether transformative action is taken or not. 'Civil society' is not to be conceived of solely in oppositional or transformative terms since it constitutes the terrain in which most of the present ideological domination takes place. Global civil society is therefore the terrain on which much of the global domination, via global cable networks, information technology and so on, occurs.

Nevertheless, spaces for counter-hegemonic action exist, offering progressive groups, located in various parts of the globe, the means to connect electronically or otherwise. Information technology is, in this sense, a double-edged sword[97] in that, as an instrument of capitalism, it can constitute an effective process of domination, but can also offer counter-hegemonic possibilities in the fostering of international alliances.[98] There is, of course, nothing in Gramsci that addresses this issue, given the time in which he lived. There is also very little in Freire's writings that touches on this issue.

An international historical bloc?

Is there validity in the suggestion that Gramsci's concept of a 'historical bloc' must transcend its 'national-popular' character to begin to signify an alliance of movements across national boundaries? I would argue that the challenge, in terms of transformative international action, is for the creation of an *international historical bloc*, characterised by an international alliance of movements, ranging from environmental to labour movements.

The inclusion of the labour movement among the list of social movements here is important, given the criticism levelled at it over the years, not least for its exclusionary character and the totalising discourse it has promoted. The perception that the movement is a 'white male bastion' is fairly widespread. Yet there is the hope that this movement can transform itself into a more inclusionary and proactive one, recognising difference as an important characteristic of the labour force, both waged and unwaged. Gramsci, in his later writings, expressed the view that the factory councils, intended as working-class agencies able to transcend the capitalist wage relation, would transform the trade union into a new proactive institution. Many, such as John McIlroy, echoing Raymond Williams,[99] have argued that the institutions which form part of the labour movement must 'be renewed from top to bottom and ... urgently connect with new causes and new movements based on feminism, anti-racism, ecology, to reconnect with the general interest.'[100]

Adult education and the politics of inclusion

I have argued elsewhere that an inclusionary politics should constitute an important feature of adult education agencies operating within the context of the labour movement. Throughout this book I have referred to my case study of a particular programme of workers' education in Malta. The programme in question is that provided by the Workers' Participation Development Centre (WPDC) at the University of Malta. The study consisted of an analysis guided by the politics of inclusion.[101] The organisational set-up of the agency concerned, its adult educators and the content of its programmes were all analysed. The work of the WPDC was evaluated in terms of the consistency between the politics it professes and the pedagogical action carried out. This work was also analysed in terms of the gender politics involved and the nature of the content of its programmes, which was regarded as being Eurocentric.

The particular approach I took in my analysis was motivated by concerns similar to those expressed by John McIlroy and by my commitment to the kind of transformative pedagogical politics advocated in this book.[102] Labour organisations cannot hope to provide an appropriate setting for the kind of adult education promoted here unless they themselves experience a transformation along the lines I have just indicated. There are, in fact, indications in the published literature that such transformations have been taking place within labour organisations in different parts of the world. Bruce Spencer, for instance, has shown how Canadian unions have embraced issues affecting the 'lifeworld' strongly associated with the new social movements.[103] In one of his works, he refers to the 'greening' of labour unions, indicating their openness to ecological politics.[104] These institutions have a long history and constitute the mainstay of that long and repressed tradition of 'independent working class education'[105] strongly represented in such works as Brian Simon's *The Search for Enlightenment*.[106] Such an opening up to social movements, which can have the kind of transformative effect on unions which Gramsci believed the factory councils could have provided, would render this tradition even richer.

Adult education with a global dimension

However, it is not only in transforming themselves along these lines that certain unions can serve as model agencies for transformative adult education. Spencer has indicated, in his most recent work, how labour unions in Canada have woken up to the challenge posed by the information age[107] to create vehicles for the fostering of global linkages and alliances.[108] He indicates, for instance, how SoliNet (Solidarity Network) constitutes the means of establishing links between members of the Canadian Union of Public Employees across Canada's six time zones.[109] But it is not only through websites that the wider alliances can be made. Spencer and others have shown how Canadian unions have strengthened the international dimension of their work in response to intensification of the globalisation of capital. They recognise that issues can no longer be discussed and confronted solely within the confines of the nation-state. Canadian autoworkers have been utilising paid educational leave (PEL) to provide the kind of empowering workers' education programme which would constitute an appropriate space to accommodate the kind of pedagogical approaches advocated in this book. The work carried out within the PEL context is well documented in the recent literature.[110] Spencer reports that, 'The program is funded by a 2 to 3 cent, per member, per hour, benefit negotiated in contracts with employers. The money goes into a trust fund and is used to pay for lost wages, travel, accommodation and the educational costs of the program.'[111] The employer has no influence on the programme[112] and, therefore, as with the 150-hour experiment in Italy,[113] the education provided is not of the vocational type. Much of the programme is devoted to discussion of the relationship between national and international issues.[114] The international dimension is considered crucial to a proper understanding of the nature of global capitalist reorganisation. It serves to foster international solidarity between exploited groups in indifferent parts of the world. In so doing, it confronts the dominant ideology of competitiveness.[115] This ideology encourages a 'protectionist stance' in the North against Southern workers, and 'cooperation' between workers and management, united into 'teams', against 'the competition'.[116]

It is in the context of such labour education that transformative pedagogy, inspired by Gramsci and Freire, can take place. Canada, and more specifically Canadian labour education, continues to provide us with some important 'on the ground' examples of ideal contexts for transformative pedagogy in an age of globalisation. Arguably one of the most significant efforts at providing an international transformative education, intended to foster solidarity between Northern and Southern workers, is the Steelworkers' Humanity Fund Educational Program.[117] According to Judith Marshall, this programme constitutes a case of education for 'globalisation from below.'[118] Provision for this fund is worked into the collective bargaining agreements, with money coming from the steelworkers (they donate a penny per hour worked), management (in 10 per cent of the contracts management matched the workers' donation penny for penny), and the Canadian International Development Agency (CIDA).[119] The fund supports projects of some thirty to forty organisations throughout the world. It is a Thinking North–South programme in which popular education approaches are used, and which involves educational exchanges of workers from North and South.[120] This strikes me as constituting an excellent example of transformative education with a global dimension.

As programmes with a global, non-eurocentric dimension become increasingly important and provide an effective context for transformative pedagogy, one should not overlook the purely local. Discussing popular education, Maria Zuniga states that there are struggles for democracy and social justice occurring in a variety of places:

> I am not talking about societies and overthrowing governments but overcoming injustice in particular kinds of situations. So yes, I think it [popular education] can be applied in different contexts. I think it can be applied in neighbourhoods. I think it can be applied in cities, in factories, in different kinds of situations where people find themselves, notably in structures which are unjust and need to change.[121]

Popular knowledge and the dominant culture

Freire's pedagogy has been used and continues to be used in different communities to foster communal empowerment. One of the best examples of Freirean pedagogy in a community setting is that of the Adult Learning Project in Gorgie Dalry, Edinburgh. It is argued in the account provided by Colin and Gerry Kirkwood that the ALP helped to enable residents of this working-class community to reflect and act upon their world. Using the codification approach, participants were able to reflect critically on aspects of their environment and then organise themselves to engage in action to rectify the situation they identified.[122] One of the positive things about this project is the organisers' awareness of the need for a synthesis which values both the knowledge possessed by experts and people's own experience. They also advocate an approach that involves rigour within a dialogical education.[123] These two elements, constantly emphasised by Freire, would be important features of a pedagogical process based on a synthesis of ideas derived from Gramsci and Freire. One of the major challenges is to encounter programmes which not only focus on the popular and the communal but which also encourage a critical engagement with the dominant culture. It is opportune to cite, in this context, the point made by Denis Haughey, who states, with respect to radical education inspired by Gramsci, that one of the competencies 'largely lacking in contemporary adult education practice … is the ability to function fluently in the language of the dominant culture so as not to be relegated to the periphery of political life.'[124]

An unfinished canvas

In this book, I have explored the possibilities that exist for building
a theoretical framework for transformative adult education on the
basis of ideas expressed by Antonio Gramsci and Paulo Freire. In
so doing, I have provided an exposition of their ideas in this regard
as they bear on a contemporary project. I have supplemented
these ideas with some of the recent literature in the fields of contemporary adult education theory, feminism, cultural studies and
critical pedagogy. These ideas have been developed within the
framework of a broad democratic socialist politics that recognises
the multiple forms of structural and systemic oppression worldwide. The nature of such oppression is subject to the changing
processes of capitalist reorganisation. Many elements in this book
warrant extensive treatment in a more exploratory form. The work
remains an unfinished canvas, the issues raised being far from
settled.

Notes

1. This chapter is developed from an article on Freire – Mayo, 1993a.
It also contains material from another article on Freire – Mayo, 1995c.

2. Torres, 1982, 1993.

3. Ireland, 1987.

4. Torres, 1990b: 274.

5. Clark, 1977.

6. Morrow and Torres, 1995: 272.

7. Buttigieg, 1992: 2.

8. See the blurb on the back cover of Freire, 1970.

9. Zuniga, 1993: 38; Arnove, 1994: 202. Zuniga describes *concertación*
as the process of

> the different social actors and social forces in the community coming
> together because, if the wealthy are reasonable, they will realise that,
> unless there is some way of people working together and having cer-
> tain kinds of possibilities for a better life, the situation will become so
> explosive that they are not going to be able to maintain their wealth
> and their power. And so those who have wealth and power must sit
> down at the table with the other social actors and try to bring about
> reasonable social change. And that's what is happening in Central
> America. (Zuniga, 1993: 38)

10. Martinez, 1998.

11. Foucault, 1980: 4.

12. La Belle, 1986: 203.

13. Freire and Faundez, 1989: 65, 66.

14. Horton and Freire, 1990: 211.

15. Coutinho, 1995: 126.

16. Coutinho, 1995: 126.

17. Coutinho, 1995: 126.

18. Ireland, 1987.

19. Jarvis, 1987a: 268.

20. Arnove, 1986: 9.

21. Hoare in Gramsci, 1977: xiv–xv.

22. Shor and Freire, 1987: 37.

23. Shor and Freire, 1987.

24. Freire, in Kirkwood and Kirkwood, 1989: 138.

25. La Belle, 1986: 18.

26. La Belle, 1986: 18.

27. Mayo, 1991a.

28. Torres, 1990a: 99.

29. Gramsci, 1977: 12.

30. Aricó, 1988; Morrow and Torres, 1995; Coutinho, 1995; Fernández Díaz, 1995; Melis, 1995.

31. Hoare in Gramsci, 1977: ix.

32. Ireland, 1987.

33. Ireland, 1987.

34. Coutinho, 1995: 134–6.

35. Shor and Freire, 1987: 39.

36. Freire and Faundez, 1989.

37. Freire, 1997a.

38. It is pertinent to remark here that part of capitalism's dynamism is its ability to coopt. Paulo Freire's ideas have, on several occasions, been adopted in contexts serving the interests of capitalism and ruling elites – see Kidd and Kumar, 1981. Organisations and regimes have appropriated the technical aspects of his method, doing away with its political dimension. The very regime that banned Freire from Brazil for sixteen years claimed to have used his methods in the government-sponsored MOBRAL campaign – Bhola, 1984: 130.

39. Taped interview with Maria Zuniga from CISAS (Centre for Information and Advisory Services in Health), Managua. I take 'institutionalise' to mean 'bureaucratise' in this particular instance.

40. Freire, 1972b: 78.

41. The term is borrowed from Corrigan, 1980: xv.

42. With respect to the TUC in the UK, see McIlroy, 1993c: 53; 1992: 300.

43. Lesirge and Mace, 1992: 353.

44. Lesirge and Mace, 1992: 354.

45. Ross and Trachte, 1990: 68.

46. Carnoy and Levin, 1985.

47. Ross and Trachte, 1990: 68.

48. Ross and Trachte, 1990: 112.

49. Ross and Trachte, 1990: 112. This section on São Paulo and the issue of mobile global capital is reproduced from Mayo, 1993a: 22.

50. See Zuniga, 1993; Arnove, 1994: 207; M. Mayo, 1997: 70.

51. Arnove, 1994: 207.

52. Zuniga, 1993: 37, 38.

53. Marshall, 1997: 59.

54. Marshall, 1997: 59.

55. Freire, in Torres, 1982: 88.

56. Freire, 1978.

57. Torres, 1990b: 273.

58. Arnove, 1986: 41; Torres, 1990a: 87, 97; Jules, 1993: 146.

59. Torres, 1982: 87. For an interesting anecdotal account of Freire's involvement in Tanzania, see Hall, 1998.

60. Cited in Unsicker, 1986: 231.

61. Arnove, 1986: 3.

62. Torres, 1990a: 95, 96.

63. Torres, 1990a: 107.

64. Saul, in Freire, 1993: 151.

65. Torres, 1990a: 9,.

66. Sultana, 1992: 298.

67. Horton in Horton and Freire, 1990: 221.

68. Freire, in Horton and Freire, 1990: 219.

69. Freire, 1991.

70. Horton in Horton and Freire, 1990: 200.

71. I refer here also to dictatorships in colonial centres which had a direct bearing on quality of life in places like Guinea-Bissau, Cape Verde and São Tomé e Príncipe, to name but three former Portuguese colonies.

72. Arnove, 1986; Carnoy and Torres, 1987; R.M. Torres, 1986; Freire, 1978, 1981.

73. Horton and Freire, 1990: 224; Hammond, 1991: 93; Zuniga, 1993: 36.

74. Hammond, 1991: 93.

75. Torres, 1993: 127.

76. Carnoy and Torres, 1987.

77. This point was made during a talk delivered by Pablo Latapí in the Department of Educational Foundations, University of Alberta, Edmonton, in autumn 1987.

78. Arnove, 1986; Arnove, 1994; Carnoy and Torres, 1987.

79. Zuniga, 1993.
80. M. Mayo, 1997: 24.
81. Marks in Gramsci, 1957: 15.
82. Freire, 1994: 23–26. I am indebted to Peter McLaren, Silvia Serra, Estanislao Antelo and Gustavo Fischman for reminding me of this passage in the first draft of their paper for a forthcoming book on Gramsci and Education and which will also appear in the *Journal of Thought*.
83. Mayo, 1991a.
84. Arnove, 1986: 55; Carnoy and Torres, 1987: 31; Lind and Johnston, 1986: 62.
85. Arnove, 1986: 58.
86. C.A. Torres, 1991; R.M. Torres, 1986.
87. ICAE, 1990: 5.
88. Zuniga, 1993.
89. Carnoy and Torres, 1987.
90. Melo, 1985.
91. Mayo, 1991a.
92. Melo, 1985: 42, 43.
93. Lind and Johnston, 1986: 61.
94. Mayo, 1991a.
95. Korsgaard, 1997: 23, 24.
96. Korsgaard, 1997: 23.
97. This point is taken from the conclusion to Mayo, 1996.
98. Hall, 1993.
99. Williams, 1983. On this issue, see also Blackburn, 1989 and Westwood, 1993.
100. McIlroy, 1993b: 227.
101. Mayo, 1997b.
102. Mayo, 1997b.
103. Spencer, 1994, 1995.
104. Spencer, 1995.
105. Sharp, Hartwig and O'Leary, 1989.
106. Simon, 1992.
107. Baldacchino, 1997.
108. Spencer, 1998a, 1998b.
109. Spencer, 1998b: 174.
110. Marshall, 1997; Livingstone, 1997; Spencer, 1998a, 1998b.
111. Spencer, 1998a: 104.
112. Spencer, 1998a: 106.
113. Yarnit, 1980.
114. Spencer, 1998a: 106.
115. Marshall, 1997: 59.
116. Marshall, 1997: 59.
117. Marshall, 1997; Spencer, 1998a, 1998b.

118. Marshall, 1997.
119. Marshall, 1997: 60, 61.
120. Marshall, 1997: 61; Spencer, 1998a: 107.
121. Zuniga, 1993: 34.
122. Kirkwood and Kirkwood, 1989.
123. Kirkwood and Kirkwood, 1989: 135.
124. Haughey, 1998: 211.

Bibliography

Abercrombie, N., B. Turner and S. Hill (1984), *A Dictionary of Sociology*, Penguin, London and Harmondsworth.

Achebe, C. (1975), *Morning. Yet on Creation Day*, Doubleday, Garden City NY.

Adams, F. (1972), 'Highlander Folk School: Getting Information, Going Back and Teaching It', *Harvard Educational Review*, vol. 42, no. 4, pp. 97–119.

Adamson, W. (1980), *Hegemony and Revolution*, University of California Press, Berkeley, Los Angeles and London.

Alden, H. (1981), 'Gramsci's Theoretical Legacy', *Convergence*, vol. XIV, no. 3, pp. 91–94.

Allman, P. (1988), 'Gramsci, Freire and Illich: Their Contributions to Education for Socialism', in T. Lovett (ed.), *Radical Approaches to Adult Education: A Reader*, Routledge, London.

Allman, P. (1994), 'Paulo Freire's Contribution to Radical Adult Education', *Studies in the Education of Adults*, vol. 26, no. 2, pp. 144–61.

Allman, P. (1996), 'Freire with no Dilutions' in H. Reno and M. Witte (eds), *37th Annual AERC Proceedings*, University of South Florida, Tampa.

Allman, P. and P. Mayo (1997), 'Freire, Gramsci and Globalisation: Some Implications for Social and Political Commitment in Adult Education', in P. Armstrong, N. Miller and M. Zukas (eds), *Crossing Borders Breaking Boundaries: Research in the Education of Adults*, Proceedings of the 27th Annual SCUTREA Conference, Birkbeck College, University of London.

Allman, P. and J. Wallis (1990), 'Praxis: Implications for "Really" Radical Education', *Studies in the Education of Adults*, vol. 22, no. 1, pp. 14–30.

Allman, P. and J. Wallis (1995a), 'Challenging the Postmodern Condition: Radical Adult Education for Critical Intelligence', in M. Mayo and J. Thompson (eds), *Adult Learning, Critical Intelligence and Social Change*,

NIACE, Leicester.

Allman, P. and J. Wallis (1995b), Gramsci's Challenge to the Politics of the Left in "Our Times"', *International Journal of Lifelong Education*, vol. 14, no. 2, pp. 120–43.

Allman, P. and J. Wallis (1997), 'Commentary: Paulo Freire and the Future of the Radical Tradition', *Studies in the Education of Adults*, vol. 29, no. 2, pp. 113–20.

Amendola, G. (1978), *Antonio Gramsci nella vita culturale e politica italiana*, Guida Editori, Naples.

Amin, S. (1997), *Capitalism in an Age of Globalization*, Zed Books, London.

Anderson, P. (1976), 'The Antinomies of Antonio Gramsci', *New Left Review*, 100, pp. 5–78.

Apitzsch, U. (1993), 'Gramsci and the Current Debate on Multicultural Education', *Studies in the Education of Adults*, vol. 25, no. 2, pp. 136–45.

Apitzsch, U. (1995), 'Lavoro, cultura ed educazione tra fordismo e fascismo', in G. Baratta and A. Catone (eds), *Antonio Gramsci e il 'Progresso Intellettuale di Massa'*, Edizioni Unicopli, Milan.

Apple, M. (1980), Review of H. Entwistle, *Antonio Gramsci: Conservative Schooling for Radical Politics*, *Comparative Education Review*, vol. 24, no. 3, pp. 436–8.

Apple, M. (ed.) (1982), *Cultural and Economic Reproduction in Education*, Routledge & Kegan Paul, Boston MA.

Apple, M. (1991), 'Education, Power and Personal Biography', Michael Apple interviewed by R.A. Morrow and C.A. Torres, *Education* (Malta), vol. 4, no. 2, pp. 28–9.

Apple, M. (1992), 'The Text and Cultural Politics', *Educational Researcher*, vol. 21, no. 7, pp. 4–11.

Araújo Freire, A.M. (1997), 'A Bit of My Life with Paulo Freire', *Taboo: The Journal of Culture and Education*, vol. II, Fall, pp. 3–11.

Aricó, J. (1988), *La Cola del Diablo: Itinerario de Gramsci en América Latina*, Editorial Nueva Sociedad, Caracas.

Armstrong, P. (1988), '*L'Ordine Nuovo*: The Legacy of Antonio Gramsci and the Education of Adults', *International Journal of Lifelong Education*, vol. 7, no. 4, pp. 249–59.

Arnove, R.F. (1986), *Education and Revolution in Nicaragua*, Praeger, New York.

Arnove, R.F. (1994), *Education as Contested Terrain: Nicaragua (1979–1993)*, Westview Press, Boulder CO.

Arnove, R.F. and H.J. Graff (eds) (1986), *National Literacy Campaigns: Historical and Comparative Perspectives*, Plenum, New York.

Aronowitz, S. (1993), 'Freire's Radical Democratic Humanism', in P. McLaren and P. Leonard (eds), *Paulo Freire: A Critical Encounter*, Routledge, New York and London.

Aronowitz, S. and H. Giroux (1991), *Postmodern Education*, University of Minnesota Press, Minneapolis and Oxford.

Arvidson, L. (1993), 'Adult Education and Democracy', in *Social Change and Adult Education Research: Adult Education Research in Nordic Countries 1991/92*, Special-Trykkereit Viborg A/S, Copenhagen.

Azzopardi, E. and L.J. Scerri (eds) (1984), *Issues: Aspects of an Island Economy*, Economics Society, Malta.

Baldacchino, G. (1990), *Worker Cooperatives with Particular Reference to Malta: An Educationist's Theory and Practice*, Institute of Social Studies, The Hague.

Baldacchino, G. (1997), 'The Information Age: Implications for Trade Unions and Worker Education', in G. Baldacchino and P. Mayo (eds), *Beyond Schooling: Adult Education in Malta*, Mireva, Malta.

Ball, W. (1992), 'Critical Social Research, Adult Education and Anti-Racist Feminist Praxis', *Studies in the Education of Adults*, vol. 24, no. 1, pp. 1–25.

Bhola, H.S. (1984), *Campaigning for Literacy. Eight National Experiences of the Twentieth Century, With a Memorandum to Decision-makers*, Unesco, Paris.

Blackburn, R. (1989), 'Introduction', in R. Williams, *Resources of Hope*, Verso, London.

Blackledge, D. and B. Hunt (1985), *Sociological Interpretations of Education*, Croom Helm, London, Sydney, Dover and New Hampshire.

Blundell, S. (1992), 'Gender and the Curriculum of Adult Education', *International Journal of Lifelong Education*, vol. 11, no. 3, pp. 199–216.

Bobbio, N. (1987), 'Gramsci and the Conception of Civil Society', in R. Bellamy (ed.), *Which Socialism?*, University of Minnesota Press, Minneapolis.

Bocock, R. (1986), *Hegemony*, Tavistock, London and New York.

Boff, L. and C. Boff (1987), *Liberation and Theology 1: Introducing Liberation Theology*, Burns and Oates, Kent.

Borg, C. and P. Mayo (1993), Review of Roger I. Simon, *Teaching Against the Grain*, *McGill Journal of Education*, vol. 28, no. 1, Winter, pp. 161–7.

Boron, A. and C.A. Torres (1996), 'The Impact of Neoliberal Restructuring on Education and Poverty in Latin America', *Alberta Journal of Educational Research*, vol. XLII, no. 2, pp. 102–14.

Bourdieu, P. and J.C. Passéron (1990), *Reproduction in Education, Society and Culture*, 2nd edn, Sage, London, Newbury Park and New Delhi.

Briton, D. (1996), *The Modern Practice of Adult Education: A Postmodern Critique*, SUNY Press, Albany NY.

Broccoli, A. (1972), *Antonio Gramsci e l'educazione come egemonia*, La Nuova Italia, Florence.

Brookfield, S. (1987), *Developing Critical Thinkers*, Jossey-Bass, San Francisco.

Brookfield, S. (1989), 'Teacher Roles and Teaching Styles', in C.J. Titmus (ed.), *Lifelong Education for Adults: An International Handbook*, Pergamon Press, Oxford.

Brookfield, S. (1993), 'Breaking the Code: Engaging Practitioners in Critical Analysis of Adult Education Literature', *Studies in the Education of Adults*, vol. 25, no. 1, pp. 64–91.

Bruss, N. and D. Macedo (1985), 'Toward a Pedagogy of the Question: Conversations with Paulo Freire', *Journal of Education*, vol. 167, no. 2, pp. 7–21.

Buttigieg, J.A. (ed.) (1992), *Antonio Gramsci: Prison Notebooks, Volume 1*, Columbia University Press, New York and Oxford.

Cannadine, D. (1983), 'The Context, Performance and Meaning of Ritual: The British Monarchy and the "Invention of Tradition", *c.* 1820–1977', in E.J. Hobsbawm and T. Ranger (eds), *The Invention of Tradition*, Cambridge University Press, Cambridge.

Carnoy, M. (1982), 'Education, Economy and the State', in M. Apple (ed.), *Cultural and Economic Reproduction in Education*, Routledge & Kegan Paul, Boston MA.

Carnoy, M. and H. Levin (1985), *Schooling and Work in the Democratic State*, Stanford University Press, Stanford CA.

Carnoy, M. and C.A. Torres (1987), 'Education and Social Transformation in Nicaragua 1979–1986', in M. Carnoy and J. Samoff (eds), *Education and Social Transition in the Third World*, Princeton University Press, Princeton NJ.

Caruso, S. (1997), 'La riforma intellettuale e morale', in S. Mastellone (ed.), *Gramsci: I 'Quaderni Del Carcere', Una riflessione politica incompiuta*, UTET Libreria, Turin.

Chu, D.-C. (1980), *Chairman Mao: Education of the Proletariat*, Philosophy Library, New York.

Clark, M. (1977), *Antonio Gramsci and the Revolution that Failed*, Yale University Press, London and New Haven.

Clark, M.C. (1997), 'Learning as a Non-unitary Self: Implications of Postmodernism for Adult Learning Theory', in P. Armstrong, N. Miller and M. Zukas (eds), *Crossing Borders Breaking Boundaries: Research in the Education of Adults*, Proceedings of the 27th Annual SCUTREA Conference, Birkbeck College, University of London.

Clover, D.E. (1991), 'Institute in Honour of Paulo Freire', *ICAE News*, no. 4, pp. 1, 6, 7.

Coben, D. (1994), 'Antonio Gramsci and the Education of Adults, Adult Education and Social Change', collection of papers presented at the European Research Seminar of the European Society for Research on the Education of Adults (ESREA), Lahti, Finland, 7–11 August.

Coben, D. (1995), 'Revisiting Gramsci', *Studies in the Education of Adults*, vol. 27, no. 1, pp. 36–51.

Coben, D. (1998), *Radical Heroes: Gramsci, Freire and the Politics of Adult Education*, Garland, New York.

Collins, M. (1977), *Paulo Freire: His Life, Works and Thought*, Paulist Press, New York.

Comeliau, C. (1997), 'The Challenges of Globalization', *Prospects*, vol. XXVII, no. 1, pp. 29–34.

Connelly, B. (1992), 'A Critical Overview of the Sociology of Adult

Education', *International Journal of Lifelong Education*, vol. 11, pp. 235–53.

Cooper, G. (1995), 'Freire and Theology', *Studies in the Education of Adults*, vol. 27, no. 1, pp. 66–78.

Corrigan, P. (ed.) (1980), *Capitalism, State Formation and Marxist Theory*, Quartet, London.

Corrigan, P., H. Ramsay and D. Sayer (1980), 'The State as a Relation of Production', in P. Corrigan (ed.),*Capitalism, State Formation and Marxist Theory*, Quartet, London.

Corrigan, P. and D. Sayer (1985), *The Great Arch: English State Formation as Cultural Revolution*, Basil Blackwell, Oxford.

Coutinho, C.N. (1995), 'In Brasile', in E.J. Hobsbawm (ed.), *Gramsci in Europa e in America*, Italian edition ed. A. Santucci, Sagittari Laterza, Rome and Bari.

Crane, J.M. (1987), 'Moses Coady and Antigonish' in P. Jarvis (ed.), *Twentieth Century Thinkers in Adult Education*, Routledge, London and New York.

Cunningham, P. (1992), 'From Freire to Feminism: The North American Experience with Critical Pedagogy', *Adult Education Quarterly*, vol. 42, pp. 180–91.

Dale, R., G. Esland and M. Macdonald (eds) (1976), *Schooling and Capitalism*, Routledge & Kegan Paul, London.

Darmanin, M. (1997), 'Women's Studies in Adult Education', in G. Baldacchino and P. Mayo (eds), *Beyond Schooling: Adult Education in Malta*, Mireva, Malta.

Da Silva, T. and P. McLaren (1993), 'Knowledge under Siege: The Brazilian Debate', in P. McLaren, and P. Leonard (eds), *Paulo Freire: A Critical Encounter*, Routledge, New York and London.

De Kadt, E. (1970), *Catholic Radicals in Brazil*, Oxford University Press, Oxford.

De Robbio Anziano, I. (1987), *Antonio Gramsci e la pedagogia del impegno*, Ferraro, Naples.

Diskin, J. (1993), 'Gramsci in Rethinking Marxism', *International Gramsci Society Newsletter*, no. 2., pp. 18–20.

Edwards, R. and R. Usher (1997), 'Globalisation and a Pedagogy of (Dis)location', in P. Armstrong, N. Miller and M. Zukas (eds), *Crossing Borders Breaking Boundaries: Research in the Education of Adults*, Proceedings of the 27th Annual SCUTREA Conference, Birkbeck College, University of London.

Elias, J. (1994), *Paulo Freire: Pedagogue of Liberation*, Krieger, Florida.

Ellsworth, E. (1989), 'Why Doesn't this Feel Empowering? Working Through the Repressive Myths of Critical Pedagogy, *Harvard Educational Review*, vol. 59, no. 3, pp. 297–324.

Entwistle, H. (1979), *Antonio Gramsci: Conservative Schooling for Radical Politics*, Routledge & Kegan Paul, London, Boston and Henley.

Escobar, M., A.L. Fernández and G. Guevara-Niebla, with P. Freire (1994),

Paulo Freire on Higher Education: A Dialogue at the National University of Mexico, SUNY Press, Albany NY.

Fernández Díaz, O. (1995), 'In America Latina', in E.J. Hobsbawm (ed.), *Gramsci in Europa e in America*, Italian edition ed. A. Santucci, Sagittari Laterza, Rome and Bari.

Festa, S. (1976), *Gramsci*, Cittadella Editrice, Assisi.

Findlay, P. (1994), 'Conscientization and Social Movements in Canada: The Relevance of Paulo Freire's Ideas in Contemporary Politics', in P. McLaren and C. Lankshear (eds), *Politics of Liberation: Paths from Freire*, Routledge, London.

Finger, M. (1989), 'New Social Movements and their Implications for Adult Education', *Adult Education Quarterly*, vol. 40, no. 1, pp. 15–22.

Fiori, G. (1970), *Antonio Gramsci: Life of a Revolutionary*, New Left Books, London.

Foley, G. (1993), 'The Neighbourhood House: Site of Struggle, Site of Learning', *British Journal of Sociology of Education*, vol. 14, no. 1, pp. 21–37.

Foley, G. (1994), 'Adult Education and Capitalist Reorganisation', *Studies in the Education of Adults*, vol. 26, no. 2, pp. 121–43.

Foucault, M. (1980), *The History of Sexuality, vol. 1*, Pantheon, New York.

Freire, P. (1970), *Pedagogy of the Oppressed*, Seabury Press, New York.

Freire, P. (1971), 'To the Coordinator of a Cultural Circle', *Convergence*, vol. IV, no. 1, pp. 61–2.

Freire, P. (1972a), *Cultural Action for Freedom*, Penguin, New York and Harmondsworth.

Freire, P. (1972b), 'Education: Domestication or Liberation?', *Prospects*, vol. 2, no. 2, pp. 173–81.

Freire, P. (1973), *Education for Critical Consciousness*, Continuum, New York.

Freire, P. (1976), 'Literacy and the Possible Dream', *Prospects*, vol. 6, no. 1, pp. 68–71.

Freire, P. (1978), *Pedagogy in Process: The Letters to Guinea-Bissau*, Continuum, New York.

Freire, P. (1981), 'The People Speak their Word: Learning to Read and Write in São Tomé and Príncipe', *Harvard Educational Review*, vol. 51, no. 1, pp. 27–30.

Freire, P. (1985), *The Politics of Education*, Bergin & Garvey, Massachusetts.

Freire, P. (1991), *Educational Policy and Social Change in Brazil: The Work of Paulo Freire as Secretary of Education in São Paulo*, audio cassette, Teach'em Inc., Chicago.

Freire, P. (1993), *Pedagogy of the City*, Continuum, New York.

Freire, P. (1994), *Pedagogy of Hope*, Continuum, New York.

Freire, P. (1995), 'Reply to Discussants', in de Figueiredo-Cowen and D. Gastaldo (eds), *Paulo Freire at the Institute*, Institute of Education, University of London.

Freire, P. (1996), *Letters to Cristina. Reflections on My Life and Work*, Routledge, New York.

Freire, P. (1997a), 'A Response', in P. Freire with J.W. Fraser, D. Macedo, T. McKinnon and W.T. Stokes (eds), *Mentoring the Mentor: A Critical Dialogue with Paulo Freire*, Peter Lang, New York.

Freire, P. (1997b), *Pedagogy of the Heart*, Continuum, New York.

Freire, P. (1998a), *Teachers as Cultural Workers: Letters to Those Who Dare Teach*, Westview Press, Boulder CO.

Freire, P. (1998b), *Pedagogy of Freedom: Kinds of Knowledge Essential for Educative Practice*, Rowman & Littlefield.

Freire, P. and F. Betto (1985), *Essa Escola Chamada Vida*, Atica, São Paulo.

Freire, P. and A. Faundez (1989), *Learning to Question: A Pedagogy of Liberation*, World Council of Churches, Geneva.

Freire, P. and D. Macedo (1987), *Literacy: Reading the Word and the World*, Bergin & Garvey, Massachusetts.

Freire, P. and D. Macedo (1993), 'A Dialogue with Paulo Freire', in P. McLaren and P. Leonard (eds), *Paulo Freire: A Critical Encounter*, Routledge, New York and London.

Freire, P. and D. Macedo (1995), 'A Dialogue: Culture, Language and Race', *Harvard Educational Review*, vol. 65, no. 3, pp. 377–402.

Freire, P. and D. Macedo (1998), *Ideology Matters*, Rowman & Littlefield.

Freire, P. with J.W. Fraser, D. Macedo, T. McKinnon and W.T. Stokes (eds) (1997), *Mentoring the Mentor. A Critical Dialogue with Paulo Freire*, Peter Lang, New York.

Fukuyama, F. (1992), *The End of History and the Last Man*, Free Press, New York.

Gaber-Katz, E. and G.M. Watson (1991), *The Land that We Dream of: A Participatory Study of Community-Based Literacy*, OISE Press, Toronto.

Gadotti, M. (1994) *Reading Paulo Freire: His Life and Work*, SUNY Press, Albany NY.

Gadotti, M. and C.A. Torres (1997), 'Paulo Freire: A Homage', *Taboo: The Journal of Culture and Education*, vol. II, Fall, pp. 96–101.

Gam, P., S. Tosse, J. Tuomisto, M. Klasson and B. Wahlgren (1993), *Social Change and Adult Education Research: Adult Education Research in Nordic Countries 1991/92*, Special-Trykkereit Viborg A/S, Copenhagen.

Geras, N. (1987), 'Post Marxism?', *New Left Review*, 163, pp. 41–82.

Gerhardt, H.-P. (1993), 'Paulo Freire (1921–)', *Prospects*, vol. 23, no. 3/4, pp. 439–58.

Germino, D. (1990), *Antonio Gramsci: Architect of a New Politics*, Louisiana State University Press, Baton Rouge and London.

Giroux, H. (1980), Review of H. Entwistle, *Antonio Gramsci: Conservative Schooling for Radical Politics*, *British Journal of Sociology of Education*, vol. 1, no. 3, pp. 307–15.

Giroux, H. (1981), 'Hegemony, Resistance and the Paradox of Educational Reform', *Interchange*, vol. 12, nos 2–3, pp. 3–26.

Giroux, H. (1983), *Theory and Resistance in Education: A Pedagogy for the Opposition*, Bergin & Garvey, Massachusetts.

Giroux, H. (1985), 'Introduction' to P. Freire, *The Politics of Education*, Bergin & Garvey, Massachusetts.

Giroux, H. (1987), 'Literacy and the Pedagogy of Political Empowerment', in P. Freire and D. Macedo, *Literacy: Reading the Word and the World*, Bergin & Garvey, Massachusetts.

Giroux, H. (ed.) (1988), *Teachers as Intellectuals*, Bergin & Garvey, Massachusetts.

Giroux, H. (1992), *Border Crossings, Cultural Workers and the Politics of Education*, Routledge, New York.

Giroux, H. (1996), *Disturbing Pleasures*, Routledge, New York and London.

Giroux, H., D. Shumway, P. Smith and J. Sosnoski (1988), 'The Need for Cultural Studies', in H. Giroux (ed.), *Teachers as Intellectuals*, Bergin & Garvey, Massachusetts.

Gore, J.M. (1992), *The Struggle for Pedagogies. Critical and Feminist Discourses as Regimes of Truth*, Routledge, New York.

Goulet, D. (1973), 'Introduction', to P. Freire, *Education for Critical Consciousness*, Continuum, New York.

Grabowski, S.M. (ed.) (1972), *Paulo Freire: A Revolutionary Dilemma for the Adult Educator*, ERIC Clearing House, New York.

Gramsci, A. (1957), *The Modern Prince and Other Writings*, edited by L. Marks, International Publishers, New York.

Gramsci, A. (1964), *2000 Pagine di Gramsci (vol.1)*, edited by G. Ferrara and N. Gallo, Il Saggiatore, Milan.

Gramsci, A. (1971a), *Gli intelletuali e l'organizzazione della cultura*, Editori Riuniti, Rome.

Gramsci, A. (1971b), *Selections from the Prison Notebooks*, edited by Q. Hoare and G. Nowell Smith, International Publishers, New York.

Gramsci, A. (1972), *L'Alternativa Pedagogica*, edited by M.A. Manacorda, La Nuova Italia, Florence.

Gramsci, A. (1976), *Scritti 1915–1921*, edited by S. Caprioglio, Moizzi Editore, Milan.

Gramsci, A. (1977), *Selections from Political Writings (1910–20)*, edited by Q. Hoare and J. Matthews, International Publishers, New York.

Gramsci, A. (1978), *Selections from Political Writings (1921–1926)*, edited by Q. Hoare, International Publishers, New York.

Gramsci, A. (1985), *Selections from Cultural Writings*, edited by D. Forgacs and G. Nowell Smith, Harvard University Press, Cambridge MA.

Gramsci, A. (1988), *A Gramsci Reader*, ed. D. Forgacs, Lawrence & Wishart, London.

Gramsci, A. (1995), *Further Selections from the Prison Notebooks*, trans. and ed. D. Boothman, University of Minnesota Press, Minneapolis.

Gramsci, A. (1996), *Lettere dal Carcere 1926–1937*, edited by A. Santucci, Sellerio Editore, Palermo.

Green, A (1990), *Education and State Formation: The Rise of Educational Systems in England, France and the USA*, Macmillan, London.

Hall, B.L. (1993), 'Learning and Global Civil Society: Electronic Network-ing in International Non-governmental Organisations', *International Journal of Computers in Adult Education and Training*, vol. 3, no. 3, pp. 5–24.

Hall, B.L. (1998), '"Please Don't Bother the Canaries": Paulo Freire and the International Council for Adult Education', *Convergence*, vol. XXXI, nos 1 and 2, pp. 95–104.

Hall, S. (1996), 'Gramsci's Relevance for the Study of Race and Ethnic-ity', in D. Morley and K.-H. Chen (eds), *Stuart Hall: Critical Dialogues in Cultural Studies*, Routledge, London and New York.

Hammond, J.L. (1991), 'Popular Education in the Midst of Guerrilla War: An Interview with Julio Portillo', *Journal of Education*, vol. 173, no. 1, pp. 91–106.

Hart, M.U. (1992), *Working and Educating for Life: Feminist and International Perspectives on Adult Education*, Routledge, London and New York.

Harwood, R. (1984), *All the World's a Stage*, Methuen, London.

Haug, F. (ed.) (1987), *Female Sexualization: A Collective Work of Memory*, Verso, London.

Haughey, D. (1998), 'From Passion to Passivity: The Decline of University Extension for Social Change', in S.M. Scott, B. Spencer and A.M. Thomas (eds), *Learning for Life: Canadian Readings in Adult Education*, Thompson Educational, Toronto.

Haviland, R. (1973), 'An Introduction to the Writings of Paulo Freire', *Adult Education*, vol. 45, no. 5, pp. 280–85.

Highet, G. (1991), 'Gender and Education: A Study of the Ideology and Practice of Community-Based Women's Education', in S. Westwood and J.E. Thomas (eds), *Radical Agendas? The Politics of Adult Education*, NIACE, Leicester.

Hill, R.J. (1996), 'Learning to Transgress: A Socio-historical Conspectus of the American Gay Lifeworld as a Site of Struggle and Resistance', *Studies in the Education of Adults*, vol. 28, no. 2, pp. 253–79.

Hobsbawm, E.J. (1983), 'Mass-Producing Traditions: Europe, 1870–1914', in E.J. Hobsbawm and T. Ranger (eds), *The Invention of Tradition*, Cam-bridge University Press, Cambridge.

Hobsbawm, E.J. (ed.) (1995), *Gramsci in Europa e in America*, Italian edition ed. A. Santucci, Editori Laterza, Rome and Bari.

Hobsbawm, E.J. and T. Ranger (eds) (1983), *The Invention of Tradition*, Cambridge University Press, Cambridge.

Hoechsmann, M. (1993), 'Resources for Memory', *Border/Lines*, 27, pp. 55–6.

Holub, R. (1992), *Antonio Gramsci: Beyond Marxism and Postmodernism*, Routledge, London and New York.

Hommen, L. (1986), 'On the "Organic Intellectualism" of Antonio Gramsci: A Study of the Concept as a Contribution to the Politics of Adult Education', unpublished thesis, College of Education, Univer-sity of Saskatchewan.

hooks, b. (1981), *Ain't I a Woman? Black Women and Feminism*, South End Press, Boston MA.

hooks, b. (1988), *Talking Back: Thinking Feminist, Thinking Black*, Between the Lines, Toronto.

hooks, b. (1993), 'bell hooks Speaking about Paulo Freire: The Man, His Work', in P. McLaren and P. Leonard (eds), *Paulo Freire: A Critical Encounter*, Routledge, New York and London.

hooks, b. (1994), *Teaching to Transgress*, Routledge, London and New York.

Horton, M. and P. Freire (1990), *We Make the Road by Walking: Conversations on Education and Social Change*, Temple University Press, Philadelphia.

Husen, T. and N. Postlewaithe (eds) (1985), *The International Encyclopaedia of Education: Research and Studies*. vol. VIII, Pergamon, Oxford.

Ireland, T. (1987), *Antonio Gramsci and Adult Education: Reflections on the Brazilian Experience*, Manchester University Press, Manchester.

Jackson, T. (1981), 'The Influence of Gramsci on Adult Education', *Convergence*, vol. 14, no. 3, pp. 81–6.

Jarvis, P. (1985), *The Sociology of Adult and Continuing Education*, Croom Helm, Beckenham.

Jarvis, P. (1987a), 'Paulo Freire', in P. Jarvis (ed.), *Twentieth Century Thinkers in Adult Education*, Routledge, London and New York.

Jarvis, P. (1987b), *Adult Learning in the Social Context*, Croom Helm, Beckenham.

Jarvis, P. (ed.) (1992), *Perspectives on Adult Education and Training in Europe*, Leicester, NIACE.

Jules, D. (1993), 'The Challenge of Popular Education in the Grenada Revolution', in C. Lankshear and P. McLaren (eds), *Critical Literacy, Politics, Praxis and the Postmodern*, SUNY Press, Albany NY.

Kekkonen, H. (1977), 'An Experiment in Outreach and the Pedagogy of Freire', *Convergence*, vol. 10, no. 1, pp. 53–7.

Kelly, U. and J.P. Portelli (1991), 'Absent Discourses: A Review Symposium on Peter McLaren's *Life in Schools* and the Author's Response', *Journal of Education*, vol. 173, no. 3, pp. 7–59.

Kester, G. (1980), *Transition to Workers' Self-Management: Its Dynamics in the Decolonising Economy of Malta*, Institute of Social Studies, The Hague.

Kidd, R. and K. Kumar (1981), 'Coopting Freire: A Critical Analysis of Pseudo-Freirean Adult Education', *Economic and Political Weekly*, vol. XVI, nos 1 and 2, pp. 27–36.

Kirkwood, G. and C. Kirkwood (1989), *Living Adult Education: Freire in Scotland*, Open University Press, Milton Keynes.

Korsgaard, O. (1997), 'The Impact of Globalization on Adult Education', in S. Walters (ed.), *Globalization, Adult Education and Training: Impacts and Issues*, Zed Books, London.

Kozol, J. (1997), 'Exiles', in *Taboo: The Journal of Culture and Education*, vol. II, Fall, pp. 176–178.

La Belle, T.J. (1986), *Non Formal Education in Latin America and the Caribbean:*

Stability, Reform or Revolution?, Praeger, New York.

Laclau, E. and C. Mouffe (1985), *Hegemony and Socialist Strategy: Towards a Radical Democratic Politics*, Verso, London and New York.

Lajolo, L. (1985), *Gramsci: un uomo sconfitto*, Rizzoli, Milan.

Lange-Christensen, E. (1996), 'Freire and Liberation Theology', in H. Reno and M. Witte (eds), *37th Annual AERC Proceedings*, University of South Florida, Tampa.

Lawner, L. (ed.) (1973), *Letters from Prison, Antonio Gramsci*, The Noonday Press, New York.

Lawton, D. (1984), 'Curriculum and Culture', in M. Skilbeck (ed.), *Readings in School-based Curriculum Development*, Harper & Row, New York.

Ledwith, M. (1997), *Participating in Transformation: Towards a Working Model of Community Empowerment*, Venture Press, Birmingham.

Leiner, M. (1986), 'The 1961 National Cuban Literacy Campaign', in R.F. Arnove and H.J. Graff (eds), *National Literacy Campaigns: Historical and Comparative Perspectives*, Plenum, New York.

Leonard, P. (1993), 'Critical Pedagogy and State Welfare: Intellectual encounters with Freire and Gramsci, 1974–86', in P. McLaren and P. Leonard (eds), *Paulo Freire: A Critical Encounter*, Routledge, New York and London.

Lepre, A. (1998), *Il Prigioniero: Vita di Antonio Gramsci*, Laterza, Bari.

Lesirge, R. and J. Mace (1992), 'Literacy and Return to Learning Programmes for Women: Shifts in Perspective', in M. Taylor and R. Bédard (eds), *Proceedings of the 11th Annual Conference of the Canadian Association for the Study of Adult Education*, University of Saskatchewan, Saskatoon.

Lichtner, M. (1992), 'Italy', in P. Jarvis (ed.), *Perspectives on Adult Education and Training in Europe*, NIACE, Leicester.

Lind, A. and A. Johnston (1986), *Adult Literacy in the Third World*, SIDA, Stockholm.

Livingstone, D.W. (1976), 'On Hegemony in Corporate Capitalist States: Materialist Structures, Ideological Forms, Class Consciousness and Hegemonic Acts', *Sociological Inquiry*, 46, vol. 3, no. 4, pp. 235–50.

Livingstone, D.W. (1995) 'Searching for the Missing Links: Neo-Marxist Theories of Education', *British Journal of Sociology of Education*, vol. 15, no. 3, pp. 325–39.

Livingstone, D.W. (1997), 'Working Class Culture, Adult Education and Informal Learning: Beyond the "Cultural Capital" Bias to Transformative Community', in P. Armstrong, N. Miller, and M. Zukas (eds), *Crossing Borders Breaking Boundaries: Research in the Education of Adults*, Proceedings of the 27th Annual SCUTREA Conference, Birkbeck College, University of London.

Lloyd, A. (1972), 'Freire, Conscientisation and Adult Education', *Adult Education*, vol. 23, no. 1, pp. 3–20.

Lojacono, G. (1977), *Gramsci, Nuove Linee del P.C.I. ed Euro-Comunismo*, Istituto

Padano Di Arti Grafiche, Rovigo.

London–Edinburgh Weekend Return Group (1979, 1980), *In and Against the State*, Pluto Press, Bristol.

Lorde, A. (1984), *Sister Outsider*, The Crossing Press, California.

Lovett, T. (ed.) (1988), *Radical Approaches to Adult Education: A Reader*, Routledge, London.

Lovett, T. (1978), 'The Challenge of Community Education in Social and Political Change', *Convergence*, vol. X, no. 1, pp. 42–51.

Lunacarskij, A. (1976), 'La Cultura nel movimento socialista', in S. Caprioglio (ed.), *Antonio Gramsci: Scritti, 1915–1921*, Moizzi Editore, Milan.

Luria, A.R. (1976), *Cognitive Development: Its Cultural and Social Foundations*, Harvard University Press, Cambridge MA.

Lynch, K. and C. O'Neill (1994), 'The Colonisation of Social Class in Education', *British Journal of Sociology of Education*, vol. 15, no. 3, pp. 307–24.

Macedo, D. (1993), 'Literacy for Stupidification: The Pedagogy of Big Lies', *Harvard Educational Review*, vol. 63, no. 2, Summer, pp. 183–206.

Macedo, D. (1994), 'Preface', in P. McLaren and C. Lankshear (eds), *Politics of Liberation: Paths from Freire*, Routledge, London.

Mackie, R. (ed.) (1980), *Literacy and Revolution: The Pedagogy of Paulo Freire*, Continuum, New York.

Manacorda, M.A. (1970), *Il Principio Educativo in Gramsci*, Armando Editore, Rome.

Mancini, F. (1973), *Worker Democracy and Political Party in Gramsci's Thinking*, discussion paper, Bologna, School of Advanced International Studies, The Johns Hopkins University.

Marks, L. (1957), 'Biographical Notes and Glossary', in A. Gramsci, *The Modern Prince and Other Writings*, International Publishers, New York.

Marshall, J. (1997), 'Globalization from Below: The Trade Union Connections', in S. Walters, (ed.), *Globalization, Adult Education and Training: Impacts and Issues*, Zed Books, London.

Martinez, E. (1998), 'Freire in the North under Southern Eyes', *Convergence*, vol. XXXI, nos 1 and 2, pp. 128–36.

Mastellone, S. (1997), 'Introduzione: Una lettura diacronica dei *Quaderni del Carcere*', in S. Mastellone (ed.), *Gramsci: I 'Quaderni Del Carcere', Una riflessione politica incompiuta*, UTET Libreria, Turin.

Mayo, M. (1995), 'Adult Education for Change in the Nineties and Beyond: Towards a Critical Review of the Changing Context'. in M. Mayo and J. Thompson (eds), *Adult Learning, Critical Intelligence and Social Change*, NIACE, Leicester.

Mayo, M. (1997), *Imagining Tomorrow: Adult Education for Transformation*, NIACE, Leicester.

Mayo, P. (1988), 'A Comparative Analysis of Antonio Gramsci's and Paulo Freire's Ideas Relevant to Adult Education', unpublished M.Ed. thesis,

Department of Educational Foundations, University of Alberta.

Mayo, P. (1991a), 'Pedagogy and Politics in the Work of Paulo Freire', *Education*, vol. 4, no. 1, pp. 20–28.

Mayo, P. (1991b), Review of P. Freire and A. Faundez, *Learning to Question: A Pedagogy of Liberation, Convergence*, vol. XXIV, no. 4, pp. 80–82.

Mayo, P. (1992), Review of M. Horton and P. Freire, *We Make the Road by Walking, Convergence*, vol. XXV, no. 2, pp. 77–80.

Mayo, P. (1993a), 'When does it Work? Freire's Pedagogy in Context', *Studies in the Education of Adults*, vol. 25, no. 1. pp. 11–30.

Mayo, P (1993b), Review of P.V. Taylor, *The Texts of Paulo Freire, Adults Learning*, vol. 4, no. 10, p. 283.

Mayo, P. (1994a), 'Synthesising Gramsci and Freire: Possibilities for a Theory of Radical Adult Education', *International Journal of Lifelong Education*, vol. 13, no. 2, pp. 125–48.

Mayo, P. (1994b), 'Gramsci, Freire and Radical Adult Education: A Few "Blind Spots"', *Humanity and Society*, vol. 18, no. 3, pp. 82–98.

Mayo, P. (1994c), 'A Comparative Analysis of the Ideas of Gramsci and Freire from an Adult Education Perspective', *The Canadian Journal for the Study of Adult Education*, vol. 8, no. 2, pp. 1–28.

Mayo, P. (1995a), 'Towards a Process of Transformative Adult Education: A Maltese Case Study', in M. Bron and M. Malewski (eds), *Adult Education and Democratic Citizenship*, Wroclaw University Press, Wroclaw.

Mayo, P. (1995b), 'The "Turn to Gramsci" in Adult Education: A Review of the English Language Literature', *International Gramsci Society Newsletter*, April.

Mayo, P. (1995c), 'Critical Literacy and Emancipatory Politics: The Work of Paulo Freire', *International Journal of Educational Development*, vol. 15, no. 4, pp. 363–79.

Mayo, P. (1996), 'Transformative Adult Education in an Age of Globalization: A Gramscian–Freirean Synthesis and Beyond', *Alberta Journal of Educational Research*, vol. XLII, June, pp. 148–60.

Mayo, P. (1997a), 'Tribute to Paulo Freire (1921–1997)', *International Journal of Lifelong Education*, vol. 16, no. 5, pp. 365–70.

Mayo, P. (1997b), 'Workers' Education and Democracy', in G. Baldacchino and P. Mayo (eds), *Beyond Schooling: Adult Education in Malta*, Mireva, Malta.

Mayo, P. (1997c), Review of P. McLaren and P. Leonard (eds), *Paulo Freire: A Critical Encounter* and P. McLaren and C. Lankshear (eds), *Politics of Liberation: Paths from Freire, Mediterranean Journal of Educational Studies*, vol. 2, no. 2, pp. 165–73.

McGinn, N.F. (1996), 'Education, Democratisation and Globalisation: A Challenge for Comparative Education', *Comparative Education Review*, vol. 40, no. 4, pp. 341–57.

McGinn, N.F. (1997), 'The Impact of Globalization on National Educational Systems', *Prospects*, vol. XXVII, no. 1, pp. 41–54.

McIlroy, J. (1992), 'The Rise and Fall of Independent Working Class Education in the UK', in M. Taylor and R. Bédard (eds), *Proceedings of the 11th Annual Conference of the Canadian Association for the Study of Adult Education*, University of Saskatchewan, Saskatoon.

McIlroy, J. (1993a), 'Border Country: Raymond Williams in Adult Education', in J. McIlroy and S. Westwood (eds), *Border Country: Raymond Williams in Adult Education*, NIACE, Leicester.

McIlroy, J. (1993b), 'Community, Labour and Raymond Williams', *Adults Learning*, vol. 4, no. 10, pp. 276–7.

McIlroy, J. (1993c), 'Tales from Smoke-filled Rooms', *Studies in the Education of Adults*, vol. 25, no. 1, pp. 42–63.

McIlroy, J. and S. Westwood (eds) (1993), *Border Country: Raymond Williams in Adult Education*, NIACE, Leicester.

McLaren, P. (1986), 'Postmodernity and the Death of Politics: A Brazilian Reprieve' *Educational Theory*, vol. 36, no. 4, pp. 389–401.

McLaren, P. (1989), *Life in Schools*, Longman, New York and London.

McLaren, P. (1991), 'Critical Pedagogy: Constructing an Arch of Social Dreaming and a Doorway to Hope', *Journal of Education*, vol. 173, no. 1, pp. 9–34.

McLaren, P. (1994), 'Postmodernity and the Death of Politics: A Brazilian Repreive', in P. McLaren and C. Lankshear (eds), *Politics of Liberation: Paths from Freire*, Routledge, London.

McLaren, P. (1995), *Critical Pedagogy and Predatory Culture*, Routledge, New York and London.

McLaren, P. (1997), 'Paulo Freire's Legacy of Hope and Struggle', *Taboo: The Journal of Culture and Education*, vol. II, Fall, pp. 33–38.

McLaren, P. and T.T. Da Silva (1993), 'Decentering Pedagogy: Critical Literacy, Resistance and the Politics of Memory', in P. McLaren and P. Leonard (eds), *Paulo Freire: A Critical Encounter*, Routledge, New York and London.

McLaren, P. and C. Lankshear (eds) (1994), *Politics of Liberation: Paths from Freire*, Routledge, London.

McLaren, P. and P. Leonard (eds) (1993), *Paulo Freire: A Critical Encounter*, Routledge, New York and London.

McLaren, P., G. Fischman, S. Serra and E. Antelo (1998), 'The Spectres of Gramsci: Revolutionary Praxis and the Committed Intellectual', *Journal of Thought*, Winter, pp. 1–32.

Meiksins Wood, E. (1986), *The Retreat from Class*, Verso, London.

Melis, A. (1995), 'Gramsci e l'America Latina', in G. Baratta and A. Catone (eds), *Antonio Gramsci e il 'Progresso Intellettuale di Massa'*, Edizioni Unicopli, Milan.

Melo, A. (1985), 'From Traditional Cultures to Adult Education: The Portuguese Experience after 1974', in K. Wain (ed.), *Lifelong Education and Participation*, University of Malta Press, Malta.

Merrington, J. (1977), 'Theory and Practice in Gramsci's Marxism', in

Western Marxism: A Critical Reader, Verso, London.

Miles, A. (1989), 'Women's Challenge to Adult Education', *Canadian Journal for the Study of Adult Education*, vol. 3, no. 1, pp. 1–18.

Miles, A. (1997), 'Adult Education for Global Social Change: Feminism and Women's Movement', in P. Wangoola and F. Youngman (eds), *Towards a Transformative Political Economy of Adult Education*, University of Illinois Press, Chicago.

Miles, A. (1998), 'Learning from the Women's Movement in the Neo-Liberal Period', in S.M. Scott, B. Spencer and A.M. Thomas (eds), *Learning for Life: Canadian Readings in Adult Education*, Thompson Educational Publishing, Toronto.

Monasta, A. (1993a), *L'Educazione tradita: Criteri per una diversa valutazione complessiva dei Quaderni del Carcere di Antonio Gramsci*, McColl, Florence.

Monasta, A. (1993b), 'Antonio Gramsci (1891–1937)', *Prospects*, vol. 23, nos 3/4, pp. 597–612.

Morgan, W.J. (1987), 'The Pedagogical Politics of Antonio Gramsci: "Pessimism of the Intellect, Optimism of the Will"', *International Journal of Lifelong Education*, vol. 6, no. 4, 1987, pp. 295–308.

Morgan, W.J. (1996), 'Antonio Gramsci and Raymond Williams: Workers, Intellectuals and Adult Education', *Convergence*, vol. XXIX, no. 1, pp. 61–74.

Moriarty, P. (1989), 'A Freirean Approach to Peacemaking', *Convergence*, vol. 22, no. 1, pp. 25–36.

Morrow, R.A. (1987), 'Introducing Gramsci on Hegemony: Towards a Post-marxist Interpretation', Paper delivered at the Colloquium on the Fiftieth Anniversary of Gramsci's death, 27 April, Department of Educational Foundations, University of Alberta, Edmonton.

Morrow, R.A. (1991), 'Critical Theory, Gramsci and Cultural Studies: From Structuralism to Poststructuralism', in P. Wexler (ed.), *Critical Theory Now*, Falmer, New York and London.

Morrow, R.A. and C.A. Torres (1995), *Social Theory and Education: A Critique of Theories of Social and Cultural Reproduction*, SUNY Press, Albany NY.

Mouffe, C. (1988), 'Hegemony and New Political Subjects: Toward a New Concept of Democracy', in C. Nelson and L. Grossberg (eds), *Marxism and the Interpretation of Culture*, University of Illinois Press, Chicago.

Mulenga, D. (1996), 'The Impact of Economic Crisis and Structural Adjustment on Education and Training in Africa', in H. Reno, and M. Witte (eds), *37th Annual Adult Education Research Conference Proceedings*, University of South Florida, Tampa.

Murphy, M. (1997), 'Capital, Class and Adult Education: The International Political Economy of Lifelong Learning in the European Union', in P. Armstrong, N. Miller and M. Zukas (eds), *Crossing Borders Breaking Boundaries: Research in the Education of Adults*, Proceedings of the 27th Annual SCUTREA Conference, Birkbeck College, University of London.

Nairn, T. (1982), 'Antonu su Gobbu', in A. Showstack Sassoon (ed.), *Approaches to Gramsci*, Writers and Readers, London.

Nelson, C. and L. Grossberg (eds) (1988), *Marxism and the Interpretation of Culture*, University of Illinois Press, Chicago.

Norris, A. (1992), 'Brazil's Death Squads Refine their Methods', *The Times* (Malta), 22 August, p. 18.

Nyerere, J.K. (1979), 'Education for Self-Reliance', *The Tanzanian Experience*, Unesco, Hamburg.

O'Cadiz, P., P.L. Wong and C.A. Torres (1997), *Education and Democracy: Paulo Freire, Social Movements and Educational Reform in São Paulo*, Westview Press, Boulder CO.

Ornelas, C. (1982), 'Cooperative Production and Technical Education in the Basque Country', *Prospects*, vol. XII, no. 4, pp. 467–75.

Pannu, R.S. (1996), 'Neoliberal project of Globalization: Prospects for Democratisation of Education', *Alberta Journal of Educational Research*, vol. XLII, no. 2, pp. 87–101.

Peters, J.M. and B. Bell (1987), 'Horton of Highlander', in P. Jarvis, (ed.), *Twentieth Century Thinkers in Adult Education*, Routledge, London and New York.

Peters, S. (1997), 'Paulo Freire's Conscientization Applied to Critical Pedagogy of Hope for Students with Disabilities', presentation at the Comparative International Education Society Conference, Mexico City, 20–22 March.

Plumb, D. (1995), 'Critical Adult Education and Identity in Postmodernity', in P. Collette, B. Einsiedel and S. Hobden (eds), *36th Annual Adult Education Research Conference*, University of Alberta, Edmonton.

Quiroz Martín, T. (1997), 'Women, Poverty and Adult Education in Chile', in S. Walters (ed.), *Globalization, Adult Education and Training: Impacts and Issues*, Zed Books, London.

Ransome, P. (1992), *Antonio Gramsci: A New Introduction*, Harvester Wheatsheaf, Hemel Hempstead.

Retamal, G. (1981), *Paulo Freire, Christian Ideology and Adult Education in Latin America*, Newland Papers no. 5, University of Hull.

Rockhill, K. (1987), 'Gender, Language and the Politics of Literacy', *British Journal of Sociology of Education*, vol. 8, pp. 153–67.

Rosenberg, S. (1992), 'Inside the Ellipses: Intervals (of) (for) Memory', *Border/Lines* 24/25, pp. 30–35.

Ross, R. and K.C. Trachte (1990), *Global Capitalism: The New Leviathan*, SUNY Press, Albany NY.

Said, E. (1994), *Representations of the Intellectual*, Vintage, London.

Scatamburlo, V.L. (1997), 'The Revolutionary Legacy of Paulo Freire', *Taboo: The Journal of Culture and Education*, vol. II, Fall, pp. 55–57.

Schedler, P.E. (1993), 'Autonomy: Solution, Transition or Possibility? Women's Emancipation and Education', *Studies in the Education of Adults*, vol. 25, no. 1, pp. 31–9.

Schedler, P.E. (1996), 'Gay Emancipation and the Information Society', *Studies in the Education of Adults*, vol. 28, no. 2, pp. 280–91.

Schenke, A. (1992), 'Refashioning Girlhood', *Border/Lines* 24/25, pp. 56–8.

Scholle, D. (1991), 'Critical Pedagogy and Popular Culture: The Language of Critique and Possibility', *Journal of Education*, vol. 173, no. 1. pp. 124–30.

Senese, G.B. (1991), 'Warnings on Resistance and the Language of Possibility: Gramsci and a Pedagogy from the Surreal', *Educational Theory*, vol. 41, no. 1, Winter, pp. 13–22.

Sharp, R., M. Hartwig and J. O'Leary (1989), 'Independent Working Class Education: A Repressed Historical Alternative', *Discourse*, vol. 10, no. 1, October, pp. 1–26.

Shaull, R. (1970), 'Foreword', in P. Freire, *Pedagogy of the Oppressed*, Seabury Press, New York.

Shor, I. (ed.) (1987), *Freire for the Classroom: A Sourcebook for Liberatory Teaching*, Boyton/Cook, Portsmouth NH.

Shor, I. (1992), *Empowering Education: Critical Teaching for Social Change*, University of Chicago Press, Chicago.

Shor, I. and P. Freire (1987), *A Pedagogy for Liberation: Dialogues on Transforming Education*, Bergin & Garvey, Massachusetts.

Showstack Sassoon, A. (ed.) (1982), *Approaches to Gramsci*, Writers and Readers, London.

Showstack Sassoon, A. (1987), *Gramsci's Politics*, Hutchinson, London, Melbourne, Sydney and Auckland.

Simon, R. (1982), *Gramsci's Political Thought: An Introduction*, Lawrence & Wishart, London.

Simon, R.I. (1992), *Teaching Against the Grain: Texts for a Pedagogy of Possibility*, OISE Press, Toronto.

Sklair, L. (1995), 'Social Movements and Global Capitalism', *Sociology*, vol. 29, no. 3, pp. 495–512.

Soljan, N., M. Golubovic and A. Krajnc (eds) (1985), *Adult Education in Yugoslav Society*, Andragoski Centar, Zagreb.

Spencer, B. (1992), 'Workers' Education in Canada and Britain in the 1990s', in M. Taylor and R. Bédard (eds), *Proceedings of the 11th Annual Conference of the Canadian Association for the Study of Adult Education*, University of Saskatchewan, Saskatoon.

Spencer, B. (1994), 'Educating Union Canada', *Canadian Journal for the Study of Adult Education*, vol. 8, no. 2, pp. 45–64.

Spencer, B. (1995), 'Old and New Social Movements as Learning Sites: Greening Labour Unions and Unionising the Greens', *Adult Education Quarterly*, vol. 46, no. 1, pp. 31–42.

Spencer, B. (1998a), *The Purposes of Adult Education: A Guide for Students*, Thompson Educational, Toronto.

Spencer, B (1998b), 'Workers' Education for the Twenty-first Century', in

S.M. Scott, B. Spencer and A.M. Thomas (eds), *Learning for Life: Canadian Readings in Adult Education*, Thompson Educational, Toronto.

Spriano, P. (1979), *Antonio Gramsci and the Party: The Prison Years*, Lawrence & Wishart, London.

Stefanos, A. (1997), 'African Women and Revolutionary Change: A Freirian and Feminist Perspective', in P. Freire et al. (eds), *Mentoring the Mentor: A Critical Dialogue with Paulo Freire*, Peter Lang, New York.

Steinberg, S., J.L. Kincheloe and K. Hausbeck (1997), *Taboo: The Journal of Culture and Education*, vol. II, Fall.

Sultana, R.G. (1992), *Education and National Development: Historical and Critical Perspectives on Vocational Schooling in Malta*, Mireva Publications, Malta.

Taking Liberties Collective (1989), *Learning the Hard Way: Women's Oppression in Men's Education*, Macmillan, London.

Taylor, M. and R. Bédard (eds) (1992), *Proceedings of the 11th Annual Conference of the Canadian Association for the Study of Adult Education*, University of Saskatchewan, Saskatoon.

Taylor, P. (1993), *The Texts of Paulo Freire*, Open University Press, Buckingham and Philadelphia.

Thomas, J.E. (1991), 'Innocence and After: Radicalism in the 1970s', in S. Westwood and J.E. Thomas (eds), *Radical Agendas? The Politics of Adult Education*, NIACE, Leicester.

Thompson, J.L (1980), *Adult Education for a Change*, Hutchinson, Kent.

Thompson, J L. (1983), *Learning Liberation: Women's Response to Men's Education*, Croom Helm, London, Sydney, Dover and New Hampshire.

Thompson, J.L. (1988), 'Adult Education and the Women's Movement' in T. Lovett (ed.), *Radical Approaches to Adult Education: A Reader*, Routledge, London.

Titmus C.J. (ed.) (1989), *Lifelong Education for Adults: An International Handbook*, Pergamon Press, Oxford.

Tonkovic, S. (1985), 'Education for Self-Management', in N. Soljan, M. Golubovic and A. Krajnc (eds), *Adult Education in Yugoslav Society*, Andragoski Centar, Zagreb.

Torres, C.A. (1982), 'From the *Pedagogy of the Oppressed* to *A Luta Continua* – An Essay on The Political Pedagogy of Paulo Freire', *Education with Production*, Review no. 2, Botswana, Spring, pp. 76–97.

Torres, C.A. (1985), 'State and Education: Marxist Theories', in T. Husen and N. Postlethwaite (eds), *The International Encyclopaedia of Education: Research and Studies*, vol. VIII, Oxford, Pergamon.

Torres, C.A. (1987), *Toward a Political Sociology of Adult Education: An Agenda for Research on Adult Education Policy-Making*, Occasional Paper series, Department of Educational Foundations, Centre for International Education and Development, University of Alberta.

Torres, C.A. (1988), 'An Analytical Framework for Adult Education in Alberta', *Alberta Journal of Educational Research*, special issue, Adult Education in International Perspective, vol. XXXIV, no. 3, pp. 269–86.

Torres, C.A. (1990a), *The Politics of Nonformal Education in Latin America*, Praeger, New York.

Torres, C.A. (1990b), 'Adult Education and Popular Education in Latin America: Implications for a Radical Approach to Comparative Education', *International Journal of Lifelong Education*, vol. 9, no. 4, pp. 271–87.

Torres, C.A. (1991a) 'A Political Sociology of Adult Education: A Research Agenda', *Education*, vol. 4, no. 1, pp. 29–34.

Torres, C.A. (1991b), 'The State, Nonformal Education, and Socialism in Cuba, Nicaragua, and Grenada', *Comparative Education Review*, vol. 35, no. 1, pp. 110–30.

Torres, C.A. (1993), 'From the *Pedagogy of the Oppressed* to *A Luta Continua* – An Essay on The Political Pedagogy of Paulo Freire' in P. McLaren and P. Leonard (eds), *Paulo Freire: A Critical Encounter*, Routledge, New York and London.

Torres, C.A. (1994a), 'Education and the Archeology of Consciousness: Freire and Hegel', *Educational Theory*, vol. 44, no. 4, pp. 429–45.

Torres, C.A. (1994b), 'Paulo Freire as Secretary of Education in the Municipality of São Paulo', *Comparative Education Review*, vol. 38, no. 2, pp. 181–214.

Torres, R.M. (1986), 'Education and Democracy in Revolutionary Grenada', *Access*, vol. 5, no. 1, pp. 1–43.

Tucker, R. (ed.) (1978), *The Marx–Engels Reader*, W.W. Norton, New York.

Turner, G. (1990), *British Cultural Studies*, Unwin Hyman, Boston.

Unsicker, J. (1986), 'Tanzania's Literacy Campaign in Historical-Structural Perspective', in R.F. Arnove and H. Graff (eds), *National Literacy Campaigns in Historical and Comparative Perspective*, Plenum, New York.

Usher, R. and R. Edwards (1994), *Postmodernism and Education: Different Voices, Different Worlds*, Routledge, London.

Usher, R., I. Bryant and R. Johnston (1997), *Adult Education and the Postmodern Challenge: Learning Beyond the Limits*, Routledge, London.

Vanek, J. (1977), 'Education and the Practice of Self Management', in *Democracy in the Workplace*, Strongforce Inc., Washington DC.

Viezzer, M. (1990), 'La Población Marginada, Objeto del Ano Internacional de la Alfabetización', interview with Paulo Freire, *Convergence* vol. XXIII, no. 1, pp. 5–8.

Walker, J.C. (1980), 'The End of Dialogue: Paulo Freire on Politics and Education', in R. Mackie (ed.), *Literacy and Revolution: The Pedagogy of Paulo Freire*, Continuum, New York.

Walters, S. (ed.) (1997), *Globalization, Adult Education and Training: Impacts and Issues*, Zed Books, London.

Weiler, K. (1991), 'Freire and a Feminist Pedagogy of Difference', *Harvard Educational Review*, vol. 61, no. 4, pp. 449–74.

Welton, M. (ed.) (1987), *Knowledge for the People: The Struggle for Adult Learn-*

ing in *English-speaking Canada: 1828–1973*, OISE Press, Toronto.

Welton, M. (1991), 'Dangerous Knowledge: Canadian Workers' Education in the Decades of Discord', *Studies in the Education of Adults*, vol. 23, no. 1, pp. 24–40.

Welton, M. (1993), 'Social Revolutionary Learning: The New Social Movements as Learning Sites', *Adult Education Quarterly*, vol. 43, no. 3, pp. 152–64.

Westwood, S. (1991a), 'Constructing the Other: Minorities, the State and Adult Education in Europe', in S. Westwood and J.E. Thomas (eds), *Radical Agendas? The Politics of Adult Education*, NIACE, Leicester.

Westwood, S. (1991b), 'Constructing the Other: A Postmodern Agenda for Adult Education', in S. Westwood and J.E. Thomas (eds), *Radical Agendas? The Politics of Adult Education*, NIACE, Leicester.

Westwood, S. (1993), 'Excavating the Future: Towards 2000', in J. McIlroy and S. Westwood (eds), *Border Country: Raymond Williams in Adult Education*, NIACE, Leicester.

Westwood, S. and J.E. Thomas (eds) (1991), *Radical Agendas? The Politics of Adult Education*, NIACE, Leicester.

Wexler, P. (1991), *Critical Theory Now*, Falmer Press, New York and London.

Williams, R. (1961), *The Long Revolution*, Penguin, Harmondsworth.

Williams, R. (1975), 'You're a Marxist, Aren't You?' in B. Parekh (ed.), *The Concept of Socialism*, Croom Helm, Beckenham.

Williams, R. (1976), 'Base and Superstructure in Marxist Cultural Theory', in R. Dale, G. Esland and M. Macdonald (eds), *Schooling and Capitalism*, Routledge & Kegan Paul, London.

Williams, R. (1983), *Towards 2000*, Chatto & Windus, London.

Young, M.F.D. (ed.) (1971), *Knowledge and Control*, Collier–Macmillan, London.

Youngman, F. (1986), *Adult Education and Socialist Pedagogy*, Croom Helm, Beckenham.

Zachariah, M. (1986), *Revolution through Reform: A Comparison of Sarvodaya and Conscientisation*, Praeger, New York.

Zammit, E. (1995–96), 'Worker Participation and Employee Empowerment: A Comparative Study of Two Enterprises in Malta', *Economic and Social Studies*, vol. 7, pp. 1–17.

Zammit, E.L. and A. Gauci (1984), 'Case Studies in Industrial Democracy: Malta Drydocks and the Mondragon Co-operatives', in E. Azzopardi and L.J. Scerri (eds), *Issues: Aspects of an Island Economy*, Economics Society, Malta.

Zuniga, M. (1993), 'Popular Education and Social Transformation in Nicaragua', Maria Zuniga interviewed by Peter Mayo, *Education*, vol. 5, no. 1, pp. 33–40.

Index